Living into Community

CULTIVATING PRACTICES
THAT SUSTAIN US

Christine D. Pohl

WILLIAM B. EERDMANS PUBLISHING COMPANY
GRAND RAPIDS, MICHIGAN / CAMBRIDGE, U.K.

Published 2012 by
Wm. B. Eerdmans Publishing Co.
2140 Oak Industrial Drive N.E., Grand Rapids, Michigan 49505 /
P.O. Box 163, Cambridge CB3 9PU U.K.
www.eerdmans.com

Printed in the United States of America

18 17 16 15 14 13 12   7 6 5 4 3 2 1

Library of Congress Cataloging-in-Publication Data

Pohl, Christine D.
    Living into community: cultivating practices that sustain us / Christine D. Pohl.
        p.   cm.
    Includes bibliographical references (p.   ) and index.
    ISBN 978-0-8028-4985-4 (pbk.: alk. paper)
    1. Christian life.   I. Title.

    BV4501.3.P635   2011
    248.4 — dc23

                                                                2011040634

Unless otherwise noted, the Scripture quotations in this publication are from the New Revised Standard Version of the Bible, copyright © 1989 by the Division of Christian Education of the National Council of Churches of Christ in the U.S.A., and used by permission.

LIVING INTO COMMUNITY

Contents

CHAPTER ONE

Introduction: Four Practices That Sustain Community

Stop wasting time running after the perfect community. Live your
life fully in your community today.

Jean Vanier, *Community and Growth*

This breakdown could have been avoided. But then, few breakdowns in community are inevitable. In this case, some folks made several poor decisions. Other people responded poorly to the poor decisions. More decisions, more responses, more trouble. Words were exchanged, positions hardened, sides drawn up. Rumors flew, and even when folks knew they were rumors, they repeated them until it was very difficult to discern what had "really" happened.

People were angry and hurt; some conversations stopped, and new alliances were formed. Only certain people knew about key meetings. A lot of energy was expended in determining motives, justifying decisions, and anticipating "the opposition's" next move. Regular activities continued, but the life was drained out of them; everything seemed hollow. Small acts and casual comments were freighted with huge symbolic meaning. Everyone felt undervalued and betrayed by someone; a number of people threatened to leave. The meltdown had taken on a life of its own.

Friends questioned one another's commitments; grumbling and weariness became highly contagious. Disagreements took strange turns; old differences and hurts came to the surface and played into the present trouble in unpredictable ways. Some people ducked, determined to weather the storm without being drawn into it. Others "defected in place"[1] — showing up when the occasion required it, but emotionally and relationally absent or detached. A few seemed to add fuel to the fire, reporting the latest outrageous development and speculating on what might happen next. Still others tried to keep conversations going and looked for resolution, but were often battered or sidetracked in the process. Several years later, members of the community continue to live with the wounds, even as they move forward.

Is this a description of a church? A school? An intentional community? A parachurch organization? An extended family? Because these breakdowns are common and painful, even general descriptions can evoke many memories. Places, events, personalities, and consequences flood our thoughts. We've been there. We remember the feelings of disappointment, hurt, helplessness, betrayal, and anger. And we often remember the sense of having been sullied by the experience. Perhaps we wanted to make things better, but found it nearly impossible in the moment. We'd been caught in the downward pull of a whirlpool that was not leading to anything good.

When these breakdowns happen in Christian communities, the costs go beyond the shattering of valued relationships, important projects, or a shared future. The best testimony to the truth of the gospel is the quality of our life together. Jesus risked his reputation and the credibility of his story by tying them to how his followers live and care for one another in community (John 17:20-23).

If we could cut through our complacency or despair, we might be shocked at what is really at stake here. The character of our shared life — as congregations, communities, and families — has the power to draw people to the kingdom or to push them away. How we live together is the most persuasive sermon we'll ever get to preach.

The beauty of loving communities does not replace the importance of the verbal proclamation of the gospel, but Jesus explicitly linked the truth of his life and message to our life together. The Word who became flesh and lived among us — full of grace and truth — expects that our relationships with one another will also be characterized by grace and truth. And so, for two thousand years, Jesus' followers have been forming communities built and sustained by love, though often also fractured by sin and corruption.

The desire to be part of communities that are vibrant, caring, and faithful keeps us working at the task of building and repairing congregations. When folks enjoy being together, share celebrations, and walk through hard times with grace and love, the beauty of their shared life is deeply compelling. Human beings were made for living in community, and it is in community that we flourish and become most fully human.

Unfortunately, experiences of moral failure, group meltdowns, personal pettiness, and partisan harshness in congregations and communities make us wonder if our efforts in building community are worth the trouble. We often invest great hope in our Christian communities, and when there are serious ruptures, it feels as if part of the kingdom has been trampled. How is it that people who want closer relationships and deeper experiences of shared life sometimes find themselves in terribly difficult situations — sorting out betrayals, broken commitments, and creeping cynicism?

Longing for Community

Growing into the likeness of Christ and into the church as it's supposed to be cannot be separated from the messiness and disappointments that are part of human relationships. We can protect ourselves from such difficulties only by cutting ourselves off from our relationships, and that is rarely a satisfactory option. Nevertheless, we can build and maintain congregations — just like we do with marriages, families, monastic communities, and businesses — in better and worse ways. Good communities and life-giving congregations emerge at the intersection of divine grace and steady human effort.

Biblical descriptions of the church as God's household, as the body of Christ, and as a new family of brothers and sisters leave many of us dissatisfied with church life that is defined by a weekly worship service and an occasional committee meeting or mission project. The biblical images suggest closer and more significant relationships and a life together that draws people in.

Religious as well as secular researchers have recently rediscovered the human need to "belong," and describe various versions of our longing for community — a place where one is known, or at least a group where everybody knows your name. Our cultural emphasis on personal freedom and self-fulfillment has left many people lonely and emotionally fragile. Many of us are looking for community.

Our yearnings to belong and our desire for lasting relationships, however, are often accompanied by uncertainty about making commitments. As one person put it, it would be so much easier if we could be "connected without being encumbered." Despite the fact that many of us claim to be dissatisfied with individualism, we cherish our capacity to make individual choices and to seek opportunities for personal growth.

While we readily recognize the ways in which the larger culture challenges Christian beliefs and commitments, we don't always notice how profoundly our expectations, desires, and practices are also shaped by our culture. We bring the values of self-actualization, individual success, consumption, and personal freedom — and the choices that result from them — to church life, just as we bring them into family and work.

The ways we've been formed by church and culture have not given us the skills or virtues we need to be part of the very communities we long for and try to create. While we might want community, it is often community on our terms, with easy entrances and exits, lots of choice and support, and minimal responsibilities. Mixed together, this is not a promising recipe for strong or lasting communities.

When I've asked students and friends to describe an experience of community, they often tell stories about a time of intense emotional bonding with a group of people: a weekend retreat that was deeply affirming, a camping trip with friends, or a short-term mission project where participants began to feel like family. Such experiences of community tend to be brief, occasional, and intense. Communities in which we grow and flourish, however, last over time and are built by people who are faithful to one another and committed to a shared purpose. Community life certainly has moments of incredible beauty and intense personal connection, but much of it is daily and ordinary. Our lives are knit together not so much by intense feeling as by shared history, tasks, commitments, stories, and sacrifices.

But communities need more than shared history and tasks to endure. A combination of grace, fidelity, and truth makes communities safe enough for people to take the risks that are necessary for growth and transformation. That same combination makes it possible for groups to handle disagreements without being torn apart and to minister to the world in ways that are far greater than the sum of the individuals involved. Shaped and sustained by gratitude, such communities grow by making room for others, whether friends or strangers.

Sorting Out What's Going On

Turning back to the opening description of a community meltdown, we could interpret that experience in several different ways. We could observe that some of the personalities involved were dysfunctional, codependent, or passive-aggressive. We might conclude that leadership styles were outdated, or that better procedures for handling disagreements should have been in place. Each of us comes to challenges in relationships and in community with some framework for interpretation, a lens for making sense of what's going on.

In this culture, we tend to use the language of psychology or therapy for interpreting interpersonal difficulties. We also turn to management models and business language when we need to figure out how to make relationships or institutions work. These approaches are useful, but they are not adequate for the challenges of building communities.

Though less familiar, we could also use more explicitly theological and moral categories, and language that connects us to the wisdom of the Christian tradition. In reflecting on what builds up and what breaks down communities, we can also ask about fidelity and keeping promises, speaking the truth, gratitude, envy and grumbling, exclusion and welcome. A framework that focuses on *practices* allows us to see issues in congregational and community life from a different angle and helps us to get at the moral and theological commitments that structure our relationships.

Practices are at the heart of human communities; they are things "people do together over time to address fundamental human needs." Every community has practices that hold it together; for Christians, practices can also be understood as responses to the grace we have already experienced in Christ, in light of the word and work of God, and for the sake of one another and the world.[2] Our practices include hospitality, making and keeping promises, truthfulness, gratitude, Sabbath-keeping, testimony, discernment, forgiveness, worship, healing, and many others.

This book will focus on several practices that are basic to human life. In families, communities, and congregations that are vibrant and sturdy, we notice certain patterns in relationships. We see folks making and keeping promises, living and speaking truthfully, expressing gratitude, and offering hospitality. Some aspect of each of these practices is evident in almost every group of people whose connections or interactions with one another are more than temporary.

Strengthening these practices won't necessarily mark us as unusual or exemplary. Unless circumstances make a particular practice very costly to us, these practices are the ordinary, taken-for-granted dynamics of good relationships. We don't usually make a big deal over keeping a promise or telling the truth unless there's a problem associated with it.

In general, practices are most powerful when they are not noticed, when they are simply an expression of who we are and what we do, a way of being in the world and relating to one another that seems "natural." But, for a variety of reasons, we can no longer assume that these practices are affirmed consistently in the wider society, nor can we assume that Christians always recognize their importance.

Each of the practices we will be exploring is important to the biblical story and to expectations about the ways in which the people of God should live. Each is also at the heart of God's character and activity: we worship a God who is faithful and true, gracious and welcoming. Theologians and philosophers have often written about the importance of promise-keeping, truth-telling, gratitude, and hospitality, though rarely in terms of their roles in sustaining community.

These four practices do not address every aspect of community life, but they do hold together and intersect in surprising ways. If we consider one particular practice, the necessity of other practices becomes apparent very quickly. When communities offer hospitality to strangers, they soon discover the importance of truthfulness, gratitude, and fidelity. Speaking truthfully is difficult and often risky in the absence of commitment or fidelity to one another. Gratitude without truthfulness looks a lot like a manipulative form of flattery.

Certain attitudes and actions shatter community life rather than sustain it, and make life together unhappy and sometimes dangerous. When we engage in betrayal, deception, grumbling, envy, or exclusion, we violate connections between us. While we might describe these as practices, they are better understood as deformations of one of the four practices. For example, betrayal depends on and perverts a larger commitment to promising, just as deception and lying are parasitic on some notion of truthfulness.

In addition to the damage they do to relationships, these deformations also affect our capacity to engage in other practices well. Small deceptions and habitual grumbling make the practice of hospitality troublesome for hosts and guests. Even something as ordinary as complaining can become a way of life that eats away at the bonds that hold a community together. Deformations threaten to undermine every practice and every community.

Promise-keeping, truthfulness, hospitality, and gratitude have often been understood as duties or obligations, things we ought to do. They are much more than duties, however; they make living in community possible as well as good, sometimes even beautiful. When we see them primarily as duties, they can seem burdensome rather than life-giving. Understanding them in terms of virtues can also be limiting because we tend to view virtues individualistically and in a static way. Considering them as practices opens up the possibility of recognizing them as the relational dynamics of grace and truth — what grace and truth look like when they are embodied in community.

It is tempting to talk and write about community life in abstract and idealized terms, but when we focus on actual congregations and communities, we often notice the failures — the betrayals, the hypocrisy, the grumbling, the closed doors. While we don't usually notice practices when they are functioning well, we surely notice when they have failed or are violated. Giving attention to practices opens up a more textured and grounded approach to community life. It also allows us to draw important insights from very ordinary experiences and situations.

An emphasis on practices also fits well with the current interest in stories and formation by connecting the attention to narrative with practical concerns about our communities and social contexts. Thus we can locate contemporary challenges related to responding to strangers or dealing with frenetic work schedules within rich traditions of hospitality or Sabbath-keeping. Furthermore, working with practices allows us to move beyond important but individually focused literature on spiritual formation so that we can also attend to the formation of good communities.

When we pay attention to practices, we are likely to notice the significance and beauty in small acts of grace and truth. We have a framework for talking about what is good and holy in our ordinary communities, and for seeing how we can strengthen places that might need it. While dealing with practical concerns, practices can also help move our discussions beyond the "tricks and techniques" approaches to leadership and forming communities. Because practices address both basic human needs and God's character and activity, discussions about them give us a way to draw together the human and the divine, the earthly and the transcendent.

Wisdom and experience teach us that what is noticed and celebrated is usually also repeated. To build stronger congregations and communities, we'll need to get in the habit of recognizing the practices that undergird our relationships and our life together. We can no longer afford to take them for granted. Instead, we'll need to become more attentive to what is good and how it is sustained, without overlooking the significance and impact of the deformations. As noted earlier, a lot is at stake. Our testimony to the truth of the gospel and to the life-giving power of the resurrection of Jesus stands or falls with the character and practices of our congregations.

Why These Practices? The Project behind the Book

More than a decade ago, I interviewed close to sixty people whose lives and communities were shaped by offering hospitality to strangers. A significant number of experienced workers said that they would not be able to offer long-term hospitality to strangers without the support of a community. I was surprised when several who were working in the most difficult circumstances — with homeless people, refugees, and undocumented workers — followed that statement with the comment that they had found sustaining community even harder than welcoming strangers. Community life is necessary, but it is also difficult. Their insights reminded me of how often we are drawn to ministry and yet underestimate the daily needs of the community that supports it.

For the past twenty-five years, scholars in theology, biblical studies, and ethics have emphasized the importance of the church as a "contrast" or alternative community, and have argued that Christians can challenge the beliefs and practices of the larger society by the beauty of their shared life.[3] The theologian Robert Webber expresses it well:

> The church is the primary presence of God's activity in the world. As we pay attention to what it means to be the church we create an alternative community to the society of the world. This new community, the embodied experience of God's kingdom, will draw people into itself and nurture them in the faith. In this sense the church and its life in the world will become the new apologetic.[4]

Despite the richness of many of these discussions, few writers discuss the challenges of actually forging alternative communities in contemporary society.

In my experience, confident assertions that Christian community is or can be the new apologetic are as troubling as they are hope-filled. The winsome and life-giving character of Christian community is often accompanied by profound difficulties arising from disagreements and betrayals. Unless participants are prepared for the inevitable challenges, when difficulties develop, they will quickly become wary of moving toward deeper involvement in any church or community. The testimony of our shared life is crucial, but it is also fragile.

I am fascinated by Christian communities and the challenges they face. My experience with various congregations and intentional communities, my extended study of hospitality, and my conversations with scholars and practitioners pointed me toward the importance of practices in community life. The current attention to community among Christian leaders, academics, and young people reinforced my interest.

Thinking about the Christian life in terms of practices has turned out to be very fruitful for renewing communities and congregations. Building on Alasdair MacIntyre's work in *After Virtue*, and under the leadership of Craig Dykstra and Dorothy Bass, various scholars and pastors have recently focused on practices as a significant way to connect theological reflection with congregational activity and life.[5] In writing about Sabbath-keeping, testimony, hospitality, discernment, honoring the body, singing, and other practices, they have drawn insights from the biblical and historical tradition and related them to features of contemporary life. Through my study of hospitality, our paths intersected, and I have found the approach to be very helpful.

In 2002, the Lilly Endowment launched a large initiative called Sustaining Pastoral Excellence. Leaders of my local church and I drafted a proposal for a project that looked at pastoral excellence within community. We were blessed in receiving generous funding for several years so that we could explore the practices of promise-keeping, truthfulness, gratitude, and hospitality in relation to pastoral and congregational strengthening.

The project allowed us to bring together twelve pastors, three leaders of intentional communities, and three professors for three days of meetings twice a year.[6] At each of the meetings, we focused on one of the practices. Every participant provided a two-page description of a recent incident in his or her congregation or community that illuminated some of the dynamics of the practice or its deformation. We used these brief essays inductively; they provided the substance — the material — out of which we gradually came to a fuller understanding of the role of promise-keeping, truthfulness, gratitude, and hospitality in congregational life.

Combined with biblical study, attention to the resources of the theological and moral tradition, and discussions of several books,[7] the essays and discussions opened up wonderful conversations and helped us form a community of wisdom and encouragement. We did not try to solve the problems described in some of the brief essays, but used the accounts as windows into understanding how various practices and their deformations interacted. The stories helped us see how contextual factors strengthened or undermined practices, and what redemptive responses to failure might look like.

This reservoir of wisdom stands behind much of what might be good or unusual about how practices are explored in this book. The insistence on being grounded rather than abstract in our considerations of community and excellence, the commitment to building our understanding of practices out of ordinary life, the decision to avoid problem-solving approaches as we reflected on the experiences of ministry, and the efforts to make our conversations a safe place for truth and reflection allowed surprising and significant insights to emerge. Because our primary conversations were among pastors and leaders of communities, readers might get the impression that this is mostly a book for leaders. But the issues are not only "leadership" concerns, they are human ones — and are as likely to arise in families as they are in congregations.

Practices provide a window into understanding community life, but they are themselves also best understood in the context of the life of a community. That's why stories or accounts emerging from actual communities are so fruitful. In stories, we encounter all of the messiness, beauty, and complexity of practices and life itself. Stories show us how the practices are interconnected. In addition, stories help move us beyond the sterility or woodenness that characterizes some of the more academic discussions of truth-telling, making and keeping promises, gratitude, and hospitality.

In the end, the task of drawing together the various strands of practical wisdom and locating them in the larger theological tradition has been mine. The book, however, was a shared project. It is the fruit of rigorous wrestling with difficult issues by a group of leaders who, given the opportunity to work on questions of importance and relevance to them, became something of a community along the way. Although our engagement was episodic and brief, it was also very illuminating. As we discussed fidelity and truthfulness, gratitude and hospitality, we also experienced them and found ourselves fed through our conversations, shared worship, and mutual care.

Attempting a major discussion of several practices in a single book is ambitious and impractical. Certainly, people have written extensively on each practice, and a thorough analysis of each could be helpful. In our experience, however, some of the most interesting and troublesome aspects of the practices and of community life in general appear at the intersection or collision of practices and deformations. So, even though we could provide only abbreviated discussions of each practice, it seemed particularly valuable to us to look at some of them together.

Given the range of practices that might have been addressed and that are important for community, some readers will surely wonder about the primary focus on four. How could we leave out the others? Are we saying that the others aren't quite as necessary for community? There's no simple answer, but there are several personal and historical reasons for the choices made.

In twenty years of studying hospitality, I discovered that truthfulness, promise-keeping, and gratitude appeared over and over again in relation to offering welcome. In my early research on making and keeping promises, it quickly became evident that promise-keeping and truthfulness were so closely linked in the biblical text and in human experience that it would be best to handle them together. Although I had previously done a great deal of work on hospitality for *Making Room: Recovering Hospitality as a Christian Tradition*, it seemed impossible to consider community without recognizing the centrality of hospitality and giving it at least limited attention. The decision to include gratitude as a practice came a little later when experiences made it clear that without gratitude, communities and families are unbearable. In addition, little has been written on promise-keeping, truth-telling, or gratitude in relation to community or within the current discussions of practices.

The more we worked on the four practices, the more we saw their interrelations and connections. Two additional practices came up frequently in our discussions. Discernment and forgiveness emerged as crucial for handling tensions among the practices and their deformations and for strengthening the other practices. They receive very limited attention in this book because quite a lot has been written about them lately and because they have a different type of role in communities. We usually turn to forgiveness and discernment when practices fail or conflict, so they seem to be something like "second order" practices — not second in the sense of being less important, but second in the sense of sequencing. Celebration and Sabbath also emerged in our conversations in relation to the other practices, and so are briefly discussed in several places throughout the book.

Of course, other reasons for limiting the study to four practices are the issue of space and the reality that one can't do everything. So in this book, I am arguing not that these are the most important four practices, but that they are central to community life and to God's character. In addition, each of the four has been described by scholars as definitive of morality — so they are central to the Christian moral tradition. Interesting and important insights can be gained by looking at them together. Taking them more seriously will not solve all of the issues in Christian life or ministry, nor will attention to practices break open every dilemma. But as we worked on these four, it was remarkable how relevant they were to many of the challenges that come up in congregational and community life.

Because I addressed hospitality as a practice quite fully in *Making Room*, I have chosen not to revisit that material in this book. Instead, hospitality will help to draw together and integrate the concluding discussion of the practices. A commitment to the practice of hospitality was common ground for the participants in the project, and it is woven through the stories and chapters. In a sense, *Making Room* provides the foundation for this book — in terms of my understanding of practices and my interest in how they interact.

Some readers may wonder why there is not more explicit attention to gender in the discussion of the practices. One answer is that gender did not come up frequently in our conversations, in the literature on the practices, or in our experience of the practices at work. These are human practices, though their expression may vary somewhat by gender as well as by culture.

But we are gendered beings, and so gender has shaped the whole project in more implicit ways. The choice to use practices as a lens for looking at community reflects a desire to be grounded in the particular and to be attentive to relational aspects of life. The group of pastors and leaders that discussed the material was diverse in terms of gender and ethnic background. Women formed two-thirds of the project leadership team, and almost half of the group. We worked inductively from shared texts, we looked closely at particular experiences and contexts, and we deliberately created safe settings for conversation. Without explicitly discussing feminist insights about communication, learning, or relationships, we chose approaches that reflected many of those concerns. And they worked well for everyone.

Getting Started

As we turn now to a closer look at each of the practices, we will be considering gratitude, making and keeping promises, truthfulness, and hospitality from various angles. The book is divided into four parts, with each part focusing on one practice and its related issues. Each section begins with an exploration of some of the biblical and theological understandings of the topic. There's much to learn from various discussions of the practice as they have developed over centuries and within different traditions. But any effort to strengthen a practice must also take seriously the challenges we face within contemporary culture. While some of the central values and structures of our society depend on these practices, other values and commitments undermine the practices significantly. It is important to consider our cultural context.

In the second chapter of the sections on gratitude, promise-keeping, and truth-telling, we will address some of the complications. We struggle with gratitude, promises, and truthfulness for a variety of reasons. We are finite, we have conflicting responsibilities, and our circumstances are subject to change. Because practices are tied to relationships, other people and other practices can affect our ability to live out a particular practice.

In the third chapter on each practice, we will explore the deformations associated with gratitude, promising, and truthfulness. In these chapters, we explore the impact of sin — in its various forms — on human relationships and community. Following the discussions of the deformations, we consider some of the ways we can strengthen each practice in our families, congregations, and communities.

The book concludes with a discussion of hospitality. It follows a similar pattern to the discussion of the other practices, but it is abbreviated and is specifically shaped to show how the practices intersect in everyday experience.

Because the book is oriented toward strengthening communities, readers are likely to benefit most if they can engage the material with others. To assist in exploring implications and applications, questions for discussion and reflection are provided at the end of the book.

We begin with the practice of gratitude because the Christian life is most of all a response to the grace we have received. Christian community begins in gratitude, is sustained by our promises and truthfulness, and is expressed in hospitality. But things are never really that linear or sequential. The grace to which we respond is expressed in God's welcome to us. That elicits and strengthens our practice of hospitality. Our promises are rooted in God's fidelity to us, and our truthfulness finds its home in the grace and truth of Christ.

PART I

Embracing Gratitude as a Way of Life

CHAPTER TWO

Grateful Hearts

Thou that has given so much to me,
Give one thing more — a grateful heart. . . .
Not thankful when it pleases me,
As if Thy blessings had spare days;
But such a heart, whose pulse may be Thy praise.

George Herbert, "Gratefulness," *The Temple*

Most of us do fairly well with occasional expressions of gratitude to God. We give thanks for our health, families, salvation, daily food, and unexpected blessings. But the seventeenth-century poet George Herbert was asking for much more — he wanted his every heartbeat to be thankfulness and praise to God. He gives us a picture of a heart — a body, a life — pulsing with gratitude.

If we really understand our lives as redeemed by costly grace, then our primary response can only be gratitude. It's at the center of the Christian life; in fact, the theologian Karl Barth wrote that grace and gratitude "belong together like heaven and earth. Grace evokes gratitude like the voice an echo. Gratitude follows grace like thunder [follows] lightning." If the essence of God is grace, Barth explained, then the essence of human beings as God's people is our gratitude or thanks.[1]

The word "gratitude" comes from the Latin *gratia*, which means "grace" or "graciousness." Similarly, in Greek, grace *(charis)* and thankfulness, thanksgiving, or gratitude *(eucharistia)* share the same root. If grace and gratitude are central and belong together, why then are they not more prominent in how we live? How often do we imagine or experience every beat of our hearts pumping out thankfulness?

Gratitude operates at several different levels: thanksgiving and praise to God, gratitude as a posture for life, and gratitude as a response to others for who they are or for what they have given to us.[2] We can respond in gratitude to specific gifts we have received or to the person who has given them to us, and we can also allow the "giftedness of our total existence" to shape the way we view our world.[3]

Although writers in the Christian and philosophical traditions have given substantial attention to gratitude, and although giving thanks is central in Scripture, we've mostly overlooked its importance as a practice for community life. Recently, however, gratitude has been recognized as important to the well-being of individuals. Web sites and organizations promote it, and psychologists proclaim its importance for our health and happiness.[4]

Gratitude is also vital to sustaining communities that are holy and good. Part of the recent emphasis on gratitude or giving thanks is surely a response to the epidemic of complaint, envy, presumption, and dissatisfaction that undermines human relationships and plagues many communities. These forms of ingratitude are deadly: they kill community by chipping away at it until participants long to be just about anywhere else. While gratitude gives life to communities, ingratitude that has become established sucks out everything good, until life itself shrivels and discouragement and discontent take over.

The apostle Paul understood the communal importance of gratitude when he encouraged the early Christian congregations to see that at the center of their life together was "giving thanks to God the Father at all times and for everything in the name of our Lord Jesus Christ" (Eph. 5:20). Ingratitude toward God and human beings is a terrible thing, but it often comes dressed in other clothing — restlessness, concerns about self-fulfillment or entitlement, and irritation at not being properly valued or recognized. Once a "culture of complaint"[5] is established, it spreads through communities and affects everyone.

Ingratitude is not only annoying and unpleasant, it is dangerous. While thanksgiving should characterize God's people, Paul describes failure to give thanks to God as idolatry. In Romans 1:21-23, Paul argues that at the root of human sin is a refusal to trust and to honor God, and a failure to give God thanks.[6] Following Paul, the reformer Martin Luther also concluded that ingratitude to God ultimately leads to a "whirlpool of vices."[7] Even ingratitude toward human benefactors has been viewed by theologians and philosophers as a serious moral failing.[8]

Gratitude and Ingratitude in Our Communities

Gratitude and ingratitude are closely tied to what we notice, and once we start focusing on flaws in a community, they quickly dominate our attention. There are always things about a community or congregation that will disappoint us, and because our expectations for the church are high, disappointment and frustration can run very deep.

A church member whose expectations for congregational life were not being met confronted the church's leadership team: "The church is moving farther and farther away from its ideals. We don't stand for anything anymore. Everything is dying, dying beneath us. I have lots of ideas on how to fix things, but nobody is listening. The staff doesn't listen, and anyway, I'm really tired and bored. Everybody is bored with the services."

When asked about what a return to the church's ideals might look like, the member replied, "Well, I don't know, but not this." Saddened and somewhat surprised by the intensity of the dissatisfaction, one of the pastors asked, "What about all the good that is going on? What about the people that we've reached? What about our own changed lives over the past several years?" And between themselves, the leaders wondered, "And what about your changed life — the three years of walking together with you toward health and healing?"

In a follow-up conversation several weeks later, the unhappy church member mentioned making plans to spend some time traveling from Christian community to Christian community to see how other believers shaped their lives together.

Beneath the critique and complaint, is there also ingratitude for the congregation and its pastors? Is the church member's dissatisfaction rooted in a lack of recognition of God's faithfulness in times of difficulty and weariness? Are the complaints legitimate about church drift and the inaccessibility of church leaders? Or, as is often the case, is the dissatisfaction a mixture of truth and ingratitude, concern and irresponsibility?

Is eagerness to visit other communities an expression of real interest

19

in getting congregational life right, or is it a reflection of a consumer mind-set that is always looking for a better deal? Are the pastors using the litany of accomplishments to provoke some version of guilt and gratitude in order to stop the complaining?

There are certainly times when leaders should be challenged about loss of vision and when they need to grow in openness to new ideas and voices, but undifferentiated dissatisfaction and grumbling undermine the energy and hope necessary to sustain community. It's not only parishioners who struggle, however; pastors also struggle with gratitude. While pastoring a Vineyard church, Kevin Rains describes his journey from ingratitude to appreciation for the ways that thanks and acknowledgment can bestow blessing. He tells several stories about moments of affirmation and gratitude that were life-giving, and describes simple rituals of blessing that acknowledge what a person means to others — before she or he is dead and the words are delivered as a eulogy.

Kevin describes how, after one of these times of deliberate blessing among the leadership team of his church, he was reduced to tears because of the deep encouragement it represented. He writes,

> Gratitude and affirmation are in short supply. Sadly, I must admit that I'm not only ingratitude's victim but also its perpetrator. Often I have shrugged off gratitude while embracing discontent. Usually I can justify this in the name of "vision" or "unmet potential." That is, until I read the following quote from Dietrich Bonhoeffer:
>
> > We think we dare not be satisfied with the small measure of spiritual knowledge, experience, and love that has been given to us, and that we must constantly be looking forward eagerly to the highest good. . . . We pray for the big things and forget to give thanks for the ordinary, small (and yet really not small) gifts. How can God entrust great things to one who will not thankfully receive from Him the little things? If we do not give thanks daily for the Christian fellowship in which we have been placed, even where there is no great experience, no discoverable riches, but much weakness, small faith, and difficulty; if on the contrary, we only keep complaining to God that everything is so paltry and petty, so far from what we expected, then we hinder God from letting our fellowship grow according to the measure and riches which are there for us all in Jesus Christ.[9]

I can only imagine if this advice were heeded by even a fraction of a local church — the effects could be revolutionary. How many times have I wished I were somewhere else where God was REALLY moving? How many times have I longed to be in a more beautiful place (with mountains or an ocean) and abandon the urban neighborhood where I live? How many times have I fantasized about the perfect fellowship where everyone got along like a perfect family. What this boils down to is spiritual pornography . . . creating a mental fantasy of a perfect place or people and not recognizing the good things all around me. This spiritual porn is my nemesis. It's poison. Thankfully, the antidote is available and accessible: equal parts of gratitude and affirmation.[10]

Kevin's experience reminds us that gratitude can be undone in surprising ways. When we yearn for some ideal of church or community, it's easy to grow increasingly dissatisfied with what we have. Although we might readily acknowledge that always wanting more possessions or money is wrong, we often overlook the danger of always wanting more success in our ministries, greater spiritual growth in ourselves or others, or more dramatic spiritual experiences. While there is tension between being grateful for what we have and striving for excellence, our cultural emphases on growth and success tend to undermine gratitude and to interpret contentment as an absence of drive or vision.

A true desire for growth in oneself or others, or in the effectiveness of our ministries, can be misshapen by a combination of restlessness, lack of fidelity, and ingratitude hiding behind a "prophetic" posture. We surely want congregations to grow in faithfulness and maturity, but they can suffer profoundly under people who misunderstand the ways to challenge a community toward deeper vision or fuller commitment.

Self-appointed "prophets" tend to stand above their own communities and offer criticism of the leadership or congregation and their less-than-perfect efforts at the Christian life. Without the generosity that comes with grace and gratitude, they find fault with every endeavor while simultaneously longing for deeper connections and more vibrant shared life. Like parents who are never satisfied with their children's achievements, such persons destroy rather than build up. Spiritual pornography takes many forms, but its saddest results are the incapacity to appreciate small gifts and the tendency to trample fragile expressions of beauty and goodness.

Hundreds of years ago, Thomas à Kempis worried about our tendency to overlook the small gifts on the way to wanting more, and urged those who longed to grow in Christ-likeness, "Be thankful for the smallest blessing, and you will deserve to receive greater. Value the least gifts no less than the greatest, and simple graces as especial favors. If you remember the dignity of the Giver, no gift will seem small or mean, for nothing can be valueless that is given by the most high God."[11]

The Route to a Beautiful Land

When our lives are shaped by gratitude, we're more likely to notice the goodness and beauty in everyday things. We are content; we feel blessed and are eager to confer blessing. We are able to delight in the very existence of another human being. In a grateful community, individuals and their contributions are acknowledged and honored, and there is regular testimony to God's faithfulness, through which the community experiences the joys of its members. Expressions of gratitude help make the community alive to the Word, the Spirit, and God's work.

Such a community is "a beautiful land" whose culture is grace and whose inhabitants see life as a gift.[12] In this land, we often find abundant forgiveness and frequent celebrations. While we might assume that individuals and communities grow toward holiness and goodness primarily through the hard work of discipline, correction, and challenge, we tend to underestimate the importance of grace. The emphasis on loving God and loving neighbor — our usual foci for discipleship — is most fruitful as it is rooted in a deep understanding of God's prior love for us.[13]

In the story of the Antioch community, as told by one of its founders, we can see how a small Christian community struggled with these very tensions. Chris Rice describes the challenges they faced in trying to live out racial reconciliation in the context of an intentional Christian community in Mississippi. During a time of crisis in their community, a friend from the outside explained to them, "The way you grow into God's love isn't by making demands of each other. . . . You do it by giving each other grace." Grace expressed as love "when it didn't seem fair, or reasonable," and "when others were being complete jerks."[14]

Their wise advisor continued,

> The truth is, we can't stand the idea of not fixing each other. But insofar as we can fix people at all, we can do it only by forgiving them, and

giving them grace, and leaving them to our loving Father. Grace assumes sin. When we ask you to accept each other, we aren't asking you to ignore hurts between you. People of grace speak the truth. But in an atmosphere of grace, truth seems less offensive and more important. It's no big deal to tell each other how you're sinning. If you talk about people's failures as matter-of-factly as you talk about the weather, they'll hear your love and not your judgment.[15]

Chris describes the community's delight when it was introduced to the recipe for a "new culture of grace." The ingredients for life in community were surprisingly simple: "It is enough to get the love of God into your bones and to live as if you are forgiven. It is enough to care for each other, to forgive each other, and to wash the dishes."[16]

When we more fully understand the grace we've received, we are able to turn outward in gratitude and generosity. Gratitude becomes "our home in the presence of God,"[17] or, in Henri Nouwen's words, an "intimate participation in the Divine Life itself" that "reaches out far beyond our own self to God, to all of creation, to the people who gave us life, love, and care."[18]

The Heart of Worship: Gratitude in Community

In the book of Psalms, worshipers are frequently invited to enter God's presence with praise and thanksgiving.[19] Remembering God's goodness and acts on behalf of the community was at the center of Hebrew worship. First Chronicles 16 offers a vibrant picture of the various dimensions of the practice of gratitude within worship: speaking of God's deeds among the people, and remembering and telling of God's blessing, wonderful works, and faithfulness.[20]

When, as a community, we remember Jesus' gift to us in bringing salvation, we are also drawn into the heart of worship. Costly sacrifice and gratitude are profoundly intertwined at the Last Supper, when "Jesus offered thanks over the bread and wine before passing it among his disciples, of whom one had betrayed him, one would deny him, and all would desert him. Still he offered thanks, saying grace by offering up both words and his very life. Jesus graced the dreadful evening of his betrayal with gratitude."[21] As the church enacts the Eucharist or "Great Thanksgiving" regularly, our small expressions of gratitude are joined with Jesus' gift of himself; together they form a life-giving liturgical expression of thanksgiving and hope.

In Paul's second letter to the Corinthian church, we can see how a cycle of grace, gratitude, and gift strengthens community and brings glory and thanks to God. Their experience of God's grace led the Corinthians to respond with gratitude, expressed by giving financial gifts to the church at Jerusalem. That, in turn, led to the Jerusalem church's response of gratitude to God for the Christians in Corinth, and the cycle of gratitude and grace strengthened all of them in their ties to God and to one another (2 Cor. 8–9).[22]

As the early Christians were learning what it meant to be a new and transformed community, Paul frequently urged them to give thanks or to be thankful. For Paul, God was always the "ultimate object of thanksgiving," but he also gave "thanks for the 'work' and 'labor' of the believers (1 Thess. 1:3) and their faithful 'partnership in the gospel' (Phil. 1:5)."[23]

Quite often, Paul's encouragement toward gratitude was part of his instructions on how to live out an identity as God's beloved and holy people, and on how to live well in community (Col. 3:15; Eph. 5:3-4, 20; 1 Thess. 5:18).[24] In Romans 12, Paul explained that the fitting response to the mercies of God is to offer one's entire self to God in gratitude and to live in community with humility, love, and generosity. In this way Paul closely linked gratitude with conduct.[25]

Similarly, in the letter to the Hebrews, the writer encouraged persecuted believers to remain faithful by remembering with gratitude the costly gift given to them in Jesus' death and by strengthening their community through love and hospitality (chapters 12–13). Fully appreciating Jesus' sacrifice should result in a willingness to bear reproach for his sake, a desire to offer a continual sacrifice of praise to God, and generous care for others. Gratitude to God and efforts to build and sustain community are closely connected in this letter. While we cannot repay God for the grace we have received, we can extend God's generosity to one another in acts of assistance and service.[26]

Becoming Gratitude Itself

The connection between gratitude to God and love for others is clear in several of John Wesley's sermons when he states that "steady good will to our fellow-creatures never flowed from any fountain but gratitude to our

Creator." "True religion," the eighteenth-century reformer explains, is a combination of "gratitude and benevolence; gratitude to our Creator and supreme Benefactor, and benevolence to our fellow-creatures." Our thankfulness to God is shown in the care we give to one another and to our enemies.[27]

Many other theologians and church leaders have also recognized the importance of gratitude to Christian identity and relationships. Of all God's earthly creatures, only humans are able to return thanks to God, argued John Calvin, who came close to equating the *imago dei* (image of God) with the act of gratitude. For him, "the whole created order has its meaning and purpose in the praise" offered to God by human beings. Calvin concluded that grateful acknowledgment of God's gifts equal piety and godliness.[28]

With a similar appreciation for gratitude, Karl Barth wrote several centuries later that God's work in our lives makes each of us a new creature and that this new creature "is grateful. It knows God, and itself becomes a new creature, by being thankful. To believe in Jesus Christ means to become thankful." For those of us transformed by grace, gratitude is not merely an act or an attitude; it is our identity.[29]

While our gratitude can be directed toward God primarily for the benefits we have received, it can also be a response to God's excellence and the "glory and beauty of God's nature."[30] Jonathan Edwards's eighteenth-century work on religious affections reminds us that gratitude is not only about gifts, but also about the Giver. In his study of Edwards's thought, Henry Knight clarifies the relationship between gratitude and praise by noting, "If gratitude is thankfulness to God for benefits received, praise could be defined as the acknowledgment of the excellency of God's attributes, and most especially God's holiness."[31] Holy gratitude includes "'thankfulness to God for his kindness to us'" arising first of all "'from love to God for what he is in himself.'"[32]

Many philosophers have also recognized the moral importance of gratitude, though their emphasis is on responding to gifts or benefits provided by another human being. The ancient philosopher Cicero viewed gratitude "not only as the greatest of virtues but as the parent of all others" — giving birth to the rest.[33] Adam Smith, a contemporary of John Wesley, viewed gratitude as a primary motivation for human benevolence and thus as an important aspect of social life and stability.[34] More recently, other philosophers have argued that gratitude is among humankind's most basic duties.[35]

25

Gratitude in the Hard Times

Practices of gratitude can be distorted when we imagine that Christians are always supposed to be smiling and cheerful, even in the face of suffering, tragedy, or grave injustice. To live gratefully is not the same as denying the misery or evil around us. Misunderstandings of the importance of gratitude can turn it into a spiritual bludgeon used to smash the heartache or grief out of people.

Gratitude involves knowing that we are held secure by a loving God, and that the God we worship is trustworthy, despite the nearly unbearable sorrow we might encounter along the way (Ps. 13). A capacity to be thankful in the midst of hard times requires acknowledging that we do not know the whole story, that we are living before it is complete, and that we are thankful for the presence of God and faithful persons in our lives. Gratitude is a crucial way in which death and destruction do not have the final word, and cannot finally define us.[36]

Gratitude is most striking when it is lived out in difficult circumstances. For many centuries, people have observed that "Christians die well." When this is the case, surely it has to do with a combination of confidence in eternal life and the fact that dying persons are surrounded by a loving and faithful community that accompanies them in their last days. One pastor in the project told of a parishioner who was dying of cancer and described several of the women in the congregation as spiritual midwives. They were fully present and helpful as the woman moved toward death and birth into her new life. The congregation and she were knit together in prayer, gratitude, and fidelity.

Another friend described how gratitude helped to "pilot his soul through a narrow channel" when the "storm of grief" threatened to overwhelm him. As he grieved the loss of his father, he also experienced deep thankfulness for the years they had shared. "The practice of thanking God for the blessings surrounding my dad's life and death has shaped my grief process," he observed. "I don't really know how people are supposed to grieve, or what 'healthy' is for this process, but I sense that I have been guided through a somewhat healthy process by the Spirit's voice reminding me of the practice of gratitude."

Whatever grieving well or "dying well" might look like, these accounts give clues to it: a capacity to remember the gifts that we have received, to trust in God's future, and to turn to a community for the strength we may not feel.[37]

Our capacity for gratitude is not connected with an abundance of re-sources but rather with a capacity to notice what it is that we do have. This is expressed powerfully in the traditional African-American prayer of grat-itude that the Lord "woke me up this morning clothed in my right mind. He didn't have to do it, but he did."

Gratitude: Out of Step with Contemporary Culture

Despite the emphasis on gratitude in the biblical texts, Christian tradition, and other great traditions, today it is often countercultural to take the pos-ture of a grateful recipient. Some of us operate with a well-developed sense of entitlement, quite certain that we deserve good things and are entitled to the best that "life" has to offer. Others of us, because we work hard, are convinced that we have earned the good that has come to us. Gratitude seems quite irrelevant.

The Strange Problem of Entitlement

Years ago, Paul Tournier observed that "no gift can bring joy to the one who has a right to everything."[38] While there is a healthy interpretation of entitlement that is tied to a sense of dignity and equality, when it is exag-gerated, it brings continual dissatisfaction and an inability to be thankful for anything.[39]

Parents of teens going through a difficult stage know how hard it can be to live with someone who has an overblown sense of entitlement. When teenagers see themselves as the center of the universe and are convinced that the world, its inhabitants, and their families owe them some kind of debt, sharing life with them can be quite unpleasant. This sense that every-body "owes me" is often accompanied by a decided absence of personal re-sponsibility. This is usually a brief phase, but there is a less intense version that persists among some adults, including Christians.[40]

Because many of us live in relatively secure environments where we can assume that there will be adequate opportunities for good work and personal fulfillment, we have come to imagine that we are entitled to this security. This differs from the experiences of many people in the world, and from prior generations, who recognized that setbacks, loss, and risks were part of life.[41] When difficulties are encountered in the midst of unrealistic expectations, frustration and complaint become common.[42]

If we think that we deserve the gifts and blessings we have received, it is easy for us to become greedy for more benefits and to overlook the needs of others. We cultivate a capacity not to notice when "our benefit has come at someone else's expense."[43] Dissatisfaction as a way of life is encouraged by a consumerist culture that feeds notions of entitlement. We want more, and we want better — better bodies, newer cars, bigger churches, more beautiful homes, finer coffee. Somehow wanting these things morphs into the sense that, really, we deserve them. A cycle of generalized dissatisfaction fuels envy, striving, and buying.[44]

Time spent outside our culture can help us see more clearly how certain assumptions have shaped us. At the end of a book describing his experience of living among poor people in South America, Henri Nouwen writes,

> What I claim as a right, my friends . . . received as a gift; what is obvious to me was a joyful surprise to them; what I take for granted, they celebrate in thanksgiving; what for me goes by unnoticed became for them a new occasion to say thanks.
>
> And slowly I learned. I learned what I must have forgotten somewhere in my busy, well-planned, and very "useful" life. I learned that everything that is, is freely given by the God of love. All is grace. Light and water, shelter and food, work and free time, children, parents and grandparents, birth and death — it is all given to us. Why? So that we can say *gracias,* thanks: thanks to God, thanks to each other, thanks to all and everyone.[45]

Self-Made and Not Indebted

Gratitude seems awkward in our culture for additional reasons. Contemporary understandings of self-fulfillment are often closely tied to individual achievement. They are not usually associated with community or grace, and for a long time, we have imagined that we are most fully human or successful when we are self-sufficient.

Gratitude is an uncomfortable reminder that we need other people and that our lives are dependent on their gifts and generosity.[46] Furthermore, the cultural emphasis on independence makes us wary about being indebted to a particular person. The cultural script that "we have made it on our own" remains powerful.

Grateful for On-Time Departures?

Gratitude fits a covenantal understanding of relationships; thankfulness is often the fruit of fidelity and a response to the love we have experienced. But much of contemporary life is structured around contractual arrangements in which each party knows what to expect and to what it is entitled. Gratitude is not our first response in situations where a person or company has delivered its side of the arrangement after we have paid our money or done our part. Satisfaction on both sides — not gratitude — is the goal of contracts.

But if grace and gratitude are a way of life for followers of Jesus, how should we respond in contractual settings or in our everyday business interactions? Think about experiences of air travel today. Perhaps because of prior difficulties, we have a momentary surge of gratitude when the plane leaves on time. But in other cases, when we've bought our tickets, arrived at the gate on time, and been responsible with our luggage — and the weather is good — how do we respond when the flight still doesn't take off? Especially when employees appear incompetent or uncooperative, or are caught in an unworkable system, our frustration levels peak. How often do we let anger take over and act as if this arena of our lives is somehow exempt from grace?

We do not stop being Christians in contractual relations. Our sense of rights and entitlement may be appropriate to our role as consumers, but the other parties do not stop being human beings. Some Christians respond very badly when contractual relations break down, as if their attitudes or behavior can be justified because they are dissatisfied. A posture of grace in the midst of trouble does not mean we are feeling grateful for the inconvenience or that we trust the airline, but it does say that we trust God in all of the circumstances of our lives.

Too Busy to Say Thanks

Gratitude and wonder are squeezed out when our lives are packed full with busyness and responsibilities. There is simply no room, no time to notice.

We experience God's gifts when we pause long enough to notice them, suggesting important but overlooked connections between Sabbath and gratitude.

Our busyness is often tied to working very hard so that what we have or receive does not seem like a gift. Our desire for "more" feeds our busyness, whether in work environments or in our efforts to hold on to a last bit of vacation. Schedules have no space to accommodate things going wrong, and we are unable to receive any gift that might come in the form of an interruption.

Our emphasis on accomplishments and efficiency makes us wary about pausing to give attention to the gifts we easily take for granted. Finding time to be thankful to God and others often seems like a nice extra rather than a vital component of our lives. But it is when we break from our regular routines and quiet the noise and activity of everyday life that we are able to make space for gratitude, and in those moments we are often surprised by the renewal and strength we find.

Despite the cultural challenges we face today, a posture of gratitude remains a beautiful witness to the transforming power of God's grace. However, in making gratitude a more central practice in our lives and congregations, we will need to consider some of the ways in which our commitment to gratitude and our responses to gifts can become very complicated. We will explore some of this complexity in the next chapter.

CHAPTER THREE

Complications in Gratitude

Give thanks in all circumstances; for this is the will of God in
Christ Jesus for you.

1 Thessalonians 5:18

While I was teaching an intensive course recently, two students in the class invited me out to dinner. Because they were from out of state, they both were staying in a nearby hotel and eating out every night during the week-long course. They wanted to show their appreciation for the class by treating me to a "really nice" meal. The invitation caught me off guard. I had no doubt that the gift was well-intentioned, but, among other things, I had not yet done any of the grading for the class. Although I think that sharing meals with students is both central to community-building and to learning ethics, this was a little different. I declined, and they were surprised. I explained some of my concerns.

Not accepting a gift can be awkward, but sometimes we find it necessary. Gifts and gratitude are connected, but some gifts make us more wary than grateful. In personal life, community, and ministry, we don't respond to every gift, situation, or giver in the same way.

The potential for difficulty comes at various points, and not all of the complexity is related to receiving gifts. When we give a gift, we voluntarily "give it away," yet we are often hurt when that gift is misused or carelessly discarded. The relational dimensions of gifts and gratitude can be surprisingly complicated.

What makes something a gift? In our general understandings, first of all, it is unearned. The person receiving it has no claim on it or right to it, and is not expected to pay for it in the future. A gift has some kind of value and is intentionally given to be a benefit to the recipient.[1]

We generally expect a recipient of a gift to respond with gratitude, and the intensity of the gratitude is often, though not always, tied to the value or cost of the gift, as well as to the pre-existing obligations between the persons involved.[2] When we are grateful, we usually find some way to acknowledge the gift without "paying it back."[3] Often, a moral relationship is formed between the one who gives and the one who receives that involves grateful behavior towards the donor and "grateful use of the gift."[4] In addition to our thankfulness for gifts and for how we have been blessed or benefited, we are often also grateful for the overall goodness of the donor.[5]

Obligated to Say Thank You?

Today, we tend to view obligatory responses as somewhat coerced. If we *should* or *must* be grateful or express gratitude, it somehow feels less genuine or spontaneous. In theory, anyway, we do not emphasize reciprocity in gift relations. In addition, as noted earlier, we dislike feeling indebted to any particular person. To be grateful is to put ourselves in the position of a recipient — gratitude reminds us that we are dependent on others.[6]

Some cultures have traditions of gratitude and gift-giving that strongly emphasize obligation. In the ancient Greco-Roman world, a person who received a gift also received "the obligation to show gratitude." In fact, the recipient was expected immediately to "'turn his or her thought to repaying.' Gift and obligation to respond [were] experienced together. Reciprocity was a core value of these societies. . . . Showing gratitude was considered a sacred obligation."[7] Giving and receiving gifts or benefits was a central way that relationships were established and strengthened.

When we are overwhelmed by the goodness or generosity of God or another human being, however, we don't usually feel "constrained or obligated to feel gratitude." We're simply grateful.[8] Focusing on obligation or debt does not adequately capture our deepest experiences of gratitude. The experience of grace reminds us that in some cases, we can't possibly try to keep the "accounts" even. There are some gifts we can never repay; at best we can only imitate them.

How do you thank a friend who is faithfully present during a long recovery after brain surgery? What kind of thanks is appropriate for a person who comes every night at two A.M. for several hours to relieve family members and to be a tender companion to one walking through a dark valley? Lydia, the recipient of this kindness, described her friend as one who was "willing to love me in my pain and suffering," whose "sacrifice became nourishment for my soul." She wrote later, "I can never repay [her] for her gift to me in the wee hours of the night. But I can live my life in such a way that I try to replicate that kind of beautiful relationship."

Communities and organizations are strengthened and sustained by the complex mutuality of helping. When a group of people gives something to an individual, it is not necessarily the case that the individual can give something back to each person in the group. He or she can, however, thank them and contribute to subsequent group endeavors, thus strengthening the community and the bonds within it.[9]

Not Expecting Thanks from Others

In community and congregational life, offering our gifts and receiving acknowledgment for them can be like a complicated group dance. We know that folks are not supposed to expect or demand a grateful response for what they have done. When they do, we conclude that they didn't give a gift; they made a loan or entered into some kind of exchange.[10] But the moral and social dynamics are actually more complicated because "good" recipients are grateful, and they do find ways to express their thanks.

In response to the grace we have experienced, we often offer our gifts — even ourselves — without expecting or needing a response of gratitude. But over the long term, it is difficult to give graciously and happily to those who do not respond to our gifts and sacrifices with any evidence of appreciation. While we must be careful about allowing the gratitude of others to motivate our ministry, the offering of thanks is an expression of respect for a relationship. Generous folks struggle when their efforts are consistently taken for granted.

Volunteers become discouraged and feel unappreciated when other church members never take their turn at fixing a common meal or cleaning up afterwards, or when some folks always take more than their share of food. The notion of a common meal begins to unravel when most of the participants see it only as a place to grab lunch. One woman who prepared a meal regularly for her community and for homeless friends wondered aloud, "Should I expect our guests to feel grateful? Should I expect them to value the relationships beyond the free meal?"

To love and persevere in situations where the people we serve are unresponsive or ungrateful requires that we understand our work as offered first to God. "God's affirmation of our belovedness," as Keith Wasserman regularly explains, "needs to be sufficient." Keith, a participant in the project, leads a community in ministry with people who are homeless. Their work does not expect or demand gratitude, but he is careful to give residents and recipients opportunities to express thankfulness. As a leader, he also provides ways for staff and volunteers to receive thanks and acknowledgment, especially when that recognition does not come from recipients.

Even when we think we have worked these issues out, our expectations regarding gratitude can sometimes catch us by surprise. As one church staff member commented, "I love to help people implement their visions. When I begin the process, I am not thinking about being thanked or appreciated. At the end, I am not even good at receiving appreciation. But if gratitude is not eventually offered, stand back. So really, what is my motivation?"

Shared Projects and Offering Thanks

While it is not necessarily difficult to express gratitude for a benefit or gift one has received personally, it is not always clear how to say thanks for individual contributions to a shared project. Even when we are the leaders or conveners of a project, giving thanks to volunteers for their contributions can at times feel presumptuous. The volunteers have not necessarily served or benefited us. To say "thank you" seems to claim a certain authority over the gift, and yet it is important to celebrate or recognize contributions in some way. Perhaps this is what Paul is doing when he thanks God upon every remembrance of Christians — sometimes for their personal help, but also in recognizing their fidelity to a shared project. He does it in a way that they "overhear" his gratitude.[11]

The Calvinist tradition addresses some of these tensions in a helpful way. In his book on gratitude, B. A. Gerrish explains, "Finally, even the good deeds of one person to another are occasions of gratitude to God, since many of God's benefits reach us only through the network of social relations." Working with the section on prayer in the Geneva Catechism, Gerrish writes,

> We are to invoke God alone in every need, and yet this does not exclude our requesting the help of others. For it is God who has conferred on them their ability to help and has appointed them "ministers" of his beneficence. Whatever benefit we receive from others we should regard as coming from God, who alone bestows every benefit through their "ministry." Then comes the interesting question (Q. 237): "But should we not be grateful to other people when they perform some service for us?" Answer: "Of course we should, precisely because God honors them by channeling through their hands the good things that flow to us from the inexhaustible fountain of his generosity. In this way he puts us in their debt, and he wants us to acknowledge it. Anyone, therefore, who does not show gratitude to other people betrays ingratitude to God as well."[12]

This is an important insight, especially for persons who, from a hyper-spiritual mind-set, argue that only gratitude to God is important, and who imagine that it is spiritual to ignore the significance of offering thanks to others.

Offering thanks and recognizing individual contributions or sacrifices within community can also be awkward because someone might be overlooked. This is especially the case with quiet, undramatic, or long-term contributions. The risks are reduced when we become more attentive to how community work gets done and when we create a culture of gratitude. Nevertheless, how we recognize exceptional individual contributions — when everyone has given something — can be tricky. It becomes especially complex when working with staff and volunteers in church, mission, or ministry.

Community visions are implemented by individuals, and the work is often unevenly distributed. While we might properly want to celebrate the communal dimension of a project, collective congratulations or thanks can discount the extra effort given by an individual who has gone far beyond her or his usual duties or responsibilities. Urging people not to care who "gets the credit" may work as a form of spiritual discipline at the personal level, but it is problematic for truthful assessment of how work is getting done in a community.

One woman, known in the church for a capacity to accomplish amazing amounts of work, explained, "I have always felt that if it was worth God's doing a miracle to make something happen, then extra work and extra enthusiasm on my part embody my gratefulness for God's willingness to include me in the project." But she also shared her struggle when, after great effort on her part to complete a project, the congregation's leaders responded with "We did it!" and immediately went on to the next item on the agenda of the meeting.

Individuals who are able and willing to see what needs to be done in a community, who pick up the pieces and fill in the gaps, often work very hard because their efforts are crucial to the vision to which they are committed. The sacrificial work of these staff members or volunteers is sometimes taken for granted by the community — people come to assume that these individuals are good at "those things" and that somehow they have more expendable time to contribute. Saddest of all is when congregations imagine that the person's time is less valuable because he or she gives it away freely.

People who can handle interruptions, surprises, and glitches well are a blessing to their community. They willingly put their own work aside to help with emergencies or unexpected developments. While a community can become dependent on the person's problem-solving skills and generosity, sometimes it also concludes that the person is unaffected by the additional work or is unfocused or lacking in direction because he or she responds well to interruptions.

At times this is gendered; for a number of reasons, women can find themselves being "organizational wives"[13] attending to mountains of details, and doing large amounts of administrative housekeeping. While this work is crucial to organizations, it is often thankless and invisible. Because of their important behind-the-scenes work, sometimes these individuals are overlooked for — or excluded from — more public teaching or leadership roles, despite their gifts in those areas.

Gratitude and Justice

For those involved in struggles for justice and human rights, any talk of gratitude can raise concerns about insensitivity to injustice, blindness to people's needs or suffering, or complicity in social arrangements that benefit oneself but hurt others. Gratitude and a commitment to justice, however, are often inappropriately juxtaposed.

Joyce Hollyday explains that we're afraid we'll be accused of being naïve or out of touch with reality if we're thankful. "It's the old 'How can we praise God for this beautiful day when there was an earthquake in El Salvador yesterday?' syndrome. We feel that if we're committed to justice, if we're committed to seeing an end to suffering, then we must be very serious about it. And heaven help us if we thank God for something as trivial as a nice day!"[14]

She contrasts this awkwardness with the attitudes she found among many of the people with whom she worked. "People of faith who have very little materially often have lives profoundly marked by an attitude of praise. 'Thank you, Lord, that I have seen another day' is a very common prayer in our neighborhood. There is a deep and heartfelt gratitude simply to be alive."[15]

In situations of misery and exploitation, gratitude is not a substitute for pursuing justice. A posture of thankfulness and gratitude roots persons in love and trust, and enables them to remember that the difficulties and injustices of the present time do not have the final word. Gratefulness to God and gratitude for life can strengthen persons for the long journey toward wholeness and justice.

But injustice and ingratitude intersect in many different ways, and one of the most discouraging can occur in efforts to re-establish community through forgiveness. Out of a commitment to reconciliation and to restoring relationships, sometimes persons or communities are very gracious toward previous wrongdoers. However, if the "forgiven" do not fully value the generosity they've been shown, those who have sacrificed their rightful claims to justice can find themselves betrayed once again.[16] Respect and mutuality are extremely important in these relationships.

Even when personal or congregational circumstances are comfortable, there are ways we can resist becoming blind to the needs and injustices around us. Our gratitude and thanks for the blessings we've experienced can be turned outward in love and service. We can respond with humility to the grace we have received by becoming a channel of God's justice and mercy in the world.

Gifts We Don't Want or Aren't Sure How to Use

Not every gift is "just what we always wanted." Some gifts are troublesome. They can derail a worthy project or undermine the ethos of a community.

Acceptance or rejection of gifts requires discernment on the part of leaders and communities. A designated gift can reshape a particular ministry and require allocations of time and resources that don't fit the community's capacity or purposes.

The director of an after-school program struggled with how to respond to a significant designated gift. The youth center had been established to strengthen students' academic competence, but it had run into serious problems with disciplining the participants. The finances were very tight, and the youth were barely under control. The gift was a trip to Disney Land for everyone in the program. It wasn't exactly what they needed at the moment. *Was it a distraction from ministry or an unexpected opportunity?* the staff wondered. What would it mean to turn down such a gift? Could staff members help one another find ways to appreciate it and fit it into the overall goals for the group?

Sometimes leaders are uncomfortable with a contribution or a gift not because of its threat to the well-being or purposes of the community, but because of its potential impact on their own status or authority. We're not sure that we want certain kinds of help — especially if the person offering it is very gifted or popular. We're afraid of being "shown up" and dismiss or overlook the gift rather than deal with our own fears and insecurities. Potential givers can be deeply hurt if their intentions are good and their commitment to the community has already been proven.

There's a lot at stake in graciously receiving what is offered by another person. Henri Nouwen observed that each of us comes "to recognize our own gifts in the eyes of those who receive them gratefully." "Only those who truly believe that they have something to offer can experience themselves as spiritually adult."[17] Even though we might not be able to accept every gift, we do need to recognize how important it is to value the gifts that are offered and, in particular, the persons who offer them.

But gifts can also reveal misalignments in relationships. A particular gift can cause us to ask, "Does he or she know us at all?" A puzzled or even angry response to certain "gifts" is not necessarily an expression of ingratitude. Gift giving and receiving can be quite revelatory, and sometimes the gifts we give speak volumes about how we perceive a recipient, even when those attitudes are quite subtle.

For example, almost every thrift-store volunteer and relief organization has struggled with receiving donations of torn and dirty clothing and broken toys. What do such "gifts" say about how the giver perceives those who shop in thrift stores or those who need relief? What is the donor assuming about the folks who sort the items and make them available? Such gifts are both an imposition and an offense, but there are rarely easy ways to address the problem. The inconvenience and insult are often simply absorbed by the volunteers.

Every Gift Has Strings

We like to imagine that the best gifts have no strings attached, but gift giving and receiving are closely connected to the deepening of relationships. The notion that gifts have no strings recognizes that gifts are different from business relationships, commercial transactions, and wages, but it also raises questions:

> If there are no strings attached to gifts, why have so many of us wanted to decline gifts from persons with whom we wished to have no further relations? Was it not precisely because we perceived that, in accepting the gift, we were consenting to such relations in a morally significant way? And if there are no obligations attached to gifts and their acceptance, why is ingratitude so universally and so vehemently condemned as a moral failure or defect?

Paul Camenisch continues, "Perhaps gift lacks the rough ropes of contract, but closer inspection will discover there the fine filaments of moral relations."[18]

When we accept a gift, we are connected to the giver in another way: "The recipient cannot strip [the gift] of its connection with the donor's will and intention, with the donor's reason(s) for giving it."[19] Nevertheless, we are particularly grateful for donors who trust us with their gifts — confident that we will use them well and appropriately. Often because they know and love us or our work, they do not want strict accounting of the gift's use, or they assume that we know better than they how it should be used.

One way that we attempt to cut the strings attached to gifts is by a "too conscientious" effort to provide repayment. To reduce the "moral relation represented by the gift,"[20] we immediately offer an equally or more valuable gift in return. This moves the relationship to a form of exchange which diminishes ongoing connection rather than forges it. Another way we try to break the connection is by accepting the gift but being unwilling to acknowledge the donor. Centuries ago, Seneca wisely warned that "one should never accept a gift if one would be ashamed to acknowledge the debt publicly (*Ben* 2.23.1); a gift should be accepted only if the recipient is willing to 'invite the whole city to witness it.'"[21]

The strings attached to gifts can be severed unwittingly in community. We show our gratitude when we honor what another person has worked on by treating it with care and respect. When someone volunteers time to maintain a church lawn or kitchen and then finds other church members carelessly tearing up the lawn or leaving the kitchen in a mess, the gift has been — sometimes inadvertently — dismissed. The person feels disrespected and unappreciated, even if there are verbal thanks at another time. In the busyness of community life, it is easy to overlook such incidents, but they quickly lead to discouraged volunteers and frustrated staff. In these cases, it is not enough to say thank you — the gift is honored by how the community treats it.

Sometimes a person attempts to use his or her gifts to control a community or its decision-making. In other cases, a volunteer or staff member can shut out the contributions of others by subtly assessing their work as never "good enough." The strings attached to gifts can strangle relationships, but in community, they can also be used to dis-empower others.

Gifts That Come to Us in Broken People

Congregations and leaders struggle with how to respond to contributions from those who are both gifted and troubled. One experienced leader observed that God "sends us help in the form of people who need at least as much help as they can give." Their neediness makes their assistance complicated, and it is not always clear how to respond to a particular combination of gift, good intentions, and personal brokenness.

A pastor recounted an incident involving Jim, a volunteer in a youth program, who was wonderful with kids, a creative and patient teacher, and an enthusiastic participant in church activities. "But Jim also comes with his baggage. He lives from crisis to crisis. He is . . . not dependable. . . . He plays the victim — acting like he often gets dishonored and deserves better than he gets. While he often expresses gratitude for the generosity of the church towards him, he can also act in a very discontented and ungrateful way. When things don't go his way, he can be so persistent about getting people to change their minds that he wearies folks and drives them away."

After a particularly difficult episode, a number of the leaders were ready to ask Jim to leave. But one of the lay leaders in the congregation encouraged the others to treat Jim himself as a gift and a human being and not simply as a problem to be solved in the most expedient manner. "Gratitude for who Jim is and what he has accomplished was brought to the attention of the others. . . . Thankfulness put us in a disposition to make wise decisions." The pastor reflected further on this experience: "Gratitude is rarely unalloyed when directed towards people. And we have a choice as to whether we will let gratitude for the person who is a gift be the predominant factor in our relationship with them or our annoyance with their flaws and sin."

Reflections on how other practices intersected with gratitude and ingratitude helped this congregation work through their concerns. As part of a promise-keeping community, the congregation and leaders chose to keep faith with Jim by refusing to let his brokenness lead them to break their "promise to care for him as a person made in God's image." Their fidelity also involved "speaking truth in love to him" — recognizing that they did him "no favors by treating him harshly or by simply leaving him in his sin."

As a community that lived truthfully, they were attentive to Jim's strengths along with their own failings. Valuing Jim even more than they valued his contributions, the congregation stood by him as he struggled with his particular combination of ingratitude and entitlement. It often kept them off balance, but they remained faithful. They were able to embrace Jim as a whole person, not just his gifts or his brokenness.

A combination of fidelity, truthfulness, gratitude, and hospitality made it possible for the community to hold on to Jim and his ministry and to help him move toward healing. But to do this, leaders had to be willing to absorb some of the brokenness and ingratitude without allowing that brokenness to become abusive. This is especially important to address if ingratitude or discontent is directed at other workers, volunteers, or fragile congregation members. Along with fidelity and truthfulness, communal discernment is crucial.

Sometimes a person's offer of her or his gifts is accompanied by such brokenness or so many unresolved issues that it puts the church at risk. For example, when a person's character flaws run very deep but his or her musical gifts are outstanding, opening a leadership role to him or her in worship is often a recipe for disaster. The pressures, opportunities, and power of public ministry can put a person in a position of being a spiritual example or model before they are ready. This is not good for the person or the congregation. The immature or troubled leader's missteps are often subjected to close scrutiny and broad public conversation. In the absence of good mentoring and discipleship, personal moral failings can leave the individual vulnerable while also confusing or misleading congregation members.

In other cases, leaders struggle to discern what stands behind a person's willingness to help, especially when it involves significant personal sacrifice. A pastor in the project spoke with gratitude about a woman in his congregation who serves regularly and quietly. She happily responds to his thanks by saying, "Don't thank me. I'm just doing this so I won't go crazy." Outside of church, her life is a mixture of difficulties and unending responsibilities. She has found "refuge and encouragement" in their community of faith, and her contributions are a response of gratitude. She seems satisfied with an occasional "thank you" from the pastor. And yet he worries that he might be taking advantage of her willingness to serve or contributing to her spiritual baggage if she is driven to this volunteering by shame or guilt. Must every motive for giving be clear before we feel free to accept a person's gifts?

Attending to the personal development of volunteers is a way that leaders can express their gratitude; otherwise, expressions of gratitude can be a way of getting more and more out of a person or benefiting from good work without addressing some important needs. All of us come to ministry with our baggage, but we are helped toward wholeness when leaders and community members are willing to engage us truthfully, respectfully, and faithfully.

Gratitude and Remembering Rightly

"You have lived a graced life." It was an odd thing to say to someone who had grown up in an alcoholic home and who continued to live with some of the scars. But hearing his overall life described as "graced" re-oriented this individual's tendency to see only the "God moments" in it.

Practicing gratitude helps us to interpret our pasts differently. A community can help individuals live into the grace that has been present in their lives, even when those individuals have not noticed it. Similarly, a person (often an outsider) can help a community see the grace that has been present but overlooked in its shared life. Gratitude can reframe the truth of our own histories and enable us to tell the stories of our lives with a different understanding of how the pieces fit together. Gratitude helps us see rightly not only the goodness and activity of God, but also the character and actions of others as well as our own.

Having been called on to serve as an interim pastor in three troubled churches within a four-year period, one leader in the project still spoke readily of the "shining moments and memorable occasions" within each congregation and proclaimed that "God is good." Concluding that the long-term outcomes did not look promising, he nevertheless recognized that the practice of gratitude had helped him "to reframe these years in light of God's awesome grace and purpose for calling me in this season of ministry." Through gratitude, truthfulness, and fidelity, he was able to identify the fruit of ministry, even in very difficult circumstances.

When we faithfully remember and recite God's acts of love and care, we corporately re-live the experiences that have shaped our histories and identities.[22] By remembering gratefully — whether special moments or overall trajectories — we see more clearly the ways in which we've been blessed. In this sense, gratitude is often a backward-looking practice — but it also shapes the future in that it allows us to build on the past in hope and confidence.

In Scripture, remembering falsely or forgetting entirely is often associated with an absence of gratitude. One of the saddest judgments passed on people in Scripture is that they didn't remember God's steadfast love.[23] There are many ways in which we continue to struggle with ingratitude, so it is important for us to discuss the various deformations of gratitude in the next chapter.

CHAPTER FOUR

Going Deeper: Exploring What Weakens and What Strengthens Gratitude

To believe in Jesus Christ means to become thankful.

Karl Barth, *Church Dogmatics*

Exploring Deformations of Gratitude

"Of all crimes that human creatures are capable, the most horrid and un-natural is ingratitude," claimed the philosopher David Hume. Immanuel Kant described ingratitude as "detestable," the essence of wickedness.[1] Linked in Scripture to the sins of idolatry, infidelity, and pride, ingratitude is also associated with spurning God's goodness. Whether it takes the form of envy, entitlement,[2] presumption, or grumbling, ingratitude has a destructive impact on individuals, families, congregations, and communities. In fact, the absence of gratitude is an important prompt for practicing discernment. Chronic ingratitude should cause us to ask, *What's going on? What's wrong here?*

Envy: A "Small Town" Sin

In his book *Grace Matters,* Chris Rice offers a painfully truthful description of the power of envy to undermine love and community. He recognizes its very close connection to the tendency to compare ourselves to others:

44

I already knew how much living in community intensified comparisons between people, because I was prone to it myself. No matter who you were, there were endless ways to see yourself on the losing end, constantly reminded that someone else got their way more often, had a nicer cat, had a child who was more advanced or got more attention, got listened to for their opinions more, or had found a marriage partner while you were single. Unfairness stared you right in the face every day around the dinner table. Living so intensely together, comparison could be dangerously and divisively habit-forming.[3]

In Scripture, envy is often listed with other sins that "destroy fellowship."[4] Because it almost always involves comparisons, envy flourishes in close-knit communities.[5] The nineteenth-century philosopher Søren Kierkegaard described it as a "small town" sin because we are usually envious of people who live near us and are like us in age, class, occupation, or of the same sex.[6]

In fact, envy strikes most powerfully in those "intimate relations where love is supposed to rule." We know that love should be central to Christian life and community, and so we deal with envy by keeping it secret. We end up being hypocritical — what we say does not match what we are feeling.[7] In this way, envy, falsehood, and deception are closely connected. When we struggle with envy, we often withdraw from relationships or become indifferent to those around us.[8]

Basil, Bishop of Caesarea in the fourth century, observed that the particular misery and torment of envy is "the pain that arises from another's good fortune. And because of this the envious man is never without pain, never without grief of mind."

> And the worst of the sickness of soul is that the sufferer cannot make it known; but with bowed head and downcast eyes he suffers torment, he grieves, he perishes of his affliction. Asked of what he is suffering, he is ashamed to reveal his disease and confess, "I am envious and bitter: the gifts of my friends are a torment to me. I grieve at my brother's happiness. . . ." For this is what he must say if he would tell the truth.[9]

Echoing Basil's insights fifteen hundred years later, the ethicist William May has noted that when envy gets hold of our lives, it "secretly" governs much of what we do; "it can be the unaccountable source of dejection," flooding our lives with avarice and malice.[10]

Just as gratitude has been described as the parent of the other virtues, envy gives birth to other sins and deformed practices.[11] It involves more than jealousy or covetousness;[12] envy reflects, as Basil wrote, the "sadness that comes from being close to success."[13] John of Damascus and Thomas Aquinas described envy as "sorrow for another's good."[14] It's not just that we want what another person has; we don't want her or him to have it. Somehow in the envier's calculations, "every good in a rival is a diminishment" of the self.[15]

Theologian Neal Plantinga distinguishes between coveting and envy: "to covet is to want somebody else's good so strongly . . . that one is tempted to steal it. To envy is to resent somebody else's good so much that one is tempted to destroy it. . . . Envy . . . carries overtones of personal resentment; an envier resents not only somebody else's blessing but also the one who has been blessed."[16]

There is a strange and perverse power in envy that has been recognized throughout the Christian tradition. Those who are envious "have a knack for creating misery *ex nihilo,* for making themselves and others worse off than they need to be."[17] In fact, as Basil noted, the envious person ultimately "consumes" himself or herself.[18]

After decades of work within communities, Jean Vanier has concluded that "envy is one of the plagues that destroys community. It comes from people's ignorance of, or lack of belief in, their own gifts. If we were confident in our own gift, we would not envy that of others."[19] We can be envious of another person's relationships, spiritual giftedness, blessings, reputation, possessions, successes — just about anything. Will Willimon, pastor and theologian, notes that among Christians, envy can even surface when "your god seems oddly more beneficent than mine."[20] At the core of envy is an absence of gratitude for the gifts we've been given.

Envy generates and reproduces misery because it is accompanied by distrust, malice, and uncertainty. When we are envious, it shows in backbiting, grumbling, and resentment. We tend to disparage and minimize the accomplishments of others, or to challenge the standards by which accomplishments are measured.[21] Envy's venom is hard to fight off — those who are envied find it difficult to respond in a way that is constructive. Sadly, even people who are amiable and obliging find that in defending themselves against envy, "they also have fangs."[22]

Leaders sometimes struggle with envy when another person receives the attention and acclaim they perceive as rightly their own. A powerful example of this comes from the Gospels. We read in the Gospel of Mark that Pilate perceived that "it was out of envy" that the religious leaders had handed Jesus over to him. The honor that Jesus had received from the crowds provoked envy from his peers, who were disturbed by Jesus' "success" and wanted to "destroy his prestige."[23]

Jesus' parable about the laborers in the vineyard captures other dimensions of envy (Matt. 20:15). The gracious employer asks his disgruntled laborers, "Are you envious because I am generous?" It is surprising how often we struggle with the generosity of others, especially when their generosity benefits someone other than ourselves. We have a highly developed sense of fairness and are often troubled even when our own good has not been diminished by the blessing another has received. Henri Nouwen wonders at how hard it is for us to "rejoice that someone other than ourselves [is] given an unexpected gift," concluding that "we can only fully enjoy God's generosity toward others when we truly know how much God loves us."[24]

During a time of testimony in a chapel service at Asbury, a very bright and gifted student stood and shared that she had recently been released from her long-time struggle with envy. She described how, in her mind, Jesus had taken her to her house and to the room in which she had locked up everyone she envied. It was packed with all her family and friends. And she testified that when Jesus helped her open the door, the people streamed out — they were free. But she simultaneously understood that it was she who had been freed. The story powerfully pictures the imprisonment that envy causes. Those who are envied are imprisoned — no matter what they do, they can't fix the problem because it is not with them. This student's story also illustrates how envy imprisons persons who are unable to be thankful for what they have received and entraps the very people they care about in a miserable cycle of envy and ingratitude.

Because envy is secret and shame-filled, we need the help of others in addressing it. Resistance to envy is developed as we cultivate gratitude, as we speak the truth to one another about envy, and as we do not call it by a "nicer" name.[25] Communities can find ways to discuss the dangers of envy, and to talk about its ugliness and misery-causing qualities. When exposed to the light of loving truthfulness, envy is, in a sense, de-fanged, and can be seen for how petty it is. Together, by grace, we seek forgiveness and learn to celebrate each person's gifts and blessings, partly because they are also understood as blessings for the whole community.

Becoming a Grumble

In our communities, ingratitude can take another deadly form — grumbling and complaint directed at God or others. In the familiar story of the Exodus, the children of Israel experience a series of extraordinary miracles in their rescue from Egypt. But soon they find themselves stuck in the wilderness, where they grumble, remember inaccurately, and take a posture of complaint against God and Moses (Exod. 15–17; Num. 11). They remember their previous situation in Egypt as better than it was, and they do not see the benefits they are receiving in the midst of a difficult situation. But even more problematic, their murmuring reflects a breaking of the covenantal bond with their God, who has rescued them and provided for them.[26]

Grumbling is highly contagious within communities, and occasional complaining and dissatisfaction can become a way of life. Complaint is often overgeneralized, and soon everything seems unsatisfactory. While gratitude makes us more sensitive to the gifts that other people bring into our lives, discontent blinds us to what we've been given.

There is a memorable section on grumbling in *The Great Divorce* by C. S. Lewis. Several people have taken a bus from the grey town to the outer edge of Heaven, where we have an opportunity to listen in on their reflections on life. Lewis captures some of their disappointment and sense of entitlement, even as they are offered a chance to leave their miseries behind. The distinction between grumbling as an occasional frustrated response and grumbling as a way of life becomes clear.

We encounter the ghost of a woman who is very unhappy and has picked up the habit of unrelenting grumbling. She doesn't seem evil, just miserable. Another character, the Teacher, responds,

> "The question is whether she is a grumbler, or only a grumble. If there is a real woman — even the least trace of one — still there inside the grumbling, it can be brought to life again. If there's one wee spark under all those ashes, we'll blow it till the whole pile is red and clear. But if there's nothing but ashes we'll not go on blowing them in our own eyes forever. They must be swept up."
>
> "But how can there be a grumble without a grumbler?"
>
> "The whole difficulty of understanding hell is that the thing to be understood is so nearly Nothing. But ye'll have had experiences . . . it begins with a grumbling mood, and yourself distinct from it: perhaps

criticizing it. And yourself, in a dark hour, may will that mood, embrace it. Ye can repent and come out of it again. But there may come a day when you can do that no longer. Then there will be no *you* left to criticize the mood, nor even to enjoy it, but just the grumble itself going on forever like a machine."[27]

It is a powerful and disturbing image — the possibility of not just being a grumbler, but allowing grumbling to become a way of life until all that is left of a person is the grumble.

Grumbling is frequently addressed in the *Rule of Benedict,* which has guided Benedictine monastic life for nearly fifteen hundred years. Because grumbling is viewed as a major threat to communal life and goodness, the Rule warns about those who grumble. But it doesn't stop there. The Rule is also attentive to circumstances that can cause unnecessary hardship to community members and includes instructions that kitchen workers should have special food and help so that their service to brothers and guests can be "without grumbling." It instructs leaders to make decisions that allow for a life in which community members can "go about their activities without justifiable grumbling" (*RB,* 35:12-13; 53:18; 41:5).

Within its concerns about complaint, the Rule allows some category of "justifiable" grumbling (*RB,* 41:5) and suggests that expectations of gratitude in community can be used to foreclose legitimate criticism. Leaders must be careful not to misinterpret truth-telling as grumbling. When an unwelcome truth about injustice, poor leadership, or irresponsibility is spoken, it is easy for those with institutional power to dismiss it wrongly as ingratitude.

Communities in which grumbling has become a major issue may find it helpful to address the problem directly, and to set aside times in which people are invited to articulate their frustrations and suggest what would make things better. When people are challenged to be explicit about problems and to expose their complaints in the light of public discussion, all can see more clearly whether the complaining is justified. In an environment of fidelity and truthfulness, people can then choose to address problems constructively.

It's easy to complain about our congregations and communities — there's always something wrong. War stories or complaints about difficult congregations can become pastors' chief topic of conversation when they gather. Dietrich Bonhoeffer warns leaders, however, not to complain about their congregations, "certainly never to other people, but also not to God."

He warns that our congregations and communities have not been entrusted to us so that we can become their "accuser" before God or other people.[28]

Because we often struggle with a sense that we're entitled to better than we've gotten, John Wesley's frank words about gratitude and grumbling are disconcerting but also important. He asks, "Are you . . . full of gratitude to Him who giveth you life, and breath, and all things? Not so, you rather spurn his gifts, and murmur at Him that gave them. How often has your heart said, God did not use you well? How often have you questioned either his wisdom or goodness? Was this well done? What kind of gratitude is this?"[29]

Using Gratitude to Get Something Else

It isn't easy to encourage the practice of gratitude within a suspicious and cynical society. Think of the annoying phone calls from the charities we support that begin with, "We're just calling to thank you for your recent generous donation." Before the caller finishes the sentence, we know that it is not just a thank-you call; within another few seconds, we expect a request for an additional donation. We are wary of expressions of gratitude that are primarily a cover for getting something else or something more.[30]

Expressions of gratitude often reinforce generous and benevolent behavior, and people who receive thanks for their gifts "are more inclined to help . . . again."[31] Charities and businesses know this; so do pastors and other church leaders. In some cases, the old saying seems to hold true that gratitude is merely a "lively anticipation of future favors."

Although temporarily effective, using gratitude instrumentally, or to get something else, subtly undermines any real relationship because it is fundamentally manipulative. Similarly, when we thank someone profusely instead of apologizing for the trouble we've caused them, or for the way we have wronged them, we are also misusing gratitude.[32]

In troubled settings, Christian leaders sometimes attempt to generate enthusiasm and group spirit by forcing expressions of gratitude or appreciation. Requiring staff prayer times that include saying something "grateful" — in situations where the leader or organization is misusing power or mistreating people — is very destructive and can sacrifice truth at the "altar" of community.

Feelings of gratitude can certainly evoke or elicit personal loyalty, and that loyalty can be converted into power. Individuals who lead by creating a sense of personal obligation can make it very difficult for others to speak truthfully to them about their weaknesses or wrongdoing. Speaking the truth in these contexts is sometimes interpreted and dismissed as ingratitude or betrayal. Emphasis on the "debt" a person or community owes to another can be a way of silencing or ignoring protest or a means of maintaining the status quo.

Although misuses of gratitude, and forms of ingratitude, are common, we can lessen their impact in our lives and communities by more intentionally embracing the practice of gratitude.

Living into the Practice of Gratitude

Gratitude begins with paying attention, with noticing the goodness, beauty, and grace around us. The practice of gratitude becomes more central to our communities when we stop feeding the cycles of complaint and orient our lives around praise, testimony, and thanks. Our communities flourish when we regularly tell stories of God's faithfulness and goodness and when we find opportunities to express gratitude and celebrate the gifts we have received. Because of God's grace and work in bringing us together in Christ and in building our congregations, we are able to participate in congregational life "not as demanders but as thankful recipients."[33]

Each Day a Small Resurrection

For followers of Christ, there are endless opportunities to offer thanks. In the early eighteenth century, the theologian William Law described the joy of greeting each new day as a small personal resurrection:

> As the morning is to you the beginning of a new life; as God has then given you a new enjoyment of yourself, and a fresh entrance into the world; it is highly proper that your first devotions should be a praise and thanksgiving to God. . . .
>
> Receive, therefore, every day as a resurrection from death, as a new enjoyment of life; meet every rising sun with such sentiments of God's

goodness, as if you had seen it, and all things, new[ly] created upon your account: and under the sense of so great a blessing, let your joyful heart praise and magnify so good and glorious a Creator.[34]

Beginning each day with an expression of gratitude to God and to those around us and ending the day recounting moments of grace and goodness would frame our daily experiences with thanksgiving.[35] Reflecting on how we can create environments of gratitude would challenge us, our families, and our communities to interpret ordinary activities differently.[36] If we think about the different dimensions of gratitude — toward God, as a way of life, and toward one another — we realize that there are infinite opportunities to cultivate it.

Recovering simple practices such as offering thanks at meals can help us with gratitude, especially when we learn to be more explicit about the gifts for which we are thankful. Some families have found it helpful to establish a permanent "thanksgiving spot" in the house, a refrigerator door or bulletin board on which to note special reasons for gratitude.[37]

We can learn from those who have already made gratitude central to their shared life. Keith Wasserman provides some details about how Good Works, Inc. (a ministry with homeless people) embodies gratitude. Every evening, when staff members, volunteers, and residents/guests gather for dinner, each one shares a brief explanation of something for which they are grateful. Keith has found that as they make time to listen to one another and to celebrate the gift of food, a different tone is set, and opportunities for conversation increase. The act of gratitude, he observes, is contagious and builds community while lowering the level of complaining. At their weekly Friday-night gatherings, which involve the larger community, people are also invited (though not required) to express gratitude for something in their lives. They begin with the children who want to give thanks. Sometimes it is for ketchup, or parents, or for being alive. For those who come, it is a valued part of the evening, and people leave feeling refreshed and encouraged.

The Good Works community has also intentionally developed ways for staff members to encourage one another and to experience their belovedness. They have instituted regular occasions — called "Surprise: This Is Your Life!" — to celebrate each individual staff member and to affirm her or his gifts and contributions. Within community, these rituals create a storehouse of gratitude and hope upon which to draw in leaner times. Because Good Works also has structures in place that allow for regular and open communication about difficulties in community life, these times of gratitude are not coercive.

Making Room for Gratitude

Special events like anniversaries, weddings, birthdays, funerals, and other significant passages provide contexts in which gratitude and appreciation can be formally and specially offered. Frequently these events involve re-membering how much we value someone and carving out space to express it. We tend to do this most fully at funerals and when people are leaving communities for retirement. These are important times, but there are many lost opportunities if they are the only times.

Although we don't want to wait for endings before we express grati-tude to others, it certainly is important to express our gratitude and appre-ciation then. Having rituals of exit like we have for entrances or beginnings is important to communities. In a context of fidelity and covenantal com-mitments, leaving a community can be very difficult, and finding ways to show our gratitude to one another can reduce the pain of changing or end-ing relationships. Taking time to express love and gratitude can also open into powerful encounters with God and God's promises of ongoing rela-tionship and care.

Congregations are much happier communities when gratitude is widely practiced. Members of several congregations have taken up a chal-lenge to speak a word of gratitude and blessing into the lives of the first several people they encounter each day. Finding ways to bless others in small, daily words of appreciation — learning to "catch them in the act of being a gift," as another person put it — can transform communities into places in which we are delighted to live.

One of my colleagues at Asbury described childhood memories of Sunday-evening gospel services that were shaped by individual testimo-nies of gratitude. She explained that through the personal testimonies, the community experienced the joys of each member, and the practice made the community alive to God's activity in the world. On some nights, each of the participants would introduce words of testimony by saying, "I want to sing because . . . [some expression of gratitude]," and then all would sing the requested hymn together. This simple practice had shaped the community.

On other nights, members would begin their stories by saying, "I want to stand tonight and give praise to God because I'm thankful." This liturgical form, my colleague noted, was how the community learned to articulate the events of their lives within the larger narrative of Scripture. Reflecting years later on their communal formation, she observed that it was very different from the impact of phone calls asking for prayer or sharing good news. The latter tend to be very individual, and do not shape a whole community in gratitude or fidelity.

Small changes in practice can shift the culture of a community. One pastor in the project decided to devote a major portion of the church's annual meeting to thanking everyone who had made a contribution to congregational life. Some churches in the Wesleyan tradition have bread-breaking services or love feasts that are times of thanksgiving and affirmation. In other congregations, the weekly liturgy includes ten or fifteen minutes for voicing thankfulness. An intentional community established an affirmation/ recognition event on the anniversary date of each staff person's decision to join the community.

"You Have Been God's Grace to Me"

Moments of crisis or potential loss often prompt expressions of gratitude. In the novel *Gilead*, Reverend Ames does not expect to live to see his young son grow up. He explains, "I'm writing this in part to tell you that if you ever wonder what you've done in your life, and everyone does wonder sooner or later, you have been God's grace to me, a miracle, something more than a miracle."[38]

Hearing from another person that "you have been God's grace to me" changes how we experience the ordinariness of our lives and the sacrifices we willingly make for the good of others. Seeing ourselves and others as expressions or embodiments of God's grace transforms life together. It simultaneously recognizes God's goodness and the ways in which we have been gifted through other persons. It involves learning not to wait until we're about to lose something we cherish before we express how much we value it.

A posture of gratitude allows us to see beauty and to receive it, to recognize goodness and to take pleasure in it, even when circumstances are difficult. So when we face loss or death, we can still find delight in the sparkle of the ocean, the sweetness of a friendship that has lasted over decades, or the bright color of a sweater.

Notes of gratitude and affirmation can be a wonderful source of encouragement. For many years, several of my senior colleagues at Asbury have written notes of appreciation to me when they came across something I had written or when they heard a presentation or sermon I'd given. They often combined affirmation with a word of gratitude about my presence in the community. Those brief notes have been treasured reminders of having received a place in a loving and generous community.

Our communities suffocate when we fail to express how grateful we are for the goodness we find there — the ordinary expressions of fidelity and love that are so easy to take for granted. But we can "pump oxygen into our communal lungs" by helping to cultivate a community that notices and celebrates the good. Judy Alexander, who is experienced in helping community life to flourish, suggested that in every meeting, it was important to "have far more positive affirmation than negative confrontation" and to "talk in our meetings about how we saw God at work in each other."[39] Other relationships, such as marriages and families, are similarly strengthened when people express appreciation to one another on a regular basis.[40]

Gratitude and Celebration

When gratitude fills our lives and communities, it spills over into celebration. Shared meals, spontaneous and planned parties, Sabbath, and worship — every culture finds ways and traditions through which to reflect corporate thanksgiving.

Like gratitude, celebration nourishes us in surprising ways, as Jean Vanier points out: "It makes present the goals of the community in symbolic form, and so brings hope and a new strength to take up again everyday life with more love. Celebration is a sign of the resurrection which gives us strength to carry the cross of each day."[41]

Vanier, in describing life in the L'Arche communities, writes that the elements of celebration that bring us into "communion with God and each other" are "prayer, thanksgiving, and good food." He explains, "Celebration is a communal experience of joy, a song of thanksgiving. We celebrate the fact of being together; we give thanks for the gifts we have been given." "Celebration sweeps away the irritations of daily life; we forget our little quarrels." He concludes that a festival "is a sign of heaven. It symbolizes our deepest aspiration — an experience of total communion."[42]

We can become more intentional about allowing gratitude to connect our community life to our liturgy, worship, prayer, and praise. The Eucharist — a communal time of eating and drinking together that is transformed into our "Great Thanksgiving" — is a distillation of gratitude. Emphasis on gratitude and celebration does not mean that we overlook lament or heartache. Gift and sacrifice are intertwined in the crucifixion and in the Eucharist, much as they are in everyday life.

As noted earlier, those for whom gratitude is a way of life are not usually people who have been spared sorrow and difficulty. They have been shaped by a deeper grace and hope. Years ago, in a shelter for asylum seekers, I found myself in a large, sparsely furnished gathering space. The walls were brightly painted, but as I looked closer, I realized that the ribbons of color were actually hundreds of names of people who had been killed in the wars of Latin America. It was a memorial developed by surviving family members, simultaneously haunting and beautiful, a tragic and powerful testimony to individual lives cut short by human destructiveness. But the space itself came alive as people gathered for a meal, turned on the radio, and began singing and dancing — people who had lost so much were finding ways to celebrate life and community on a regular basis surrounded by love, loss, memory, and hope.

Joyce Hollyday tells the story of a church worker who had spent several years with refugees in Latin America and had discovered how the refugee camps were structured. "As soon as the refugees began to make a new camp, they set up three committees. There was the committee of education and the committee of construction. And there was the . . . 'committee of joy.' Celebration was as basic to the life of the refugees as teaching their children to read or building a latrine." One refugee challenged the church worker for being overly focused on her tasks, and said, "'You're not serious about our struggle. Only people who expect to go back to North America in a year work the way you do. You cannot be serious about the struggle unless you play and celebrate and do those things that make it possible to give a lifetime to it.'"[43]

We tend to think of celebrations as enjoyable but not central. Communities and congregations that last, however, especially in difficult settings, practice and embody gratitude and celebration. Because celebration expresses the meaning and joy of community in a "concrete and tangible way," "it is an essential element of community life."[44]

In his book *Life Together*, Dietrich Bonhoeffer helps us appreciate the celebratory element in daily shared meals. In the fellowship of a meal and "in their wholehearted joy in the good gifts of this physical life," followers of Jesus "acknowledge their Lord as the true giver of all good gifts; and beyond this, as the true Gift; the true Bread of life itself; and finally, as the One who is calling them to the banquet of the Kingdom of God. So in a singular way, the daily table fellowship binds the Christians to their Lord and one another."[45]

As he continues his reflections on meals, gratitude, and celebration, Bonhoeffer connects them to the experience of Sabbath rest:

> The fellowship of the table has a festive quality. It is a constantly recurring reminder in the midst of our everyday work of God's resting after His work, of the Sabbath as the meaning and goal of the week and its toil. Our life is not only travail and labor; it is also refreshment and joy in the goodness of God. We labor, but God nourishes and sustains us. And this is reason for celebrating. . . . Through our daily meals He is calling us to rejoice, to keep holiday in the midst of our working day.[46]

Being attentive to practicing Sabbath — and to rest as an expression of gratitude — also allows us time to notice what is good. Sabbath is both a response of gratitude and a context for gratitude.

Gratitude and thanksgiving help to make all of the other practices more beautiful. When gratitude shapes our lives, fidelity is more likely to be joy-filled, truth is life-giving, and hospitality is offered with generosity and joy. Similarly, gratitude flourishes when the other practices are vibrant. In the next three chapters, we will explore the important practice of fidelity or making and keeping promises.

PART II

Making and Keeping Promises

CHAPTER FIVE

Promises, Promises

Without being bound to the fulfillment of promises, we would never be able to keep our identities.

Hannah Arendt, *The Human Condition*

In my grandfather's moral universe, the place of deepest disgrace was reserved for people who didn't keep their promises. From the time I was a young child, I can remember his frequent, solemn warning: "Don't forget — never forget — your word is your bond." I didn't know what a bond was for a long time, but I quickly figured out what he meant. If you say you'll do something, you'd better do it, and the only assurance you need from a good person is his or her promise.

My grandfather was born at the beginning of the twentieth century, and he kept his word through some very difficult years — especially during the Great Depression. Not only did he keep his promises, but on several occasions he intervened to help other people — family members and friends — fulfill the commitments they had made. Often he offered his help at significant personal sacrifice. When my grandfather died in 1989, he had seen huge changes in the world, but the change that grieved him most was the increasing carelessness he saw about fidelity and promise-keeping. More than duty or obligation, making and keeping promises were for him central to a person's character and integrity.

Today we have cleaning agents, margarine, and personal-health products with names like Pledge, Ensure, Promise, and Depends. Despite its importance to most theological and philosophical traditions, our moral vocabulary related to fidelity and promising has been trivialized. Partly as a result of the continual hype of advertising, our culture is jaded about making and keeping promises. Whether referring to diet plans, detergents, or running shoes, the promises are quite incredible, and mostly we know better than to believe them. We laugh when politicians make impossible promises to whatever constituency they are courting. We're familiar and often comfortable with a complicated legal system which makes sure that individuals and companies both keep their promises and have ways to get out of them — whether marriage vows or refrigerator warranties.

Despite how cynical we have become about the likelihood of fidelity today, many of us continue to make and keep promises. As ethicist Lewis Smedes observes, people "choose not to quit when the going gets rough because they promised once to see it through. They stick to lost causes. They hold onto a love grown cold. They stay with people who have become pains in the neck. They still dare to make promises and care enough to keep the promises they make." Smedes continues, "If you have a ship you will not desert, if you have people you will not forsake, if you have causes you will not abandon, then *you are like God.*"[1]

We don't ordinarily think about the connections between the practices of God and our faithfulness to certain promises and people. But the God we worship and serve is one who has made promises to us, lives in a covenantal relationship with us, and is faithful even when we are unfaithful. Promise-making, promise-keeping, fidelity, and commitment are central to how we relate to God and to how God relates to us. We live by faith in a God whose character is steadfast love, so it should not surprise us that making promises and keeping promises are also at the heart of what is best in our human relationships. As a result, as Smedes has noted, many husbands and wives care for one another not only when things go well, but also when their marriages hit very rough patches. Pastors and congregations remain steady through both the good times and the hard times because of the commitments they have made.[2]

The "Tough Fibers" of Promise-Keeping[3]

One morning I was deeply moved by a brief interview I heard on the radio. At 101 years old, a woman named Clarisse was caring for her 89-year-old brother, who had suffered multiple strokes, and her 95-year-old sister, who had advanced Alzheimer's disease. When the interviewer asked her why she did it, Clarisse responded that she had made a promise to the Lord that if he kept her able, or for as long as she was able, she would care for them, and had been doing so for years. Neither of Clarisse's siblings were able to speak. The interviewer asked what she thought they would say if they could. She responded that she had no idea, but probably they would say "Thank you."

Hers is a remarkable yet everyday story of faithfulness — promises that shape our lives and our futures, personal commitments that knit together love, life, and sacrifice. The ethicist Margaret Farley captures this well:

> The history of the human race, as well as the story of any one life, might be told in terms of commitments. . . . At the heart of this history . . . lies a sometimes hidden narrative of promises, pledges, oaths, compacts, committed beliefs, and projected visions. At the heart of any individual's story, too, lies the tale of her or his commitments — wise or foolish, sustained or broken, fragmented or integrated into one whole.[4]

Promises provide the internal framework for every relationship and every community — they function like the "hidden supports in a well-built house."[5] We don't generally notice or call attention to them when they are providing structure to our relationships, though we certainly notice when they collapse.

Life together depends on the "tough fibers" of promise-keeping, to use Smedes's phrase again. Things as ordinary as the predictability of carpools and having refreshments for the church coffee hour each week involve making and keeping promises. International peace talks and airline schedules assume that individuals and institutions both make and keep promises. Marriages and building projects move forward based on the promises people have made.[6]

Commitments and promises that have been tested and proven are at the root of our ability to trust one another, and without some measure of trust, it is difficult to do much of anything. It is hard to put ourselves and our energy into something if we can't count on fellow participants to do what they have said they will do. No team can work effectively when people are fearful about betrayal by fellow team members or when deep hurts resulting from broken promises have not been addressed.

The promises we make set up expectations — often fairly ordinary expectations — but people arrange their behavior and their choices based on these expectations. If for some reason we can't keep a promise, or if we break it thoughtlessly, experiences of betrayal and disappointment can be acute, depending on how important the promise was. But even when promises are minor and the reasons for breaking them justifiable, people sometimes feel disappointed or betrayed. Promises are deeply connected to our ability to sustain hope, and broken promises and betrayals are the stuff of tragedy — great and small, epic and very personal.

In the Scriptures, we can readily see the connection between the practices of promising and gratitude; thanksgiving is both an act of fidelity and a response to fidelity. Based on God's covenantal promises and faithfulness in the past, the people of God are able to look into an uncertain future with hope, trust, and gratitude. Ingratitude is similarly connected to broken promises and infidelity. Murmuring among God's people is viewed as an expression of unfaithfulness to the covenant or as breaking the covenantal bond.[7]

What Are We Doing When We Make and Keep Promises?

When we make a promise, we voluntarily obligate ourselves "to perform some future course of action," often for another person's benefit.[8] In doing this, we reach into an uncertain and unpredictable future, with the intention of binding "ourselves to someone or something."[9] It is our intention in the present that then shapes or affects the future.

Keeping our promises is closely tied to personal integrity. We lose part of ourselves when we don't keep our word. In her book *Personal Commitments*, Margaret Farley explains, "To give my word is to 'place' a part of myself, or something that belongs to me, into another person's 'keeping.' It is to give the other person a claim over me, a claim to perform the action that I have committed myself to perform. When I 'give my word,' I do not simply give it away. . . . It claims my faithfulness, my constancy."[10]

Although I had learned the importance of keeping my promises when I was young, only when I started to study the topic did I realize how complex it is. Philosophers have been fascinated by the practice of promising for centuries, exploring how it is that human beings can "engage our wills in the process of getting the future to turn out as we planned." Promising is a powerful "expression of the self," yet it is also a relational activity.[11]

We make and depend on promises because we know that, as human beings, we are often inconsistent, and we find it hard to live and love without some assurances. Commitment, as Farley notes, "is love's way of being whole while it still grows into wholeness," and promises help us to "stabilize our loves in the midst of the fickleness of our feelings."[12] In the words of philosopher Hannah Arendt, when we make and keep promises, we create "islands of predictability" amid the "unpredictability of human affairs" and the "unreliability" of human beings.[13]

The stabilizing impact of promises is evident in everyday life. If we haven't made a promise, or if we don't take seriously the one we have made, it often seems easier and more sensible to move on or move out when serious difficulties arise. In situations where we have given our word or made some commitment — even when things are very hard — we are more likely to stay.

To make a promise involves recognizing that, under most circumstances, it should be kept. If taken seriously, the words of a promise carry within themselves some of the force of an action.[14] We can make promises and commitments without saying "I promise," and sometimes when we say "I promise," we mean to emphasize a point or a commitment rather than express an intention about the future.[15] We can make promises formal by putting them in a written contract or by speaking them in wedding vows, but in other cases we don't even use words — we just nod or show agreement in another way.[16]

Not surprisingly, things can go wrong. Sometimes we are unclear in the promises we make, or the other person misunderstands us, or each understands the nature of the promise or promising differently. Because much of our communication takes place at the nonverbal level, we don't always read each other's cues correctly.[17]

Promising is usually "bidirectional" — the practice involves more than one person making or keeping a promise. Generally, we also count on the other person, the *promisee,* to have reasonable expectations and to recognize the uncertainty of the future.[18] In fact, almost all of our promises and commitments are provisional and partial in some ways; it helps when all the parties understand the "assumed" conditions. The philosopher W. D. Ross gives a simple example: If I promise to go for a walk with a friend, there is a basic assumption that he and I will be well enough to walk that day. Even promises that don't seem to have conditions attached usually have assumptions within them — and we don't necessarily spell out what we assume (e.g., the physical capacity to do what we promised).[19]

Using the words "'I promise to . . .' normally binds one to do the thing promised, but it does not bind unconditionally or absolutely." The binding force of a promise "depends on the conditions under which the promise is made . . . [and] it does not bind one to do the thing promised whatever the cost to oneself and others."[20] However, because promises usually set up expectations, "The more likely it is that the promisee will seriously rely on the promise being kept, the more important it is that the promisor should keep it."[21]

As the French philosopher Gabriel Marcel explains, "Fidelity can never be unconditional, except when it is Faith." Nevertheless, our fidelity and our significant promises aspire to "unconditionality." He writes,

> It is as though my oath were accompanied by this prayer: "May heaven grant that I shall not be led into temptation, that is to say that no event shall cause me to think myself authorized to deny my promise on the pretext that the implicit conditions on which it rests have been changed in a way I could not foresee when I made it." I cannot perhaps go beyond this prayer without presuming too much on my own strength: but still it must be really sincere, and I must maintain within myself the will to fight against this temptation if it ever assails me.[22]

Although promising and fidelity are closely related, there are some differences. While fidelity or faithfulness generally involves being able to remember something of the past, in making and keeping promises, we also need to have some ability to conceive of the future and have some capacity for language.[23] The philosopher John Rawls distinguishes between them by viewing promising as an important and convenient practice of ordinary life and viewing fidelity as a basic principle for living.[24] Other philosophers see promising as a basic duty that is dependent on a "normative concept of commitment" or fidelity.[25] There is surprisingly little overlap between philosophical discussions of promising and theological discussions of fidelity, but certainly, promise-making and promise-keeping are central dimensions of fidelity.

Different Kinds of Promises

We make promises in different ways. Some of them are formal — like vows, oaths, and covenants. But many more of our promises are informal, the stuff of everyday interactions — "We'll be there for your party at seven o'clock"; "I'll pick up the kids after school"; "I'll lead the small group for the next three months."

There are explicit promises — the ones we spell out. I'll do this or that. I'll be there. We'll finish the work in time — you can count on us. When we make a specific promise, we notch up the expectation level by being explicit.[26] But there are many other promises that are implicit. We don't say them out loud; they aren't specifically articulated; but somehow expectations are set up by what we have previously done or said. For example, unless stated otherwise, if we have had a significant role in a group project, fellow participants usually expect us to continue with them to its completion. In keeping our implicit promises, we weave a strong fabric of everyday fidelity.

Not all of our promises are bilateral or one-to-one. Sometimes we make promises to a group, and the group makes promises or commitments to us. In other cases, we make a vow that is a self-imposed commitment to do something which doesn't necessarily involve others.[27] When vows include other parties, such as in marriage, baptism, ordination, and citizenship, they are often public events that have rich traditions, witnesses, and ceremonies to celebrate the event and to mark its importance.

Not every promise we make is good. We can promise (usually in the form of a threat) to do evil, or make commitments to an ideology or a group that has destructive practices and intentions. Our promises need to be fitted into the larger commitments of our covenant with God. The biblical and historic Christian tradition frames our understandings of both fidelity and promises.

People of the Promise

God abounds "in steadfast love and faithfulness, keeping steadfast love for the thousandth generation" (Exod. 34:6-7a). Even when we fail to keep our promises to God, God is faithful. The Christian faith is rooted in promises, and we as Christians understand ourselves as people of the new covenant, the new promise.[28] A covenant-making, promise-keeping God has formed a people of promise, born by God's own fidelity.

The context for our promising is, as noted earlier, our inability to know and control the future and the unpredictability of our circumstances. Even more, however, it is God's steadfast love and faithfulness that frames the practice. The biblical story itself is a long account of promises, covenants, and God's fidelity. Whether in creation or with Noah, Abraham and Sarah, or Moses, we see God's promises at work. Covenants are renewed and extended over generations. We read in Psalm 25:10 that the covenantal relationship between God and God's people is comprehensive: "All the paths of the LORD are steadfast love and faithfulness, for those who keep his covenant and his decrees." Again, the psalmist proclaims, all of God's work "is done in faithfulness. . . . The earth is full of the steadfast love of the LORD" (Ps. 33:4-5).

When they reached the Promised Land, the people of God were reminded to remain faithful to God — their covenantal response to God's faithfulness and rescue was to be fidelity and obedience. The language of love, promise, and fidelity overflows in a passage from Deuteronomy: "It was because the LORD loved you and kept the oath that he swore to your ancestors, that the LORD has brought you out with a mighty hand. . . . Know therefore that the LORD your God is God, the faithful God who maintains covenant loyalty with those who love him and keep his commandments . . ." (Deut. 7:8-9).[29]

Like the ancient Israelites, we are not always faithful and do not always remember God's kindness. For Israel, *to remember* involved remaining within God's covenantal promises and relationship; it meant holding on to God's faithfulness. Similarly, in forsaking the Lord, the people of God abandoned rather than held fast to the covenant promises.[30]

God's promise or covenant is unconditional and is sealed in the death of Jesus, and yet human response also matters because "there is something about the goal of the Covenant that cannot be realized without it." That goal involves mutuality between God and human beings, and true mutuality "depends on the free response of human persons."[31]

In a wonderful burst of confidence in the midst of uncertainty, Paul tells the church at Corinth that in Jesus, "every one of God's promises is a 'Yes'" (2 Cor. 1:20). "The promise of the new covenant points to the person of Jesus. He stood at the climax of all promises (2 Cor. 1:20); in him all promises find their fulfillment (Luke 24:44)."[32]

The language of promise also pervades the second letter of Peter. Followers of Christ are kept by and in Jesus' promises, and, although other people might wonder at how long we wait for the fulfillment of some promises, we know that "the Lord is not slow about his promise," but only patient (2 Pet. 1:4; 3:4, 9, 13). "The promises of Jesus are part of the larger set of gifts that Jesus bestows on believers in order to provide the means that they need to live in a godly fashion."[33]

The Gospel of Matthew ends with Jesus' promise: "I am with you always, to the end of the age" (28:20). The substance of that promise is repeated in Hebrews 13:5: "I will never leave you or forsake you." These promises and a faithful response have allowed many Christians to face difficulty and death without wavering for two thousand years. If we do not grasp God's faithfulness and the importance of our own fidelity, it is impossible to make sense of great sacrifices for the kingdom.

Vows, Oaths, and Chastened Promising

The importance of making promises carefully and keeping the promises we make is reinforced by biblical and theological teachings; this is true whether the promises are to God or to other human beings. The psalmist notes that faithful people "stand by their oath even to their hurt" (Ps. 15:4). In Deuteronomy 23:21-23, the people of God are warned:

> If you make a vow to the LORD your God, do not postpone fulfilling it; for the LORD your God will surely require it of you, and you would incur guilt. But if you refrain from vowing, you will not incur guilt. Whatever your lips utter you must diligently perform, just as you have freely vowed to the LORD your God with your own mouth.

Thomas Aquinas defines a vow as a voluntary "promise made to God."[34] In his discussion of vows, Thomas quotes Ecclesiastes 5:4-5: "Whatsoever thou hast vowed, pay it; it is much better not to vow, than after a vow not to perform the things promised." He explains, "For one to be accounted faithful one must keep one's promises."[35]

While recognizing the importance of fidelity, Jesus also explicitly warns us about our promises and oaths. The future is in God's hands, so to imagine that we can control it by making promises or vows can be presumptuous. This is part of the point of Jesus' instructions in Matthew 5:33-37 about not making vows. Instead, Jesus calls on his followers to let our "Yes" or "No" be sufficient. The concern is picked up in the book of James when the writer warns believers to remember that they do not even know what the next day might bring, and in humility should make their plans with this caveat: "If the Lord wishes, we will live and do this or that" (James 4:13-16).[36]

Nevertheless, a willingness to make commitments to one another remains at the heart of our deepest relationships. A sense of our own frailty and dependence on God can help us with these tensions. In his essay on the importance of promises to family life, theologian and educator Craig Dykstra explains that "it is promise-making, not promise-keeping, that constitutes the family." Though we tend to emphasize promise-keeping, making promises to one another allows us to form families.[37] Dykstra's comments on the family are relevant to forming and sustaining other kinds of communities as well. He explains:

> It is not the failure to keep promises, in and of itself, that destroys family. Such failure happens in every family and can be expected. Family can remain family in the midst of unfulfilled promises. What destroys family is the collapse of promise-*making*. It is when the very making of promises is no longer believed and believed in that families die. The failure to keep promises and the collapse of promise-making are, of course, related. The continual failure to fulfill promises acts as a corrosive to the promise-making, so that there may come a time when the lack of fulfillment destroys the very meaning and significance of promise-making.[38]

We are helped in making and remembering some of our most important promises by church liturgies that locate our promises in the community of faith and make them public.[39] Baptism is a liturgical practice filled with promises and promising. In it, we recall the promises God has made to us, and, in response, the person(s) being baptized, or the parents for their child, also make promises. Through baptism, persons "are also being incorporated into the family of the church. We promise to be faithful members of a particular congregation and to seek the fellowship of the church wherever we may be." We promise to be disciples of Jesus, following him into "the new life (the new way of life) that God promises and makes possible through him."[40] We "renounce the devil and all his empty promises." In many baptismal services, the congregation then responds with additional promises.[41]

Promising: Out of Step with Contemporary Culture

While we might agree that making promises and keeping promises are important to personal integrity and human relationships, features of contemporary life challenge the practice. We are wary of making commitments that bind us or limit our freedom.

Keeping Our Options Open

Contemporary culture places a premium on individual freedom and the capacity to choose. We cherish the nearly unlimited choices we have about many things, and we like to keep our options open. When we make promises and commitments, we foreclose some good opportunities. This could be true of marriage, shopping for a house or a shirt, or joining a particular congregation. We hesitate to make final decisions because something better might be just around the corner.

In a recent conversation with a young friend about promising, I realized how changes in cell-phone use and texting have increased our culture of choice and affected our friendship practices. She has a wide and cherished friendship network, but she and her twenty-something friends rarely make plans ahead of time to get together. They might tentatively suggest an event or activity, but they don't firm up anything until the very last minute, because they can check in with one another from wherever they are at the end of the workday. At that point they make a decision about whether or not to meet.

While valuing the spontaneity that is possible with this approach, my friend also recognized that one could quickly get the impression that each friend was waiting to make sure that he or she had the full range of options for that night laid out. Each was hesitant to commit to one thing or person only to find out a few minutes later that something else would have been better. Because our experiences of being chosen are as important to us as being able to choose, this has the potential to undermine relationships in significant ways. And ironically, continually having opportunities to choose among an endless array of options is not necessarily best for us. In our finiteness, closing off some options can actually be a blessing.

The culture of choice may also be part of what stands behind the increasing difficulty in getting people to respond to invitations for major events. In the past, giving a timely answer to a formal invitation was understood as basic etiquette, but today, many people wait until very late to respond, if they do so at all. A more tentative approach to relationships and commitments has a snowball effect — it becomes more and more difficult to plan group events and count on participation because so many factors are up in the air until the last minute.

The focus on multiple options may also help explain why many churches struggle with getting people to commit to, and to stay with, programs of any duration. One pastor's description of efforts to sustain a youth program in a moderate-sized church captures the challenge. She explained that many of the parents said that they "really liked the program and found it valuable for the church and for their children." In most cases, however, sports practices, music lessons, and school activities trumped scheduled youth-group programs. She observed, "Families want the program to be available to them when it suits their schedule," but they don't seem to understand how difficult their unpredictable attendance and participation are for the youth program itself.

Although the program got "great evaluations" and strong verbal support from parents, volunteers became discouraged when families seemed to pick and choose events with little recognition of the time and sacrifice required to make those events available. In some of these situations, volunteers may rightly wonder why their commitments and promises to the youth and the program do not seem to elicit a similar fidelity from the people who benefit from the program. Is it that some congregation members see themselves, even in church, primarily as consumers rather than as coworkers in community? Are there implicit promises we make to one another when we begin a project together or when we benefit from it? Is part of the difficulty also that families regularly face the challenge of conflicting obligations and expectations?

Distrust of Institutions

Fidelity and promising are more difficult when we don't trust people in leadership roles or when we are wary of important institutions. Whether the authorities are in government, church, corporations, or school, many of us distrust their motives and question their intentions. We're often looking for the subtext or the "real" agenda.

Government officials and business executives regularly make promises that they cannot or will not keep. Institutions with moral authority — whether governmental or religious — sometimes betray the trust of the people whose loyalty they expect. Stories of church leaders who have used positions of spiritual and moral authority for personal gain are depressingly common, and clergy misconduct erodes the little confidence some people have in institutions. Those who have been betrayed are wary of further commitments and the institutions that embody them.

In some cases, we are simultaneously idealistic and cynical about institutions. When it comes to marriage, government, and church, we often have high and unrealistic expectations of what they can deliver. At the same time, as a society, we have less respect for them than in previous times. We are left with significant ambivalence about our commitments to and within these institutions.

Especially when dealing with large institutions, we make our promises or commitments to an anonymous promisee. When we take out a loan or agree to certain provisions in a contract, we interact with representatives of an institution who serve in a highly defined role. Because we don't usually form lasting relationships with these representatives, a decision to break the promise we've made with them seems to have little interpersonal cost. We might be constrained by potential legal consequences, but not by relational ones. A conversation between a pastor and a young person who had recently embraced Christian faith shows how cynicism about institutions, notions of freedom, and irresponsibility can interact.

Jason, as he anticipated his new Christian calling, was thinking about defaulting on some large loans by filing for bankruptcy. The pastor pointed out that when he had "received his loans, he had made a promise to repay them, and thus had a moral obligation to do so." Jason agreed, but then said, "I did that a long time ago, when I didn't know what I wanted to do with my life. Should I be forced to live by that now, when God is changing everything in my life?"

Jason explained that when he'd shared his plans with some other Christian friends, several had affirmed his idea of declaring bankruptcy and advised, "If it is legal, then do it." They justified their stance by dismissing commitments to the government, "which is itself basically dishonest."

The pastor then asked if declaring bankruptcy was not in this case dishonest, as Jason was not having insurmountable financial difficulties. Jason replied with obvious frustration: "I'm trying to serve God by living among the poor in our community, and I feel like I'm being punished for doing the right thing." The pastor asked whether Jason saw a difference between being punished and being expected, as a mature adult, to honor an obligation.

He then helped Jason consider who might be affected by his decision: the government, future loan applicants, and other community members who were making sacrifices to pay back their loans. Jason eventually chose not to try to declare bankruptcy and found a way to work among poor people while he paid back his loans.

The pastor's approach was direct and effective: he personalized the debt and helped Jason understand the reality and importance of his promise. He recognized that Jason's careless attitude toward paying large debts could have an impact on others within the community who were struggling with similar responsibilities. He also helped Jason reflect on who bears the cost of a broken promise when it is to a large institution. Jason gradually saw the importance of keeping commitments over time, even when changes in life plans make keeping certain promises more costly.

Recognizing the importance of fidelity and promises in our lives helps us resist some of the cultural pressures that undermine our commitments. But there are additional difficulties in making and keeping promises that we need to consider before we can help ourselves and our communities move toward deeper maturity and responsibility in the practice of promising.

CHAPTER SIX

Complications in Promising

The history of the human race, as well as the story of any one life, might be told in terms of commitments.

Margaret Farley, *Personal Commitments*

Things can become surprisingly complicated when we try to make or keep a promise. Conflicting values and promises, conditional commitments, human finiteness, and many other factors reshape, undermine, or challenge the practice.

From "Doing My Duty" to "What Works for Me"

Like my grandfather, many people in prior generations understood what it meant to be good primarily in terms of personal integrity, virtue, doing one's duty, fulfilling obligations, or following certain principles. Today, many of us tend to be more pragmatic and utilitarian when we think about how to make good moral choices. We ask, "What action will have the best result?" "Will it work?" and "What's the bottom line?" This shift in ethical orientation has affected how we think about promising.

When we make decisions based on which action produces more "good," it's hard to see why we wouldn't break a promise if, by doing so, we could accomplish something better. But such an approach undermines the whole practice of promising and makes it very hard to sustain the commitments and relations necessary to community. The philosopher John Rawls argues that there are reasons we don't keep promises, but "among them there isn't the one that, on general utilitarian grounds, the promisor (truly) thought his action best on the whole." If a person, in breaking a promise, simply says that he or she thought that overall it was best, we would be inclined to question whether or not that person "knows what it means to say 'I promise.'"[1]

Although moral arguments that a person must never break a promise seem overstated, and "the possibility of doing some much greater good" or the possibility of avoiding certain bad consequences might lead a faithful person to break his or her promise, "the whole purpose of a promise . . . is to exclude arguments based on a mere balance of convenience, or even of good." When a person makes a promise, we don't usually assume that he or she means, "'I promise but . . . before I keep the promise I shall review the situation and then determine whether or not the effects would be better if I break it; and if so, I'll break it.'"[2]

In fact, a commitment to keeping the promises we've made saves us from continually asking ourselves whether, in a particular situation, we might accomplish a small amount of additional good by breaking the promise.[3] But when utilitarian calculations are combined with decision-making based on how we feel at a particular moment, the whole practice of promising becomes much more fragile, and every decision becomes more complicated. A continual focus on feelings and results obscures the relationship of promising to our character, integrity, and responsibility. When we are careless about making and breaking promises, we lose sight of the ways in which trust in our relationships and our communities is undermined.

There are certainly times when breaking a promise is justified; for example, in order to respond to someone's sudden distress or because circumstances have made it very difficult to follow through. However, our responsibility related to that promise hasn't ended simply because we're justified in breaking it. Centuries ago, Thomas Aquinas wrote, "If that which a man has vowed becomes impossible to him through any cause whatsoever, he must do what he can, so that he have at least a will ready to do what he can."[4]

When we cannot or do not keep a promise, often an apology or explanation is needed.[5] It's helpful to find a way to honor what the original promise was about, although perhaps in a different framework.[6] The practices of confession and forgiveness become important when we face the challenge of redeeming broken promises and living with the consequences of sometimes difficult choices. Because broken promises often erode trust, restoring confidence by acknowledging and attempting to repair the break is crucial.[7]

Covenants and Contracts: Two Models of Promising

In the biblical tradition, promises and covenants are closely connected, but today we tend to link contracts with many of our promises. Contracts build into a promise the possibility of breaking it and the subsequent consequences — tied to whether or not each or all of the parties are satisfied. We sign contracts for major purchases and employment, and contracts are implicit in contemporary political life. A contractual understanding is appropriate in many areas, especially in purchasing goods and services, and in some business relations, but it is not an adequate framework for structuring the most important promises in our lives.

When we think covenantally about promises, we tend to locate our promises in a larger story and in mutual accountability. Covenantal understandings of promising reflect a set of shared commitments and rarely have exit clauses. Contracts, on the other hand, deliberately define the relationship narrowly, and, once obligations are fulfilled, the exchange is complete — it's finished. In covenantal settings, relationships are extended and deepened.[8] Covenants tend to be comprehensive and vulnerable in ways that contracts are not.

We can get at some of the difference between contracts and covenants in how we understand marriage. Historically, the Christian tradition has viewed marriage as a covenant that involves the couple, their families, the church, and God. Although a marriage covenant can be damaged beyond repair by one or both members of the partnership, there are clear expectations of lifelong fidelity and mutual responsibility. The covenant, promises, or vows that the couple make with one another and God are sometimes all that holds them together through difficult times.[9]

In marriage contracts, the economic dimensions of the relationship are given priority — what property belongs to each individual, or what one or the other will take with them if the marriage fails. In a contractual understanding of marriage, if one or the other partner doesn't "deliver," the arrangement can be dissolved.

The Consumer Mind-set

When we view ourselves as consumers, we tend to think contractually. If we bring that orientation to the church or the classroom, it changes how we understand relationships. A consumer mind-set means that commitments are limited and oriented around filling personal needs. When church members approach their pastors — or college students their teachers — as consumers, they assume, "I'm paying, and therefore I'll decide how much I invest and what I want from you." But these assumptions shrink important relationships to economic transactions.

Are college students primarily purchasing a service from a professor or a school, or are they and their teachers involved in a covenant of learning? When students carelessly turn in incomplete or inadequate work, or when professors are unprepared for class or don't return students' work, it is not just that the services rendered are inadequate. The relationships are devalued and undermined.

A consumer mind-set also stands behind the casual "switching" among church attendees who regularly move from congregation to congregation. Leaders become discouraged and feel betrayed when they have invested significant time and energy in a person or a family, only to have them quickly move on to another community "because their needs aren't being met." Frequent "moving on" to another experience reflects a careless view of relationships and mutual commitment. Although those of us who are leaders need to remember that the kingdom is far bigger than our particular congregations or projects, it is easy to see in switching not only a lack of commitment but also an absence of gratitude for the community and its gifts.

Mixing the Two Models

Most Christian organizations appear to operate with covenantal expectations. In churches and schools, as well as in mission and social-ministry agencies, we expect strong commitment to a shared vision and task, and we put a high priority on the community and God's work through it. We often depend on staff members to make personally sacrificial decisions for the sake of the vision or group. We frequently talk about being a "family."

Part of our contemporary confusion — especially in staff and congregational relationships — is that we actually work with a hybrid of covenantal and contractual expectations. In employer/employee or in staff/parish relations, although we value our shared undertakings and the sense of partnering with God, we often turn to contract when we encounter difficulties. When we must make tough budget decisions or deal with layoffs, we shift abruptly to contractual models that add up benefits and losses but give little attention to a shared narrative, intertwined lives, and previous sacrifices.

The result is a sense of betrayal and loss, especially by the people who have experienced the sharp edges of contract. Sometimes when persons are laid off, they are given little notice and told to gather their things. They receive formal letters terminating employment spelled out in the language of severance pay, ending dates, and warnings about legal action. They are rightly confused and angry when covenantal themes that had shaped their tenure within a community — themes of fidelity, community, gratitude, and sacrifice — seem to evaporate when an alternative model kicks in.

This is a significant reason that work relationships sometimes end badly in Christian settings. All the language of vision and shared undertakings seems like a mockery when communities do not find ways to honor relationships and sacrifice as employment arrangements or staff positions are terminated. Christian organizations are obviously not exempt from the need for cutbacks, employee evaluation and discipline, and hard choices, but it often seems that the processes used for those difficulties are separate from the day-to-day covenantal framework.

Ironically, an absence of the carefully defined details of contracts can also make Christian workers vulnerable. Their fidelity can be misused; employers, pastors, or congregations can be harsh or even abusive with staff members that they know are committed to the larger vision. If we're fearful that people will leave, it is hard to build anything, but if we are sure of their loyalty and commitment, it is easy to misuse it. Part of the reason we turn to contracts is to protect vulnerable people from abuses of power.

In settings in which contractual and covenantal expectations are combined, we can presume on employers and employees in other ways. If the goal of the community or organization is good or important, there can be underlying expectations that sacrifice is appropriate and gratitude unnecessary. Sometimes congregations assume that in "kingdom work," concerns about justice in working conditions or pay are inappropriate. In other cases, it is assumed that shallow expressions of gratitude are adequate substitutes for equity and justice. These assumptions make it hard for persons to raise legitimate concerns about injustice.

I'm Out of Here

Our mobility creates additional problems for promising and commitments. It's not just that people often move for their jobs or for personal advancement — it is our expectation that this will happen that makes it hard to build and sustain strong communities. It's difficult to see the point in investing time and energy in a particular group of people if you or they don't plan to stay together. Unless we are part of a very transient community that understands frequent moves to be a way of life (as in the military), we are reluctant to invest in building close relationships that won't last.

Commitment to a place and a people means that relationships can be formed that are able to withstand trials and disagreements, but often people move in and out of congregations and communities before deep roots are established. When expectations of mobility are combined with a consumer mind-set, people are very likely to leave when things get difficult.

Fidelity to a person includes correcting him or her or even addressing wrongdoing in a specific way. But if people are in the habit of leaving communities whenever there is conflict or disagreement, offering correction with accountability becomes almost impossible. Some folks simply move on if they don't want to deal with correction or aren't willing to change what they have been doing.

Our mobility can also heighten other problems. The possibility that people will leave during a crisis often further destabilizes an unstable situation. When communities face severe disagreements or internal tensions, members sometimes threaten to leave if the "other side" doesn't "get its act together." Even when those suggesting they'll leave are interpreting the problem correctly, this is a very problematic threat. It further heightens the emotional tension and fear of loss, and it proves to be a very difficult threat to undo. It is often much better to stay long enough to help with rebuilding and healing.

Benedictine monks and sisters take a vow of stability — a lifelong commitment to a particular group of people in a particular place.[10] This is a powerful context for fidelity because each member of the community can assume that folks won't leave during the hard times and that they will walk through each difficulty together. I was surprised recently when a young Benedictine woman explained that she had joined the order because she saw that the elderly sisters were dying well. This was, at its heart, a statement about individual and community fidelity. The sisters, committed to one another and to Christ, had a place in community that held them to the end. Stability allowed for the maturation of promises and commitments.

But sometimes, even with a lifelong commitment, distance grows between a person and his or her community. Often it is a quiet and subtle tension — people who don't want to break their commitments or vows might choose to "defect in place."[11] Monks may stay in their community but stop coming to common meals and prayers; faculty members may continue to teach classes, but they leave campus immediately after their teaching is over. A community may want to respond constructively, but it is difficult if the person has essentially exited. Often the community does not want to resort to harsh measures that require participation in the things people should want to do. Finding ways to re-open communication, offering pastoral care that is attentive to new ways for the person to connect within the community, and providing opportunities to reconsider and evaluate commitments/vows are important in these situations.

In denominations where pastors are moved to a different church or churches every few years, issues of mobility and fidelity are complex in other ways. Laypeople may hesitate to make deep, long-term commitments when they don't know what the next leadership change will bring. On the other hand, institutionalized and regular leadership change can function as a safety valve for communities in troubled times. It is important that both pastors and lay leaders help church members bond to one another and to the congregation more than to the appointed leaders. This allows members to sustain a congregational identity and vision while enduring frequent changes.

"Conditions that Defeat a Promise"

We make promises in the midst of already existing commitments and relationships, never in a vacuum. Our promises are part of the ongoing story of our lives, and because our stories aren't finished, promises are necessary but often also vulnerable. We struggle with commitments that conflict with each other as well as with our human limitations — we simply can't do everything even when we want to. These and other challenges contribute to what philosophers call "conditions that defeat a promise" — the reasons our promises sometimes fail.

Changes in circumstances can make it impossible to fulfill a promise;

unforeseen events or unexpected incapacity can excuse us. Parents promise their children a day at the amusement park, but one of the children wakes up in the morning feeling sick; a congregation promises to host a dinner for the community, but the building is damaged by a storm; and so on. Often the excusing conditions involve events beyond our control.[12]

In other cases, a substantially more pressing responsibility or obligation comes up after we've made a promise, and we are justified in breaking our original promise. Sometimes conflicting obligations can be anticipated, but not always. People who have multiple roles (parents, spouses, pastors) regularly find themselves in the midst of conflicting responsibilities.[13] It can be helpful, in facing these conflicting claims, to use some of the criteria from Just War Theory to weigh the two claims. If I start out assuming that I should keep my promise, is there, in this case, a sufficiently important reason to break it? Is this other or new obligation substantially more pressing or important? Is my intention to address this new situation rather than to just get out of my original promise? Does my decision seem proportional — what will be the impact of breaking the promise versus meeting this other obligation? Have I considered other ways I might fulfill both obligations? Is breaking my promise my last resort, or are there alternatives? Is this a need only I can meet?[14]

Occasionally promises are coerced, made under duress, or based on incomplete or inaccurate information. Sometimes there are major misunderstandings, and in other situations, promises involve deliberate deception. In these cases, the promisor is not usually held to his or her promise, although there might be legal ramifications.

Sometimes the promisee releases us from a promise.[15] I promise to take care of a friend after her surgery, but she recovers so quickly and well that she releases me from my promise and sends me home. In other situations, the promise we have made no longer fulfills "the purposes of the larger commitment it was meant to serve."[16] For example, members of a missional small group promise to meet twice weekly to strengthen their relationships, but gradually discover that the amount of time required for the gatherings undermines their responsibilities to the church and the neighborhood.

We tend to assume that the promisee is the one who benefits from the promise, but the person making the promise also often benefits.[17] Because a promise involves the futures of both, it is helpful in cases where we face "defeating" conditions that those affected sort out the difficulties together.[18]

Fierce Disagreements

Some promises are not made to persons; rather, they involve fidelity to historic traditions or particular beliefs. When our fundamental commitments are challenged, the entire structuring of our lives can seem at risk. Christians who disagree over matters of theological or moral significance can turn on one another with extraordinary fierceness. Communities, not to mention individuals, do not always handle disagreements well, especially when they are related to important beliefs or commitments.

In a religion that is centered in love and a crucified savior, our attacks on brothers and sisters with whom we disagree are deeply troubling. We are, in a sense, undone by our very strengths — we take our deepest commitments seriously. This fidelity, however, does not always guide us in how to disagree or seek resolution. Disagreements are often personal and interpreted as betrayal.

It is impossible to build community if people are not willing to stay in conversation or "at the table" during times of significant disagreement. Our inclination may be to shut down or shut out those who challenge us at tender or important places, but we cannot find resolution without staying with the relationship, at least for the time it takes to understand the differences fully. Although some differences may run so deep that they affect fundamental identity and communal purposes, people often sever ties before they attempt to understand disagreements or their significance.

The Bible uses the image of devouring in its description of our "adversary, the devil" who is prowling in search of someone to devour (1 Pet. 5:8). The rich and powerful are described as devouring the poor (e.g., Mark 12:40; Luke 20:47). Paul writes to the Christians in Galatia that if they continue to "bite and devour one another," they may find themselves consumed (Gal. 5:15). In church and community fights, the language of devouring is sometimes miserably appropriate. Our commitment to feeding on Jesus as the bread of life is replaced by a frenzy of devouring one another. In our efforts to gain the upper hand, to hold on to resources "for the kingdom," or to win the theological or moral argument, we can lose sight of our larger fidelities to Christ, holiness, and love.

I am not suggesting that Christians should never disagree robustly or that tolerance should become our highest value. Good arguments, shaped by love and fidelity, can build community. Efforts to understand alternate viewpoints before we dismiss them are acts of respect, and challenging one another on important commitments and loyalties can be evidence of love and faithfulness. Sometimes, differences are significant enough that they represent alternative or even incompatible visions, and separation is necessary. Nevertheless, *how* we deal with people with whom we disagree on important matters reveals our own deepest commitments.

Multiple or Conflicting Fidelities

When pastors or congregations reach out to a troubled person, they hope to offer love, space to grow, and opportunities to discover his or her gifts. When folks are not healed quickly, however, congregations face the challenges of dealing with people who are easily hurt or offended, or who respond with anger, violence, or manipulative behavior. Pastors and leaders have multiple or conflicting fidelities here — to the well-being of the congregation and to the persons who lack the skills to fit into the community easily.

When we reach out to "people on the margins," we soon realize that some folks are on the margins because they have experienced a great deal of infidelity and betrayal in their lives. The process of restoring them to community involves steady, long-term faithfulness, welcome, kindness, and discipline. But it isn't easy — trust is hard-earned, some folks test the limits of fidelity, and others have expectations of the community that are impossible to fulfill.

Questions of fidelity become more complicated when visions, purposes, and beliefs to which we have been committed change or evolve over time. A project may be started in response to a particular need or vision for ministry. Over the years, however, it can develop in other directions, and in these cases both flexibility and discernment are needed. Are such changes an appropriate response to external circumstances, or are they evidence that we are drifting away from the original vision?

If we have been serving in a ministry with homeless people for years, but recently the homeless people have been forced out of the neighborhoods near our church, what changes do we need to make to stay faithful to our homeless friends? Sometimes revisions of our original commitments are needed to preserve our larger fidelities.

We face other challenges with conflicting loyalties when we have made promises to a community, church, school, ministry, or denomination, but that group or its leadership shifts its allegiances in significant ways. Our promises have been made in the context of larger commitments related to the identity, values, and visions that we hold dear. When the institution makes changes in its fundamental commitments and still expects loyalty, persons who want to be faithful to their commitments and to their communities struggle with fulfilling the previous vows and promises they have made. Promises can suddenly seem at odds with each other, and much prayerful discernment is needed to move forward.

Other challenges emerge during times of organizational transition. When beloved leaders leave and new people come in, loyalties are often complicated. When tensions mount up, we wonder, "Is it possible to bring in new senior leadership and keep existing associate pastors on staff?" Folks sometimes feel that they must "choose sides" and be loyal to one pastor in a multi-staff situation. A new senior pastor or executive director is in an awkward position when he or she must demand loyalty before it is earned or grown naturally.

Among parishioners and staff, unnamed loyalties to past leaders can be landmines for the new leadership. When there are tight bonds or close-knit small groups within a church, it is easy to traffic in misdirected fidelity — when groups become secretive or define themselves by whom they exclude. Especially when a leader has left under awkward circumstances, the potential for tangled loyalties is high. The new leader sometimes inherits mayhem if a previous pastor has been engaged in serious wrongdoing but members of the congregation do not believe it and resent the changes made. Often it is helpful to name and discuss the complicated loyalties. The new leader may need to ask for loyalty (at least to the position) until the tensions have been worked through.

Making Promises or Expectations Explicit

During times of transition in a community, it is important to find opportunities to make implicit promises more explicit. Misunderstandings are particularly likely when communities and congregations are incorporating new people or new leadership. Explicit discussions about expectations and commitments can be illuminating and helpful because, when assumptions are not spelled out, people can have different expectations without even knowing it.

Transitions in leadership tend to bring issues of faithfulness and promises to the surface acutely. Newcomers and those who have been in a community for a long time can struggle over who has access to money or how resources are used. Misunderstandings emerge over vision, relevant history, and shared practices. Often this is addressed in the vocabulary of fidelity. What some members see as adjusting to changing times or circumstances is interpreted by others as a betrayal of historic community commitments.

Within congregational life, it is important to provide opportunities to reflect corporately on the promises we've made to one another and to God in baptism, membership, and within the larger church tradition.[19] When a community reflects on its commitments and expectations within a context of love and flexibility, it is better able to benefit from the changes brought by new people or new leadership.

The complexity of implicit assumptions is also evident when, in an effort to be open to different personality types or to unexpected moves of the Holy Spirit, some leaders are willing to live with a high degree of flexibility and ambiguity. They and their communities tend to reject hierarchical relationships and emphasize equality, friendship, or partnership instead. In most cases, however, there are still lines of accountability and ultimate authority — though they are softer and often less obvious.

Informal or nonhierarchical staff relationships and substantial individual freedom can work well if each staff member is fairly mature and has a well-developed sense of personal responsibility. Things generally go more smoothly, however, if each person is aware of the implicit expectations and the actual internal authority structures. But more often than not, the inexperienced staff member or volunteer misses or misreads invisible lines of authority or misunderstands expectations because they have not been clearly stated. The person does not have the experience or framework to supply the missing information. What seems like freedom leaves the more inexperienced person quite vulnerable.

Conditional Promises

While our promise-making and promise-keeping are always somewhat provisional and incomplete, there are times that we choose to keep commitments more open-ended. If we are very uncertain about the future or about the people involved, we sometimes make conditional promises: "If certain conditions are met, then. . . ."

In the context of ministry, we might want to give a new person the benefit of the doubt, or make the most generous arrangements until they prove unworkable. Often we want to allow opportunities for growth or change, and we decide to take risks. We don't necessarily know how God will use a person, so we don't want to close doors, even if the situation seems risky or we see red flags. On the other hand, we don't necessarily want to enter into agreements without the capacity to reconsider them if things really do not work out.

One participant in the project described his experience. As a newly appointed pastor in a church, he was asked by the former interim (retired) pastor if he could stay on in the congregation. Recognizing the risks, the new pastor responded with a conditional promise: "If you are on board, you can stay." Gradually, in this case, it became clear that the former pastor was not "on board" but instead was subtly holding on to control and to parishioners' loyalty. Numerous small acts of infidelity undermined the new pastor. When the problem was addressed, the retired leader was deeply hurt, and some of his supporters were very angry. Messy loyalties and conditional promises collided.

Conditional promises are difficult because they imply some kind of ongoing evaluation of whether the conditions have been met. People can feel as if they are permanently on trial. Unless arrangements are put in place ahead of time that allow for revisiting the fulfillment of the conditions and the promise, it is easy for the entire situation to explode.

If there are conditions, it is important to spell them out so that all the parties know the expectations. However, this can also be quite awkward and sometimes leads to a proliferation of rules. Ongoing and frequent conversation about mutual responsibilities seems crucial to keeping communication open in these circumstances.

Living with Promises We Don't Like

A covenant is generally made up of a set of promises or commitments. Sometimes we disagree with, or are troubled by, individual promises or specifications within a larger covenant. We wonder how best to amend particular promises while being faithful to the covenant, community, or vision. These are not usually promises related to major moral issues or theological beliefs, but often involve lifestyle distinctives.

Traditions prone toward defining morality in terms of obedience to rules can seem harsh and unyielding about commitments. In response, communities moving away from legalistic approaches sometimes give very ambiguous signals about the importance of certain promises. In some cases, they move forward by ignoring, or winking at, certain behaviors or infractions. Folks do not necessarily recognize that they are simultaneously undermining larger notions of fidelity and promise-keeping. Fears about "legalism" can result in careless interpretations of promising.

What do we do with promises that we find troubling or inconvenient after we've made them or after we've had to live with them for a while? How should we live when we have agreed to abide by an "ethos" whose requirements we don't fully embrace? When people who know that they are expected to keep a particular promise deliberately break it, how do they talk to themselves morally about what they are doing?

For some communities within the Wesleyan, holiness, and evangelical traditions, a commitment to not using alcohol has been a requirement for membership or employment for generations. A number of responses have been common. Many individuals choose not to drink because they agree with the policy. Others abide by the requirement whether or not they personally agree with it because they recognize the importance of living truthfully and of having made a promise to a community. Others parse the restriction carefully — they don't drink in work or church settings or with certain people, but they do drink in other circumstances. A few folks violate the pledge and drink openly.

Community responses also vary. Some leaders "overlook" certain breaches of promise. Others secretly offer "special" individuals exemption from promises that most folks are expected to keep. In other communities, the commitments are enforced quite strictly. Even when we are hard-pressed to see drinking or not drinking as important to Christian identity, keeping one's word and respecting the commitments of a community are crucial to integrity.

Years ago, I had a conversation with a man who had been a modern-day hero in the civil rights movement within his own country. During the most intense years, he often smoked a pipe to relax. He had been invited to spend a year on an "alcohol and tobacco free" campus, and in an effort to be hospitable, some of the leaders gave him permission to smoke his pipe in the privacy of his campus apartment. His response was quite instructive. "I've been through too much to sneak around and undermine my integrity over this. I'll abide by the rule like everyone else." His response helped me understand how he had endured decades of pressure in working for social change.

Occasionally we so deeply disagree with a commitment or promise that we conclude that to keep it is to "break faith" with true biblical views on the subject. In these cases, a truthful and direct approach with the community seems important. If the problem is a real moral issue, we may need to follow Martin Luther King's advice for civil disobedience — taking action that is public, loving, and willing to accept the penalty.[20] But in other cases, where the disagreement is less fundamental and we deeply value the community, we will need to abide by promises while working to change the ones with which we disagree. It may be less appealing, but in that way we honor our commitments to the community.

In the grand scheme of things, restrictions on drinking and smoking can seem like leftovers from a repressive time. We may long for freedom or want to focus on more important things; we may see the rules as hindrances to evangelism and outreach. Nevertheless, it is important to remember that faithfulness and integrity flourish when there is both truthfulness and promise-keeping. Most of our deliberate promise-breaking also involves deception.

Releasing Persons from Promises

As we try to keep our promises, it is important to discern between being faithful in hard places and allowing a project to die when that is appropriate. Our call is fidelity to God rather than to results or success, but other factors are relevant, like capacity, available resources, and changed circumstances. When we have invested a great deal of work or hope in a project or community, it is hard to trust that some things are good for a time, but then can be let go. Sometimes we need to find ways to end programs or to close institutions with integrity and in a manner that honors previous contributions and sacrifices.

When we let something go or "die," we often struggle to interpret the meaning of the energy that has been expended in building it. Especially if the commitment has been costly but also hasn't yet borne the fruit we expected, we wonder about the "spoiled" sacrifice. At times, concern about how much has been invested keeps us at a project for too long.

"When was it OK to leave a situation?" asked Chris Rice as his community struggled to continue. "A bedrock belief for us, even when we failed at it, was fidelity to a people and a place." He explained that in their experience, "leaving was always desertion; it was always divorce." Chris explained further, "'I have never felt comfortable that within our circle there seems to be no good way to go. The only Antioch category for someone leaving is negative.'" In close-knit communities, departures often make it feel like there is unfinished business. Leaving the community without breaking the relationships is a crucial challenge.[21]

In my own experience, some departures have been far more painful than others. Years ago, I was part of a congregation that had a hard time welcoming folks whose lives remained troubled even after they had become Christians. Because of the work I was doing, such folks were the ones I wanted to bring with me to church. After a while, I concluded that, for everyone's sake, I should move to a congregation that had a stronger vision of hospitality at the margins. When I told the pastor, he responded, "There are only two reasons people leave a church. Either there is something wrong with them, or there is something wrong with the church. And there's nothing wrong with the church." His view made the break much more difficult. Though not often stated quite this straightforwardly, this assumption underlies many attitudes toward departures.

When projects that have required significant faithfulness and sacrifice are completed, it is important to take time to celebrate what the completion represents. In other situations, when projects and programs are ending because they are no longer helpful or viable, it is also important to take time to recognize contributions, express gratitude, and celebrate what has been accomplished. Otherwise, people limp away with a deep sense of loss and disappointment.

Sometimes an entire community is considering its own dissolution. Chris Rice shares the advice his father offered him as the Antioch community walked through a time of discernment. "'One of the most difficult decisions to make is when to close or transform a group,' he wrote, 'when its purpose has been fulfilled, when those who are a part of it no longer have the will, the vision, the desire, or the resources to keep it going. This is especially difficult when the group has been successful, is known, and has generated expectations for others.'" But there are times when this is the right choice, and Chris noted, "To dismantle community without dismantling our relationships could only be done the way we had built this place — patiently, with care."[22]

Dismantling a project without tearing up the relationships involved is challenging in the best circumstances, but it is also a reminder that our small efforts are not the final word. God's grace and fidelity go with us into the future.

In addition to the complexity and complications we encounter in making and keeping promises, sometimes our communities are broken apart or destroyed by deliberate forms of infidelity or betrayal. We will explore such challenges in the next chapter.

CHAPTER SEVEN

Going Deeper: Exploring What Weakens and What Strengthens Promising

For one to be accounted faithful one must keep one's promises.

Thomas Aquinas, *Summa Theologica*

Exploring Deformations of Promising

In a group home, rewards for good behavior were based on a point system. Three residents had excelled one week and were promised an evening out and personal time with Carolyn, a staff member. They had prepared eagerly for the event and then waited and waited. Carolyn never came to pick them up, nor did she call them to explain what had happened.

Later, another staff person contacted Carolyn, who said that she had been too tired to do anything else that evening. When challenged about the disappointment the residents had experienced, she responded, "Well, we don't always get what we want, do we? Tell them we'll do it another time." There was no other time, and it was one more disappointment in lives already shaped by multiple betrayals. Not surprisingly, the next week at the group home was terrible. The residents' behavior was angry, sullen, and uncooperative.

Betrayal

When we break promises, we also betray relationships and erode community. Small betrayals often do a surprising amount of damage. They involve other broken practices — deception instead of speaking the truth, absence instead of welcome, grumbling and envy instead of gratitude.

Betrayal within Community

Theologians have frequently viewed betrayal as a grave sin. For John Calvin, unfaithfulness or infidelity is at the root of the fall — and ambition, pride, and ingratitude are some of its bitter fruit.[1] In Dante's *Inferno,* the ninth and lowest circle is for those who betray what they should be most faithful to.[2] Despite recognition of its gravity, we have tended to overlook the impact of betrayal on community life — that is, until we are faced with its deeply destructive consequences.

How do we explain to ourselves what we are doing when we are unfaithful to a spouse, cheat on church finances, or misuse our power? Do we tell ourselves that "this situation is different" or that "they don't understand my needs"? How do we justify our actions — even to ourselves? People rarely anticipate the impact of their infidelity on family members, parishioners, students, onlookers, or God's kingdom. The self-deception at the heart of betrayal allows us to ignore its terrible cost to community.

Our fidelities are often deeply intertwined in Christian communities. When a married couple begins a church plant, their marriage and the future of the church become linked. If, after several years, the couple divorces, the community is also at risk for being torn apart because of the relationships that are affected. The one rupture cannot be isolated; it bleeds into other marriages and friendships. The community then struggles to sort out faithfulness under these new circumstances.

When we are on the receiving end of failed promises but do not see a justification or excuse for them, we feel betrayed. Our deepest betrayals are tied to failures in our most significant relationships and commitments. Betrayal is devastating to our trust and sense of justice, and sometimes to our faith.

Christian workers often underestimate our own capacity for sin. We sometimes overlook small infidelities or deceptions, assuming they won't matter in the grand scheme of things. Because we are involved in important work "for the kingdom," we imagine that accountability and fidelity somehow matter less. Ironically, the self-confidence that derives from being connected with God's purposes in the world can make us very vulnerable to careless expressions of infidelity.

Clergy misconduct is a particularly destructive form of betrayal. The role of pastor is associated with the entire congregation, with the larger identity of the church, and with God. People don't necessarily separate these, and when someone in an institutional role betrays central promises, trust is undermined quite generally. Congregations that have been betrayed by the misconduct of their leaders often take years to recover. Subsequent pastors struggle to find and address the wounds scattered throughout the congregation. Patterns of behavior that have resulted from the broken trust are often hard to interpret.

Because of the impact of betrayal on trust and relationships, we are often harsh with those who break significant promises or violate commitments. But most of us fail in some commitment — sometimes in small and occasionally in great ways. In the messiest situations, there are multiple betrayals, and it is not necessarily clear who betrayed whom. Instead of responding to sin or human weakness redemptively, some communities "shoot their wounded." The most fragile folks are often also the most vulnerable in these settings. How we respond to betrayal and continue in love becomes a major test of individual and communal character.

Redemptive responses to misconduct involve patience, confession, correction, forgiveness, and accountability within community. Sometimes it is appropriate for the community to ask whether it had a role in the betrayal. Would the failure have been less likely if structures of accountability had been in place? A couple who provided welcome to a troubled teenager realized that they had made it too easy for him to steal from them when they left their checkbook out in the open, and when they frequently left him alone. Forging checks was his responsibility, but they also acknowledged their own lack of wisdom in not protecting him from some temptations.

Fidelity in small things adds up to a way of life that is whole; betrayal breaks our lives and relationships into pieces. The gospel, however, does not suggest that a life of faithfulness, love, and service will protect us from disappointments and betrayals.

Biblical Images of Betrayal

On the cross, Jesus bore our betrayals, infidelity, and sin. His disciples failed him miserably, and we, like them, fail and betray and need forgiveness. Judas's act often first comes to mind when we think of betrayal — betraying a friend with a kiss. Blood money, remorse, death, suicide — all the dramatic elements of treachery and infidelity are condensed into one short account. But the other disciples provide us with a more familiar version of betrayal — the garden variety of fear, boasting, desertion, and denial. The story would be almost comic if it weren't so sad.

After he ate the Passover meal with his disciples, Jesus told them that they would desert him. Peter, in his love and his ignorance, said that would never happen — even if everyone else did, even if he had to die with Christ, "I will not deny you." All the other disciples agreed: We'll never be unfaithful. But Jesus responded that before the daybreak, Peter would deny him three times (Matt. 26:31-35).

Peter doesn't seem to have realized that his acts of betrayal would be in very undramatic settings. He didn't deny Jesus in front of the Sanhedrin or in a speech to the ruling authorities; he did it in front of servant girls and bystanders. Frightened by the unfolding events, Peter lied and betrayed; he did not keep his promise to Jesus. He compounded his lies with oaths and with increasingly passionate denials. When the cock crowed, he realized what he had done, and he wept bitterly (Matt. 26:69-75).[3]

Despite their unfaithfulness, Jesus did not abandon Peter and the other disciples. After his resurrection, Jesus met them on a lakeshore and cooked breakfast for them — breakfast for friends who had deserted him. The Gospel of John gives us a tender glimpse into the moments of forgiveness, healing, and restoration. Jesus particularly met Peter at the point of his brokenness — his failed fidelity — and drew him back into relationship and ministry (John 21:15-19).

All four Gospel writers provide an account of the disciples' betrayal and desertion of Jesus; those betrayals are part of the story of our redemption. Additionally, in Jesus' trial, Pilate knowingly betrays an innocent man, and betrays his responsibility as a ruler to provide justice. Herod, many of the religious leaders, and the crowds all contribute to this archetypal story of betrayal.

But the biblical accounts also remind us that being betrayed does not mean that we have failed. Jesus' fidelity took him to Gethsemane, betrayal, and death. In ministry, we too can find ourselves betrayed by those we love. When we offer welcome and care to someone who then steals from us, it is easy to feel as if we have failed. When we befriend children who live on the streets, help them to begin to flourish in a new life, and then find that some go back to their old situations, we feel betrayed. But, much like the Gospel accounts, neither our stories nor theirs are finished, and our primary calling to faithfulness should shape what we count as success.

Abandonment

Closely connected to betrayal, even in the story of Jesus and his disciples, is abandonment or desertion. This can be as major as a person who denies the faith under persecution, or as minor as an individual who leaves a particular church during a difficult period. Congregations struggle with how to respond to these folks and re-incorporate them within community.

In the early church, there were major disagreements over what to do with the believers who had, under persecution, displayed weakness, denied the faith, or sacrificed to other gods. Especially in settings where other believers had suffered a great deal in order to remain faithful to their beliefs, disputes arose over whether and how persons who had "abandoned" the faith in hard times might be re-admitted to the Christian community and into the Eucharist.[4] Eventually, a willingness to welcome people (after penance) prevailed.

In the contemporary West, few of us have had to face overt persecution for our faith, and our fidelity has not often been tested. We have not prepared people well to stay the course; in fact, part of the difficulty with fidelity and promise-keeping in the church today is that we don't tell people there is a cost to following Jesus that involves sacrifice, commitment, and cross-bearing (Luke 14:27).

More familiar today are church members who leave their congregations during times of difficulty but then want to return after things have settled down again. Especially in small towns, where congregations are dealing with a fairly small and stable population, this can be difficult for those who remained faithful to the congregation. One pastor in the project shared his story. For a year and a half after a major church meltdown due to the previous pastor's misconduct, the congregation suffered greatly from diminished prayer, attendance, gifts, and service. He recalled, "The mission of the church was largely abandoned," and members who remained felt burdened and hurt. They wondered how brothers and sisters who had "pledged their participation" could willingly choose to "abandon ship."

In order to move forward, the congregation needed to find ways to forgive friends who had left. It was crucial that trust be restored. The new pastor spent three months preaching and teaching from the book of Nehemiah on "rebuilding the walls," addressing repentance, restoration, and service. He gently encouraged the community to let go of some of the symbols that had represented their divisions.

Though framed in spiritual language, another expression of abandonment is "putting it all on the altar," a desperate attempt to break free from commitments that have become overwhelming. Years ago, I was part of a wonderful congregation with an extraordinary ministry to refugees. We did not, however, have any sense of limits or boundaries, and gradually the level of responsibility for several hundred recently arrived refugees became unbearable. The staff and congregation members grew very weary. Our intentions had been good, and we had made a lot of commitments — more than any small community could fulfill.

This weariness coincided with a current wave of charismatic teaching about "putting it all on the altar" — giving everything back to God. It sounded not only spiritual but very appealing; we could give everything to God! The only problem was that we'd made commitments to people's well-being, and renouncing our commitments by abandoning them to God had the potential for gross irresponsibility. We could put our dreams or ambitions "on the altar," but not the people we had promised to give a new home.

In the end, we did not abandon our promises; we persevered, and gradually the responsibilities eased. But in the absence of Sabbath-keeping and wisdom about limits, we had become very vulnerable, and along with us, the people for whom we'd taken temporary responsibility.

Other acts of infidelity are less overt. When someone has been hurt, but we don't have the necessary capacity or energy to remedy the situation, sometimes we simply allow the person to float away from the community. Silence and inattention provide a convenient cover for irresponsibility and abandonment.

In a results-oriented culture, we struggle with the patience necessary for fidelity. We imagine that it is better to move on to more satisfying or fruitful projects than to stay with those that do not seem to be yielding much fruit. Of course, sometimes this is appropriate, but Eugene Peterson offers a word of warning: "Impatience, the refusal to *endure,* is to pastoral character what strip mining is to the land — a greedy rape of what can be gotten at the least cost, and then abandonment in search of another place to loot."[5]

In the biblical text, there are limits to fidelity. Jesus instructs disciples to shake the dust off their feet as they leave some villages that have shown no interest in the good news.[6] The practice of discernment[7] is key in knowing whether and when it is time to move on, or to leave behind certain good commitments in order to follow Jesus more fully. But in our fast-

MAKING AND KEEPING PROMISES

paced, results-driven communities, we need to at least question the prevailing impulse to quickly move on to the next thing.

Promises We Shouldn't Make and Shouldn't Keep

In Mark 6:14-29, John the Baptist's death follows immediately upon a promise that never should have been made.[8] John was in prison because King Herod's wife had found his truth-telling annoying. She disliked John's assessment of her relationship with Herod, and she wanted him out of the way. Herod, though disturbed by John, also knew him to be a "righteous and holy man." Herod "liked to listen to him"; he found John engaging, though he did not respond to his words with a change in lifestyle.

Herod did, however, respond to a very "pleasing" dance by his wife's daughter. He promised her anything she wanted — up to half his kingdom. She went to her mother for advice and asked immediately for John's head on a platter. It was a revolting request, morally outrageous, simultaneously petty and terrible.

Despite the outrageous nature of the request, because of his own pride and weakness, and "out of regard for his oaths and for the guests," Herod "did not want to refuse her" (Mark 6:26). John was beheaded because of a promise to a girl who provided pleasing entertainment at a birthday party.

Herod was weak and morally stupid; he was worried about — and captivated by — the wrong things. He knew John was good and imprisoned him anyway, and then had him killed. Knowing was not enough; pleasure, sensuality, and pride triumphed. Herod betrayed the authority entrusted to him, and keeping his promise became an excuse for terrible behavior.[9]

The content of our promises matters — not just that we keep them. When we follow through on a promise that should never have been made, we do not convert it into something good.[10] The emphasis on keeping promises should not be used as a "way of making immoral acts seem to be not only morally acceptable but morally obligatory."[11]

Misplaced Fidelity

Gang loyalties often include strong structures of promising, but our promise-keeping is deformed when we are faithful to the wrong persons or things. Unless human fidelity is located in the larger context of fidelity to God, our loves and loyalties will not be rightly ordered.

Unquestioning loyalty to a person or cause is very dangerous because human demands for faithfulness can be idolatrous or manipulative, and abuses of authority and power are common. This is painfully evident when a pastor or leader becomes the sole authority in a community, demands total allegiance from the members, and claims subtly (or not so subtly) that allegiance to the leader is equivalent to allegiance to God. Any questions, alternate views, or challenges to leadership are then interpreted as infidelity to God. Only by placing human loyalties within a covenantal context framed by loyalty to God and mutual responsibility can communities be protected from such abuses.

In addition, our fidelity to certain subgroups within a community can undermine loyalty to the larger community. As Jean Vanier, in *Community and Growth,* has observed, both friends and enemies are a danger to community. When a group of friends closes in on itself and commands special loyalties, the negative impact on the larger community can be significant.[12]

We can see the destructive power of this when a small group within a church conducts secret meetings to discuss whether a congregation can "move forward" under a particular pastor's leadership. Loyalty to a small group can leave its members feeling very empowered because they are knit tightly together and are "in the know." Sin is deceptive, and intense personal loyalties can blind us to the ways we are harming others.[13] Even when a small group is attempting to preserve the faith or tradition, if the means they use include secrecy and deception, they ultimately undermine any good they are trying to accomplish.

To be faithful to God, sometimes we must forsake prior loyalties and promises. Wisdom is needed for knowing how to undo or rework promises that should not have been made, and how to help new believers recognize that some of their promises must be honored because they matter humanly. The apostle Paul takes human promises seriously when he encourages believers to keep their marriage covenants with non-believers (1 Cor. 7:12-16).

At times, we struggle with faithfulness to persons because we both care for them deeply and disapprove of their actions or conduct. We struggle particularly with those who mistakenly assume that love for them requires unquestioning allegiance and affirmation detached from moral judgment and guidance. But fidelity without any expectations of the other person is not necessarily helpful, and always "being there" for a person or a community can reinforce destructive patterns and relationships. Choices here can be agonizing, and only as we keep our loves rightly ordered are we able to make difficult but responsible decisions.

Secrecy and Confidentiality

Promises of confidentiality are violated regularly in many communities. The violations are often introduced with "Please don't repeat this, but . . ." Gossip and half-truths are spread in the name of prayer requests. In some cases, promises to keep information confidential should not have been made. Usually, however, confidences should be kept as an expression of fidelity and trustworthiness.[14]

Other forms of information that are interesting but also potentially destructive are often best simply absorbed. It can be satisfying to "be in the know," and empowering to have the latest information in a crisis. When that information is selectively shared, however, some of the power comes by exclusion. Limiting access to information can be used to tell partial truths and to secretly shape responses in particular directions. A wise and good person absorbs rather than repeats information that simply adds fuel to the fire.

When we are secretive about breaking promises, deception and betrayal are intertwined.[15] Especially if communities have entrusted particular persons with responsibility to carry out a task or mission in a defined way, they depend on those persons to keep their promises. This is most important when such designated persons are not under public scrutiny. Congregations entrust their children to a youth camp expecting that the staff will abide by the established rules regarding staff behavior, exposure to risk, and so on. Failures in these areas are serious violations of trust.[16]

Irresponsibility or Grace?

A commitment to offering grace can add to our uncertainty about the ways in which we should hold persons accountable for their behavior, betrayals, or abandonment. We can mistake passivity for patience and fidelity; and especially if concerns about truthfulness are not addressed, we can allow destructive patterns to continue indefinitely.

In one case, the fear of a church member's temper tantrums eventually controlled the decision-making process in the church. Because the pastor and congregation did not confront him, they became complicit in their own destruction. As the abusive member observed to the new pastor who was only gradually learning the complicated dynamics of that congregation's life, "I was the power in the church 'til you came along."

In small congregations, the inclination to tolerate or overlook problems and manipulative or abusive behavior can be high, especially if the person is needed for the skills they bring or the resources they supply. Without truthfulness and accountability, however, fidelity is ultimately destructive.

Trust and forgiveness sometimes stand in tension with moral and legal responsibilities. We do not want to anticipate deception or betrayal, but we also cannot leave situations wide open for it to happen. It is important that structures are in place for staff and volunteers to account for things like their use of money or church credit cards. Background checks for nursery and child-care workers can feel awkward, but they are an effort to protect the most vulnerable.

While we want to celebrate spontaneity, freedom, and creativity, it is also important to link these traits to practical expressions of fidelity such as showing up prepared, keeping good records, and anticipating predictable difficulties. As one free-spirited friend who was also learning the importance of promise-keeping commented, "Style may explain me, but it doesn't excuse me."

Making and Keeping Promises Carelessly

The philosopher Søren Kierkegaard uses Jesus' parable in Matthew 21:28-31 to reflect on the risks in our practices of promising. In the parable, the two brothers respond differently to their father's request to work in the vineyard. One refuses but later changes his mind and goes to work; the other brother says he will go but does not. Jesus asks, "Which of the two did the will of his father?" Kierkegaard writes,

> Though the yes-brother was not a deceiver when he said "Yes," he nevertheless became a deceiver when he failed to keep his promise. In his very eagerness in promising he became a deceiver. When you say "Yes" or promise something, you can very easily deceive yourself and others also, as if you had already done what you promised. It is easy to think

that by making a promise you have at least done part of what you promised to do, as if the promise itself were something of value. Not at all! In fact, when you do not do what you promise, it is a long way back to the truth.

Beware! The "Yes" of promise-keeping is sleep-inducing. An honest "No" possesses much more promise. It can stimulate; repentance may not be far away. He who says "No" becomes almost afraid of himself. But he who says "Yes, I will" is all too pleased with himself. The world is quite inclined — even eager — to make promises, for a promise appears very fine at the *moment* — it inspires! Yet for this very reason the eternal is suspicious of promises.[17]

If we are not thoughtful about the promises we make, and if we ignore our own limitations or the costs involved, we are likely to become habitual promise-breakers. "Even if a promise is fairly trivial, a cavalier attitude towards the obligation to keep it is not." Such an attitude reveals much about a person's integrity, "in much the same way as does cheating at a trivial game."[18] We learn quickly in community that the reliability of a promise is tied to the reliability of the person making the promise, and we are foolish to trust habitual promise-breakers to follow through on what they say.[19]

It is easy and often personally affirming to say "yes" to requests for our presence or assistance. In one congregation, the senior pastor was unable to say no to parishioners' requests. Frequently he came back to other staff members with some version of this question: "I know I should have asked first, but can you find a way to do this?" Staff members were in continual turmoil trying to fulfill promises they hadn't made, promises that should not have been made. Because the pastor wanted to be liked and wanted to avoid conflict, he did not set any boundaries, but then also displaced the fallout on an increasingly weary and frustrated staff.

Without some recognition of our limits, we soon find our commitments in conflict with each other. Rather than deal with the interpersonal challenges of saying "no" initially, we make promises we can't keep. Then, in the crush of conflicting obligations, we chop off commitments like we're hacking at brush we're trying to clear.

Sometimes we make promises in order to smooth out relationships in the moment, or to make endings or departures easier. "We'll get together soon." "I'll be in touch — I promise." In such cases, and in times when we haven't counted the cost involved in keeping a particular promise, it would be more faithful and truthful not to make a promise than to make one carelessly and break it.

People who take their responsibilities and commitments very seriously, however, can find these discussions about keeping promises burdensome. They already keep their promises, and feel overwhelmed by the responsibility. The challenge for these folks is often in the area of making promises — are they recognizing their own limitations? Are they being pressed into more and more roles because they "come through" even when the costs are mounting up and the community should be finding other ways to accomplish its purposes?

Living into the Practice of Making and Keeping Promises

Communities that practice fidelity help us see God's faithfulness more clearly. Jean Vanier explains,

> In our time, when there is so much infidelity, when there are so many broken marriages, so many disturbed relationships . . . so many people who have not been faithful to their promise to love each other, more and more communities need to be born as signs of fidelity. . . . The communities whose members live faithfully a life-long covenant with God, among themselves and with the poor . . . are signs of the fidelity of God.[20]

Much of the work of keeping our promises within families, congregations, and communities is undramatic and mundane. Even so, we can discover "the gift and grace in . . . the book-keeping, the meetings, the chores, and the welcome." The communities we long for, as Vanier notes, are being "born of our fidelity to the present."[21] There are a number of ways we can help our communities live well into this practice.

Counting the Cost and Honoring Faithfulness

When we emphasize the importance of making and keeping promises, we need also to help people learn to assess the kinds of commitments they should make. One pastor realized that he could help volunteers in the church anticipate whether they would be able to keep the promises they made. He learned to ask them, "Well, what kind of week is ahead for you? What can you expect?" Gradually he guided them into being able to discern when it was right to say no to certain opportunities. In another congregation, the pastor had learned not to make commitments if she was unsure the congregation would be willing to keep them, even when they involved fairly simple things. She found it helpful instead to engage in a steady effort to bring people onboard before taking on any new project.

In our efforts to strengthen the practice of promising, it is important to be careful about the commitments we ask for from others. As noted earlier, commitments should be rightly ordered within our covenantal relationship with God. Many people have a nagging sense that they should be doing more — but they are working with a very unwieldy notion of what they should be doing. A renewed emphasis on our most important promises could be profoundly freeing for them.

Because it is often taken for granted, promise-keeping is usually overlooked when it is functioning well. Recognizing acts of fidelity, and occasionally naming ordinary ones as important, can strengthen the practice. We can reflect on stewardship as an expression of being faithful with resources and as an act of fidelity to God, community, and past and future generations. Similarly, when we reflect together on church membership as entailing significant promises, even life-altering commitments, we challenge consumer attitudes toward congregational life.

Keeping promises can be very costly. In contemporary culture, however, self-sacrifice — which is often about faithfulness in the hard places — is sometimes seen as dysfunctional. We need to become more careful about how sacrifice is interpreted. Caring for a child with severe disabilities, for example, or an aging parent who needs more and more attention, can affect the caregiver's health, relationships, career, and capacity to do other things. When caregivers become weary, congregations should have more supportive responses than telling them that they "need better boundaries" or should take a day off. Faithful support of the caregivers makes their long-term sacrifices more bearable. Their care is an expression of fidelity that is deserving of respect and honor from the community.

Surely discernment is needed when our fidelity and our limitations crash into each other. There are times when our commitments overwhelm us, and we need wisdom and help. Years ago, Edith Schaeffer, co-founder of L'Abri Fellowship, observed that "it is not sinful to be finite."[22] Patterns of rest and renewal within community are crucial to sustaining fidelity over the long term.

Recognizing the Blessing of Consistency

Though it seems very ordinary, consistency in showing up for worship or small-group meetings provides the communal context in which our work is accomplished and our relationships are strengthened. Many of us value spontaneity more highly than consistency, but when the church carries out its daily or weekly activities, it is keeping its promises.

In the midst of a crisis that is filled with confusion, it can be helpful to be faithful to the tasks we know need to be done. We can take care of our families, parishioners, or students; we can shoulder our responsibilities even as storms rage around us. Eventually the storms subside, and we find that the damage has been limited by our consistency in daily tasks.

Although we might be wary of structures and institutions, they are also expressions of fidelity over time and can provide a consistency that helps us to persevere even when perseverance is inconvenient or not very satisfying. Legal requirements that must be observed, responsible accounting practices, and bank regulations are structures that help sustain both fidelity and truthfulness. Some folks view these as unnecessary intrusions into the Christian life, but often such persons are naïve about how the people of God can be tempted in the areas of money, sex, and power.

Promises and structures may constrain our behavior, but they also anchor us so that we can pursue what we most desire or value. Jean Vanier has observed that "the essential nourishment" of healthy communities "is fidelity to the thousand and one small demands of each day."[23] It is an important insight — that promise-keeping and fidelity are fundamentally nourishing. They are life-giving — not first of all troublesome or costly, but nourishing.

Patience and Accompaniment

Allowing time for commitments to develop and promises to be fulfilled is at odds with a culture that demands immediate results. Taking time for discernment regarding difficult questions related to fidelity is sometimes mistaken for weakness or uncertainty. A willingness to "stay with the process" or to stay in connection with a community during difficult or uncertain times allows progress to be made in spite of the messiness. Although giving things "time" does not guarantee that we will move forward or find healing, slowing processes down often provides opportunity for giving attention to relational issues.

There are some problems that cannot be completely fixed, however, and some wounds that cannot be fully healed. Patient, grace-filled accompaniment is part of fidelity; being there when what we can offer is our presence and our love, but no immediate solutions. After decades of experience with this, Vanier has concluded: "The more we live community life, the more we discover that it is not so much a question of resolving problems as of learning to live with them patiently. Most problems are not resolved. With time, and a certain insight and fidelity in listening, they clear up when we least expect them to." "But there will always be others to take their place!"[24]

"You won't give up on me, will you?" asked one young friend in particularly difficult circumstances. Over and over again, her fear of being abandoned surfaced. She worried that she had used up her chances and her friendships as she walked very slowly through a dark valley. She sensed that people were getting weary of her litanies of despair. In fact, we do tend to expect people to get better, especially if we give them our attention and our help. We trust that they will honor our investment of time and energy by improving, and we often grow impatient if it doesn't happen quickly. But as we walk alongside people with chronic or terminal illnesses or other disabling conditions, learning the grace of accompaniment is an enormous gift.

Some promises take longer than our own lifetime to come to fruition. The Scriptures recognize this — in Hebrews 11, we read of the many faithful men and women who died without receiving what was promised. It would come to them, but not in their lifetime. We do not necessarily see the full fruit of our testimony or faithfulness.

Telling and Re-Telling Our Stories

Re-articulating the vision and commitments of a community on a regular basis helps founding members and those who have recently joined understand why things are done in certain ways. Discussions of the vision of the community can be an expression of faithfulness and can help maintain focus amid changed circumstances or needs. Especially in mission-driven congregations, re-affirming covenantal commitments encourages people to attach to the community and not just to particular individuals within the community.

In re-telling the story of a community, especially its creation account, we preserve and celebrate its history, commitments, and values. Remembering is a communal practice, and such re-telling provides the next generation with ongoing opportunities to internalize community stories and values. When we tell the biblical story as well as the stories of our traditions, congregations, and communities, we are reminded of who we are and to whom we belong. Our activities are then situated in a fuller and richer context.

After I finished a workshop with Salvation Army officers on the historic Christian tradition of offering hospitality to strangers, one man was visibly moved. He told me that for decades he had provided beds and breakfasts to thousands of homeless men without a sense that his work fit into any larger story. He had been faithful; he had kept his commitments and provided care for a multitude of people. But when he learned that Christians had valued (and engaged in) such practices for two thousand years, it changed how he viewed his own work and strengthened his resolve to serve in difficult places.

Fidelity is strengthened and the next generation of disciples is being shaped when we take time to review the story of our faith in communion and baptismal services, in new member classes and formation programs. When we draw closer connections between church rituals and the practice of promising, both are strengthened.

Making our commitments public can stabilize our promises. The promises associated with marriage and baptism are difficult for any human being, and it is naïve to think that anyone can keep them without the help of a community. In the case of marriage and baptismal services, the moments of individual promise-making are also reminders to the community of their own prior vows and commitments and serve as an opportunity to renew them. In this way, individual and corporate promises are mutually reinforcing.

A covenant service developed by John Wesley is used by some churches annually on New Year's Eve or another date to reinforce promises made personally and within the congregation. Together, the people recite the following covenant:

> And now, beloved, let us bind ourselves with willing bonds to our covenant God, and take the yoke of Christ upon us.
>
> This taking of his yoke upon us means that we are heartily content that he appoint us our place and work, and that he alone be our reward.

Christ has many services to be done; some are easy, others are difficult; some bring honor, others bring reproach; some are suitable to our natural inclinations and temporal interests, others are contrary to both. In some we may please Christ and please ourselves; in others we cannot please Christ except by denying ourselves. Yet the power to do all these things is assuredly given us in Christ, who strengtheneth us.

Therefore let us make the Covenant of God our own. Let us engage our heart to the Lord, and resolve in His strength never to go back.

Being thus prepared, let us now, in sincere dependence on His grace and trusting in His promises, yield ourselves anew to Him.[25]

Relying on God's Grace and Power

We can turn our fidelity into a demigod so that our efforts at faithfulness become a strange form of works righteousness. Keeping promises is reduced to an expression of sheer grit that is about me and my determination: "I keep my commitments." With such a perspective, we miss the grace and empowerment that come from trust in God, and fall prey to an exhausting form of idolatry. We close ourselves off from experiencing both gratitude and forgiveness.

It is only by the power of the Holy Spirit, the grace of God, and promises of Jesus that we are able to keep our promises and commitments in the hard places. When we or others fail, only grace can bring us to the point of forgiveness, and only grace can make our attempts at accountability life-giving rather than stifling.

The capacity to make and keep promises is central to all of the other practices, but promising is connected to living truthfully in particularly important ways. Truthfulness and fidelity form the structure of community and constitute trust, which is at the heart of our relationships. In the next three chapters, we will explore important dimensions of living truthfully.

PART III

Living Truthfully

CHAPTER EIGHT

Truth-Filled Lives

Teach me your way, O LORD, that I may walk in your truth;
give me an undivided heart to revere your name.
I give thanks to you, O Lord my God, with my whole heart,
and I will glorify your name forever.
For great is your steadfast love toward me. . . .

Psalm 86:11-13

In this psalm, David prays with gratitude to walk in God's truth with "an undivided heart." His words capture the wholeness of a way of life shaped by the transforming experience of God's steadfast love. Communities of people who love truth, live faithfully, and respond gratefully are rare, but they embody much of what the church is called to be and to do.

Christians who yearn for more vibrant congregational life often look to the book of Acts and the first Christian communities for a vision of shared life and its fullness. In Acts 2–4, we read that the earliest believers gathered in homes, devoted themselves to teaching and prayers, ate together, and lived in such a way that thousands came to faith in Jesus. Their preaching was bold and effective, accompanied by signs, wonders, healings, and generous sharing with those in need. Under the power of the Holy Spirit, there was a tight connection between close-knit community, powerful outreach, life-changing preaching, and miraculous healing.

These powerful images of congregational life, described in the first four chapters of Acts, do not prepare us for the incident recorded in the subsequent verses. As we longingly imagine what it might have been like to live in such a community, suddenly we are drawn into one of the more bizarre stories of early church life.

At the end of chapter 4, we learn that Barnabas, like other brothers and sisters who owned land and property, voluntarily sold some and gave the proceeds to the apostles for distribution to those in need. Then Ananias (chapter 5) sold some of his property and brought the income to the community. In this case, however, he secretly withheld a portion of the proceeds from the sale and donated the rest. Within a few minutes of offering his gift, he was dead. What happened? Things only got worse. Sapphira, his wife, had agreed to his secret withholding of some of the money, and when later confronted, she lied about the price they had received. She too was dead within a few hours. Not surprisingly, the author of Acts reports that "great fear seized the whole church and all who heard of these things" (Acts 5:11).

What happened to the beautiful community? Losing members to sudden death for minor infractions isn't usually included in the list of signs and wonders we'd like to see replicated in contemporary congregations. The responses seem disproportionate. Peter had betrayed Jesus and lied about his relationship with him, and yet now Peter was a leader in the community. What made Ananias's and Sapphira's deception so much worse or so different? At least they were sharing a portion of their resources with the community.

What in their acts could have warranted Peter's response that Satan had filled Ananias's heart and that he and Sapphira had put "the Spirit of the Lord to the test" (Acts 5:9) in their lies? No one was required to put all their money into the shared pot — it was voluntary. The couple could have reserved some of the profits for themselves. But they had chosen deception: acting as if they were giving everything while holding back at the same time. Deception and lying had moved directly into the heart of community life.

There may have been additional issues at work in this event, but a central part of the story is about the extraordinary danger of deception within Christian community.[1] And, for us, part of the value of this strange account is related to how early it appears in the life of the church. Deception, lying, and half-truths endanger communities and undermine our best efforts — they have from the beginning. Large and small, they break communities apart, distort our relationship with God, and separate us from one another. We can be thankful that our garden varieties of deception aren't often met with immediate death, but we can also benefit from the warning that this story offers. Minor deceptions often appear to serve our purposes, but they can also be very destructive.

Because we want to be good or at least appear to be good, because we compare ourselves to others and often come up short, and because we want what we want but can't always admit it, we are prone toward hypocrisy, duplicity, and deception. It's a vulnerability that many religious folks face. In the close connections of community life, the pressure can be significant to keep up appearances, enhance our spiritual image, and cover our failures or perversions.

We struggle with truthfulness and simultaneously take it for granted. It is very hard to do anything together if we cannot assume that people are going to be truthful with us, but we don't usually notice the practice unless something has gone wrong.[2] As Thomas Aquinas observed centuries ago, "It would be impossible for men to live together, unless they believed one another, as declaring the truth one to another."[3]

Despite the importance of truth and truthfulness, we might be inclined to agree with the Old Testament prophet who cried that truth "stumbles in the public square." Isaiah's description of his day echoes into our own experience of contemporary public life: people rely on empty arguments and speak lies; "there is no justice in their paths." "Righteousness stands at a distance," honesty is excluded, and even the court system is corrupted by lies, empty pleas, and unjust suits (Isa. 59).

Whether the culprits are petty criminals or well-placed corporate executives, pastors, priests, doctors, or political leaders, dishonesty and spin are common. We live with a powerful combination of false promises and false speech that has led to a significant loss of public truthfulness. As a result, many people have become deeply cynical about truthfulness in government, businesses, and churches, as well as in other moral and religious institutions.

If we take seriously God's assessment in the book of Jeremiah that the human heart is "deceitful above all things"[4] (Jer. 17:9), then perhaps we shouldn't be surprised by the condition of our world. But redeemed communities are called to a different life — one where we put away falsehood and speak truth with our neighbors, remembering that we belong to one another (Eph. 4:25). Perhaps, as Lewis Smedes has noted, the lie that Ananias and Sapphira told to the Holy Spirit and the community was dreadful because it "broke the bond of unity in the new creation."[5] Followers of Jesus are called to a common life of grace and truth.

Truth-Shaped Living

What does a community or congregation look like that loves truth or lives truthfully? What would truth-shaped living be like? Philosophers and theologians have reflected frequently on the nature of truth, but when they explore truthfulness, their discussions often center on whether a person should ever lie. The discussions are also quite narrow when we assume that truth-telling primarily involves telling someone something they don't want to hear. The importance of truthful living is much bigger than these issues.

In claiming to be "the way, and the truth, and the life" (John 14:6), Jesus connects truth with himself and with the path that he "embodies, exemplifies, and teaches."[6] We live truthfully as we fully embrace the purposes of God, experience the Holy Spirit as the Spirit of truth guiding us into truth, and as we know Jesus, who is full of grace and truth (John 14:17; 15:26; 16:13; 1:14). To know Jesus as the truth does not mean that we ignore the more abstract discussions about propositional understandings of truth, but it does mean that the personal and relational aspects of truth and truthfulness deserve full attention. We want to live and love truth.

When we allow God's grace, truth, love, and righteousness to be the framework for interpreting community life and relationships, then individuals and congregations are in a better position to address their sins and failures. Because of grace, we can see more clearly and acknowledge more truthfully the gap between our goodness and God's. We can also more confidently face our need to repent and change.

The relational dimensions of truthfulness are evident in Old Testament commands against lying. We are warned, "You shall not bear false witness *against your neighbor*" and "You shall not lie *to one another*" (Exod. 20:16; Lev. 19:11; italics added).[7] Lying and deception harm others, while truthfulness in relationships gives evidence of our renewal in the image of God. As Paul explains in Colossians 3:9-10, "Do not lie to one another, seeing that you have stripped off the old self with its practices and have clothed yourselves with the new self, which is being renewed in knowledge according to the image of its creator."[8]

People who love truth build others up with it rather than using it to tear them down; much of our truth-telling should involve affirming what is right and good. When Paul writes to the early church about moving toward deeper unity and maturity, he connects love and truth closely. "Speaking the truth in love" is at the heart of growing up in every way into

Christ (Eph. 4:1-15). Being truthful is not only about speaking hard things, but discerning the whole picture with gentleness, humility, and patience.

As mentioned earlier, we often worry more about appearances than we do about truth. A community that is truthful will not necessarily be tidy. There will be loose threads and rough edges because members are unwilling to hide their problems or to cover over wounds lightly, saying "'peace, peace' when there is no peace" (Jer. 6:14). Pastors often feel pressure to project a certain image and keep up appearances even when the reality is more troubled. One friend observed, "As I grew into the role (of pastor), I found myself both more confident and less able to be honest about my difficulties, weaknesses, and feelings. I found this contradiction vexing. How could serving God's people make me feel less Christ-like?" He concluded sadly that he had become increasingly worried about how he would be perceived.

Truthfulness + Fidelity = Being True

When we describe a person as being "true to her word," we mean that there is a close correspondence between what she says and does, and that her individual life has integrity. Her "true-ness" is often evident in her keeping promises. Because of this, she is viewed as trustworthy and reliable — someone we can count on because of her truthfulness and fidelity. The corollary, as Kierkegaard noted, is that "when you do not do what you promise, it is a long way back to the truth."[9]

A "true friend" is treasured because he or she is dependable, faithful, and proven, even in the hard places.[10] A close connection between truthfulness and fidelity is important at the individual as well as the community level because faithfulness in making and keeping promises is central to a community's ability to speak and hear the truth.

We tend to view truth-telling as a one-time event and truthfulness as "consistency between our mind and our message,"[11] but truthful living also involves forbearance, forgiveness, mutuality, and patience. In the Psalms, the Hebrew word *'emeth* was often translated as "truth" in the King James Version. In more recent translations, it is frequently translated as "faithfulness."[12] Its rich range of meaning includes stability, truth, trustworthiness, faithfulness, and verity. Especially in regard to God's character and action, when we look at truthfulness, we see its nearly inseparable connection with faithfulness (see Romans 3:3-4).[13]

The overlapping meanings of trustworthiness, reliability, truth, and faithfulness are central in thinking about truthful living, as Miroslav Volf explains:

> The idea that truth sustains community while deception destroys it is woven into the very notion of truth that we encounter in the biblical traditions. [In the Old Testament especially,] truth "was used of things that had proved to be reliable. . . . 'Reliability' would be the best comprehensive word in English to convey the idea. Truth is that on which others can rely.[14]

It is not surprising, then, that any capacity "to speak the truth in love" depends on fidelity and on taking our relationships seriously. In speaking as well as in living truthfully, our words and actions are an expression of our faithfulness to individuals, the community, and God.

Dimensions of Truth and Truthfulness

Complex and nuanced biblical understandings of truth and truthfulness are sometimes pulled apart in philosophical and theological attempts to provide precise definitions. This fracturing obscures the fact that numerous aspects of truth are operative in most communities. Volf explains,

> It is unfortunate that theologians who stress "truth as faithfulness" sometimes think they need to discard "truth as accordance with 'reality.'" . . . This is surely a false alternative, just as the alternative between "lie as an offense against trust" and "lie as an offense against truth" is a false one. . . . In biblical texts the notions of "reliability" and of "truthful speech" frequently appear together and are inextricably intertwined, though neither can be reduced to the other.[15]

Understandings of truth as reliability and truth as factual accuracy are complementary.[16]

Truth and truthfulness involve even more than reliability and factual accuracy, however; and our desire to know the truth is confirmed and embodied in our willingness to submit our lives to it — as it is revealed in Christ.[17] Paul argues in Romans 1 that God's truth is available to us, but when we choose our own wisdom and idols instead, we exchange the truth about God for a lie, and we choose a way of death rather than life. In our infidelity and ingratitude, we choose falsehood over truth.

A quick look at insights from other theologians who have addressed truth and truthfulness brings to light several additional emphases in the Christian tradition. In the twentieth century, Dietrich Bonhoeffer reflected deeply on the meaning and practice of truth and truthfulness when he was faced with the challenge of living faithfully in the midst of the deception and coercion of the Nazi regime.

In his comments on truthfulness, Bonhoeffer emphasized context and God's purposes because the large lies of Nazism were reshaping social reality, and small acts of resistance to the evil often involved deception. He wrote that telling the truth "is not solely a matter of moral character; it is also a matter of correct appreciation of real situations. . . ." To tell the truth means something different "according to the particular situation in which one stands. Account must be taken of one's relationships at each particular time."[18]

Charles Wellborn further describes Bonhoeffer's reflections on truth and truthfulness:

> Bonhoeffer took as his central concern the question, "What is truth?" Is truth simply a replication of the facts or is it something more than that? He sought to put the understanding of truth within a larger context — the loving purposes of God in the world. Well aware of human sinful tendencies, Bonhoeffer did not discard the moral injunction that it is right to tell the truth. Rather, he refused to identify truth with bare facts. Truth is always and everywhere, Bonhoeffer thought, consistent with the compassionate purpose of God, as revealed in Jesus Christ.[19]

Bonhoeffer's understandings of truthfulness and deception differed from the conclusions that Augustine had reached approximately 1500 years earlier. Although both men reflected on truthfulness in relation to God, Augustine argued that it was never right to lie, no matter the context or the relationship. His emphasis on rightly ordered love and his concerns about misdirected desire help us understand his numerous discussions about lying and duplicity. Augustine closely links speech to truthfulness and lying. Paul Griffiths explains that for Augustine, speech is a gift of God, and its proper use is "a return of gift to giver" by speaking truthfully in the form of confession and adoration.[20] To use speech in order to lie is to turn away from God and misuse the gift.

Thomas Aquinas captured multiple dimensions of truth and truthfulness in his discussions of truth in *Summa Theologica.* Truth is an aspect of virtue ("one is said to be truthful"); it has a relational dimension (it is "directed to another"); and it pertains to what is in accord with reality (it "sets up a certain equality between things").[21]

A few decades ago, The Truth and Reconciliation Commission in South Africa confronted the challenge of working with multiple aspects of truth. In a book of essays on truth-telling, Tristan Anne Borer explains that to facilitate truth-telling after major public atrocities, it is important to recognize that "the idea of a single truth is a false one. Rather, we might more profitably think of various truths. In South Africa, for example, the TRC was guided by four notions of truth: factual or forensic truth, personal or narrative truth, social truth, and healing or restorative truth." We can, she notes, draw these four notions into two "truth paradigms": forensic and narrative truths. While forensic truth is associated with "facts about past actions," narrative truth involves the personal, social, restorative, and experiential aspects of truth-telling.[22]

We can also understand various aspects of truth by distinguishing between "knowledge" and "acknowledgment." Borer explains, "Knowledge is akin to forensic truth — the factual aspect of truth. Forensic truth is the only type of truth . . . that is an end in itself — that end being the creation of knowledge about the past. Narrative truth, in contrast, is a means to a different end, such as healing or affirming the dignity of victims and survivors. In this sense, narrative truth closely resembles acknowledgment."[23]

To pursue reconciliation after any major rupture in relationships, it is helpful to work with both understandings of truth — we need knowledge, the facts — and the personal or communal acknowledgment of experience, hurt, betrayal, and loss. Only in this way can truth and truth-telling be fully connected to both justice and healing.[24]

Truthfulness: Out of Step with Contemporary Culture

Concerns about truthfulness are undermined by contemporary emphases on image, success, litigation, and personal affirmation. Cynical and dismissive attitudes toward truth are evident when the main question asked is whether something will "fly" rather than whether it is true.[25] Living truthfully may be important to personal integrity and communal relationships, but we seem to be functioning in a social environment with a fairly high level of dishonesty and distrust.[26]

Photoshopping Our Lives

When friends Photoshop their vacation pictures and photos of fashion models bear little resemblance to actual human beings, it is hard to know what counts as "true" or why it even matters. When resumes are "enhanced," credentials are routinely overstated, and steroids are used "to even the playing field," it is not easy to compete without joining in.

Many of the new technologies make deception easier. We can create alternate personas, fabricate stories, and disseminate them easily. But even without the assistance of technology, many of us, in telling our stories, "add details and omit inconvenient facts; we give the tale a small, self-enhancing spin; that spin goes over so well that the next time we add a slightly more dramatic embellishment; we justify that little white lie as making the story better and clearer — until what we remember may not have happened that way, or even may not have happened at all."[27]

Our commitment to living truthfully is also regularly challenged by the experience that whoever offers the most clever sound bite seems to win. Because winning is often seen as more important than whether something is true, fewer and fewer people are willing to acknowledge their mistakes. Fears of litigation make truthful speech and practices more complicated and at times difficult, although the legal system can also be a structure that holds errant persons accountable.

With the general loss of confidence in the notion of truth, there are fewer external standards against which people measure themselves. Tender consciences are gradually seared, made to feel silly because they are concerned about such "minor" mistakes as an overstatement or a misrepresentation here or there. In some circles, dishonesty and "casual lying for no apparent reason" have become quite common.[28]

We often cover over our dishonesty by giving it more benign names, according to Ralph Keyes: "We no longer tell lies. Instead we 'misspeak.' We 'exaggerate.' We 'exercise poor judgment.'" We are "economical with the truth," or lack "artfulness" in our responses.[29] When we become preoccupied with impression management, we ask about what "spin" we can put on the current problem or how we might manage the fallout. The move from impression management to lying is often made easier when jargon and specialized language are employed.[30]

It is difficult to resist impulses to spin situations in ways that are self-serving but not truthful. This may be a special temptation for Christians who want to have a good testimony or who do not want to bring dishonor to church or community. We sometimes choose to stretch the truth or to omit aspects of the truth that are relevant but awkward or unbecoming. Because we are so familiar with the practice, we don't necessarily even notice the dishonesty.

Whatever It Takes

When we embrace a "whatever it takes" approach to problem-solving, we discover that dishonesty is frequently rewarded. A "can-do" or pragmatic approach, so characteristic of contemporary culture, tends to ask first whether something "works." But this is an inadequate moral framework for addressing truth and dishonesty. If the job is important enough or the outcome good enough, people are often comfortable employing and over-looking small deceptions and lies.

"Getting the job done — whatever it takes" has a certain ring of commitment and energy, but it leaves major moral questions unanswered. In particular, it ignores the important insight that the "end is pre-existent in the mean[s]" — and that wrong means will ultimately undermine a worthy goal.[31]

One place where dishonesty shows up with disturbing frequency is in the current casual attitude toward cheating at the high school and college levels. Students themselves marvel at the number of classmates who engage in some form of cheating. Occasionally I encounter a seminary student who cheats by turning in a paper that is patched together from material taken from sources without credit, or by turning in another student's work as his or her own. When I confront them, the most disturbing response for me is that he or she had "done what it took to get the job done; the week had been full of church responsibilities."

In most of these cases, students do not recognize the gravity of the choices they've made. They have been significantly shaped by casual attitudes toward dishonesty and by the orientation to quick results that are prevalent in the larger culture. Some had been rewarded for doing "whatever it took" to get ahead in business and had told themselves that this was no different. Somehow they had not connected their academic dishonesty with larger questions of Christian character or even with violating biblical commands against lying.

There is enormous hypocrisy in our culture as people are outraged over the latest discovery of dishonesty in the life of a public figure while overlooking similar patterns in their own lives. But it is particularly disturbing to find this loss of truthfulness among those preparing for ministry. How will they handle pressures in ministry if they are cheating in seminary to get the job done? How will they respond to the next requirement or roadblock? If pastors are dishonest, how will they ever challenge their congregations to love the truth?[32]

Sometimes we are persuaded that a cause or a result is so important that we are willing to use deceptive means to gain a person's attention or cooperation. We don't call it deception, but we probably would if someone else were doing it. So in evangelism and fund-raising, sometimes we only gradually reveal our real purposes. In other cases, we characterize our opponents unfairly and distort their views because we believe our concerns are so important. When we do this, we corrupt our own message, disrespect the persons we are trying to persuade, and undermine our own integrity.[33]

Concerns about Self-Esteem

In response to styles of parenting and education that expected a lot from children but provided little support or encouragement, more recent childrearing philosophies have emphasized the importance of strengthening children's self-esteem. As a result, parents and teachers sometimes overstate children's gifts and skills and praise their accomplishments in order to help them "feel good" about themselves or their contributions.

When affirmations are not truthfully connected to actual achievements, however, children can be misled in several ways. They are often unprepared for the more rigorous demands that will come. Presumption and feelings of entitlement can creep in along with the falsehood.

Increasingly dependent on affirmation, children, teens, and sometimes parents are angered by subsequent critical but truthful evaluations. Emphases on excellence are held in difficult and uncertain tension with expectations of affirmation for substandard performance. Truthful evaluations and evaluators are seen as a problem. The need to address or challenge cultural pressures about success is largely overlooked.

This is not to say that we should return to harsh and unyielding assessments. It is important to recognize that different people need different levels and forms of encouragement and affirmation. But self-esteem does not come from flattery and dishonesty; it comes from true accomplishments that are truly valued by a community. There are various ways to encourage someone and to value their contributions without resorting to falsehood. Saying something to make people "feel good about themselves" is not an expression of love if it is not also truthful; it is ultimately patronizing and destructive.

Fragmentation and Community

Many of us experience daily life in fragments. The places where we live, work, worship, study, shop, and play rarely overlap, and in many cases the people within these settings are different. This is a mixed blessing. We can be a "different" person in each setting, emphasizing particular values and engaging in various practices. This can be helpful in allowing freedom for different aspects of our personalities, gifts, and interests to flourish.

Such fragmentation of our important communities, however, often results in a loosening of human connections. This makes it easier to be dishonest in one sphere while functioning normally in the others.[34] A familiar version of this is the highly involved churchman who does not bring his Christian commitments to work or to the leisure activities he chooses.

It is easier to deceive ourselves and others in anonymous settings where relationships are very limited.[35] In close communities with overlapping relations, it is more likely that deception will become apparent quickly. Fabricated stories are difficult to sustain and keep straight when people see us in more than one setting.[36]

As noted in the previous discussion of promising, confrontation or correction is difficult when people can move on easily to another community if they don't like the challenge. They avoid or dismiss truthful words or expectations by quickly shifting to a setting that is more anonymous and less demanding.

Close and overlapping communities are difficult in other ways. If we desire to tell the truth to each other, we need to know the truth about one another, but such "intimate knowledge" of one another is sometimes dangerous. As Chris Rice explains in his book titled *Grace Matters*, his community faced the challenge of "how to use greater exposure of vices and weaknesses in a way that built up rather than destroyed our friendships, to bring them into the light without the glare becoming unbearable."[37]

Relational bonds are strongest when our communities overlap and our lives are intertwined with others in several spheres — when we live, work, play, and worship with some of the same people. But that very intertwining can also make it hard to speak the truth because it will be very costly. Problems spill from one sphere into another. Finding ways to overcome fragmentation without resorting to totalizing communities is a challenge for Christians who want deeper, more accountable relationships.

Living truthfully in contemporary society is difficult on many levels, but as Christians we are called to it. We are challenged, as individuals and as congregations, not only by current cultural practices and expectations, but also by human frailties, contextual uncertainties, and practical ambiguities. These are the subject of the next chapter.

CHAPTER NINE

Complications in Truthfulness

For most of us truthfulness comes very hard.

Lewis B. Smedes, *Mere Morality*

Living truthfully is difficult. Because human beings are fallible, finite, and diverse, our efforts at truthfulness can be complicated and sometimes misguided. Even when our intentions are good, things do not necessarily go smoothly. Our perspectives and understandings are incomplete, and we live between the recognition of our limitations and the gift of God's unfailing truth.

Facing the Costs

It can be risky to take the lead in creating a truthful environment. When we publicly acknowledge our frailties or temptations, other people, if they choose, can take advantage of our transparency and vulnerability. If, in the larger setting, most folks hide their sins and mistakes and expect their leaders to be flawless, a person's honest admission of struggle can undermine confidence and invite criticism.

Additionally, we sometimes worry that our witness to the power and truth of the gospel will be discredited if we reveal the troubled or troubling aspects of our lives and communities. We want people to think we are good and good at what we do. We fear that if they knew the "truth" about us, they would be deeply disappointed or disinterested in the good news of Christ. Duplicity is a common response when expectations are impossible or unyielding.[1]

While there are clear challenges in being truthful about ourselves, addressing hard truths in another person's life can also be costly because it can threaten the relationship. Fear of tension and loss often inhibit our willingness to speak truthfully. If we ignore the important role that tension or disequilibrium can play in growth, our fears often lead to non-action or complicity. In other cases, we are caught between wanting to be truthful and wanting to protect someone else or their vulnerability.

We are also hesitant about speaking truthfully because we are not always sure we know what is true. We worry that we don't know the whole story or situation and that we might be mistaken about the facts or the interpretation of them. In other situations, the line between truth-telling and tattling seems unclear. We do not want to develop a reputation as the truth police. Sometimes, however, we are simply lazy, and we do not care enough about individuals, the community, the truth, or our own integrity to take on the challenges of being truthful.

The Clay-Pot Phenomenon

Because truth-tellers and truth-receivers are imperfect human beings, there are a number of ways that a desire for truthfulness can go awry. One pastor in our group explained, "Part of the human condition . . . is that the search for truth-knowing and the practice of truth-telling are carried on by folks who are finite and fallible, and thankfully, transformable. Our experience of truth is mediated — like treasure in clay pots — or more like truth through clay souls."

"Telling the truth in love is, in my experience, the practice that the church carries out most poorly," noted another pastor. "We either shrink back from telling it because we don't want to drive people away, or we approach people with both guns blazing because we don't care about driving them away. . . . But you can't be a pastor with a passion for healthy community for very long without learning to develop this skill."

He described a recent situation at his church as an opportunity to engage in truth-telling. A member asked if she could teach a class that she thought would be of benefit to the community. He explained his dilemma:

"The problem is that this individual, while undoubtedly gifted in many ways for teaching, has a number of significant character issues. . . . She is a chronic church-hopper . . . she is quite harsh . . . people often feel abused and damaged by her. She is something of a bully . . . [but also] . . . quite sensitive."

In response to the woman's request to teach the class, the pastor met with her and raised two key issues: her erratic pattern of church attendance and her harsh and abusive manner. She responded well to both concerns, and the pastor agreed that she could teach the four-week class. But the undertaking did not go well at first. She blew up at the group when the attendance was poor. Though she apologized for the first incident, she became very angry again the following week. Group members then confronted her on specific issues, and she led the final session well.

A person's gifts and flaws often come packaged together, and it is important to discern the difference between "weakness and wickedness" — this woman was open to growth, just difficult. Finding ways, as pastors and as congregations, to hold on to persons while speaking truthfully to them depends on deep commitments to love, fidelity, and truthfulness.

Without fidelity, truth-telling can be harsh and sometimes devastating. It is easy to be critical of others and to identify their flaws, especially if they have caused us difficulties. Without fidelity to, or appreciation for, the person or the community, we are often only addressing or acknowledging part of the truth when we call attention to those flaws.

The practice of truthfulness can be undermined by unresolved hurts and unacknowledged interpersonal irritations. Awkward efforts at being truthful can be made more difficult by inexperience, unrecognized envy, and personal brokenness. Sometimes our eagerness to tell the truth is connected to a desire for retaliation: sin drives our truth-telling, and "truthfulness" hides our sinful motives.

Certain questions can help us explore our motives in telling the truth or in keeping it secret. For whom is this truth helpful? Who benefits when it is told or hidden? Who is harmed? Why do I or we want it known? If our ultimate purpose in truth-telling is helping persons and communities grow toward maturity in Christ, then our motives need to be centered in a desire to strengthen people in goodness and godliness.[2]

Wrong intentions or self-serving motives can turn the practice of truthful speech inside out. As Elmer Brown pointed out decades ago, "We shall hardly find anything more exasperating or harder to set right than the untruthful meaning which has been conveyed by telling the exact truth in such a way as to put it in a false light. The worst kind of a lie is the truth told wrong."[3] Such is the nature of carefully crafted gossip and dissemination of facts that are accurate but misleading.

Even when we want to be good and our motives are quite exemplary, however, we can find ourselves in moral dilemmas where no action we take is free from harmful impact. This is often associated with larger situations in which much harm has already been done, or in which relationships are very entangled by power dynamics and injustice. These are extremely difficult circumstances that require humility, internal truthfulness, and confession before God. Not being able to avoid harm does not absolve us from responsibility; rather, it drives us to our knees.[4]

Miroslav Volf's insights on the impact of our faith, limitations, and sinfulness on access to the truth are as applicable on the grand scale of knowing "the truth" as they are at the level of truthful interpersonal communication:

> The belief in an all-knowing God should inspire the search for truth; the awareness of our human limitations should make us modest about the claims that we have found it, however. We "know in part" (1 Corinthians 13:12) first because we are finite beings. . . . We "know in part," second, because our limited knowledge is shaped by the interests we pursue and filtered through the cultures and traditions we inhabit.[5]

While we might recognize that "there is such a thing as a simple, human, and situated truth, that in a creaturely way corresponds to the divine truth," we do not generally have access to "pure facts" and cannot usually reconstruct totally objective narratives of events. Often, as Volf notes, "our desires and interests, the desires and interests of our communities . . . make us see what we suspect we will find and believe what we want to believe."[6]

Power Dynamics

We should be wary of contemporary arguments asserting that behind every truth claim is an expression of power. Living and speaking truthfully can be difficult, however, when there are significant power differences among persons, or when one person or group has control over the resources that another needs. Whether we are speaking into a situation of entrenched power, or we are the ones holding power, truth and truthfulness can be undermined by the desire to protect ourselves or to control others.[7]

There are many different forms of power that can be used for good or evil, and power dynamics affect every community. Although no one can manage the truth in an ultimate sense, human beings can use their power to silence dissent or prophetic voices — at least temporarily. Fears about how others might use their power can diminish our inclination to tell the truth.

"In order to know truly we need to want to exercise power rightly," notes Volf.[8] Some Christians do not grasp this insight because they are unwilling to acknowledge that they have power. To recognize the power dynamics at work among persons and groups seems too "unspiritual" for Christian community, yet many of us do have personal and institutional power. When we do not acknowledge the power we have, use spiritual language to mask the power dynamics, or wield power indirectly through manipulation, it can be very difficult for others to address the interpersonal dynamics or speak the truth.

In hierarchical settings, where the person or group in charge has significant power over the livelihood, tenure, or future of others, it can also be difficult for those with less power to speak truthfully. When pastors are dependent on the goodwill of their supervisors, governing boards, and congregations for their jobs, their vulnerability is very real when they speak the difficult but true word.

Persons with power can recast circumstances so that any form of criticism or truth-telling from others is interpreted as complaint, infidelity, or ingratitude. Individuals who attempt to speak truthfully can find that their motives and spiritual life are questioned. In Christian circles, justifiable protest can be crushed by using religious language that obscures acts that are primarily about exerting or consolidating power.

Sometimes persons in authority are permitted to demand truthfulness or fidelity from others, but do not live by those practices or commitments themselves. By claiming spiritual superiority, such leaders create empires built on spiritual intimidation and secrecy. Because many of us have seen or experienced the abuse of spiritual authority, we can become overly hesitant to exert any kind of authority ourselves, and then fail to offer necessary corrections or speak truthfully.

In interpersonal interactions, the individual with more power is often able to prevail with his or her version of "the truth." This is especially the case when interactions are contested but have been private, and no one else has access to the details. Individuals and groups use their power in different ways, however, and sometimes persons with institutional authority are also committed to confidentiality or grace. They do not defend themselves or the organization against accusations or unjust claims leveled by the person who has "less" power. In certain cases, those with little institutional power can gain the ear and sympathy of the community by telling partial truths about the injustice done to them.

In our desire to be charitable or to seek justice, we occasionally excuse victims of evil, oppression, or falsehood from living truthfully. We overlook their "small frauds and falsehoods" because victims are in a struggle with "big lies and distortions." But, as Volf notes, in the end this enthrones "precisely the enemy it set out to fight — the power of deception." He contrasts this with the biblical prophets, who "refused to be drawn into the war of dissimulations."[9] The prophets challenge us to persevere in the truth even in the most difficult circumstances.

Nonverbal Communication, Truthfulness, and Context

The way in which we say something is part of what we say to another person. Much of our communication is nonverbal, and we communicate both content and emotion in our encounters. As Daniel Goleman explains in *Emotional Intelligence,* "Just as the mode of the rational mind is words, the mode of the emotions is nonverbal. Indeed, when a person's words disagree with what is conveyed via his tone of voice, gesture, or other nonverbal channel, the emotional truth is in *how* he says something rather than in *what* he says."[10]

A commitment to speaking the truth in love helps us recognize the human care that is necessary if we want to share truth in a way that can be heard. Sometimes we might need to organize and write out our thoughts ahead of time. Because the tone and texture of our voice are important to what people hear, however, most difficult expressions of truth-telling should be face-to-face. When written communication is permanent but abstracted from an emotional context, it is easy to misunderstand; hastily written e-mails and text messages are particularly problematic.

As Paul Lehmann points out, "Where and when and how one speaks what one knows is . . . part and parcel of how we define the truth."[11] Attentiveness to the context, larger story, and nature of the relationships is crucial in truthful communication. Transitional periods are particularly primed for trouble with truthfulness because there has rarely been sufficient time to build trust among persons or between a group and its leaders. Old or misdirected loyalties can limit the flow of truth.

When roles within a community change, relational ruptures are more likely. Power dynamics, friendship, and the ordinary challenges of transitions come together when a staff person is moved to a supervisory capacity. He or she is suddenly responsible for overseeing persons who had previously been co-equals and often friends. In one case, a fragile friendship dissolved when a staff person could not handle having a friend become "the boss," but also could not name his difficulties with it publicly. Instead, he found numerous ways to challenge the new arrangement indirectly: criticizing the leadership, the programs, the church, and generally spreading discontent.

Styles of Truthfulness

Truth-telling or truthfulness is not limited to taking an in-your-face approach that assumes we are most truthful when we are very straightforward and frank. There are cultural differences in how we speak truth, and some patterns of truthfulness are more indirect. As Emily Dickinson wrote, "Tell all the Truth but tell it slant/Success in Circuit lies. . . ."[12] Those who are exclusively familiar with a direct approach might miss the truth when it is expressed less directly — for example, in the form of a question.

In some cultures, concerns about respect and shame lead persons to avoid the kind of confrontation that is often associated with truthfulness in American culture. Although many in American society value directness and openness, it can be deeply offensive in other societies. While direct approaches can be helpful in putting difficult issues front and center, each style of truth-telling needs to be sanctified and purified by love.

Sometimes a person is relentless in his or her pursuit of truth and comes across like a bull in a china shop. Intemperate and harsh, such a person assumes that bluntness is the same as truthfulness. But there is often an entire spectrum of truth and things that are true, and the choice to narrow attention to one problem or flaw means overlooking other truths that could rightly be acknowledged.

Directness is not the same as aggressiveness. In conversations between persons of different statuses, those with less power or status are often expected to avoid direct challenge, correction, or statement of their opinion. When such persons speak directly, others sometimes view it as aggressive or angry rather than as simply truthful. Historically, gender expectations about niceness have made it difficult for women to speak directly without being perceived as unfeminine or angry; this is the case even in cultures that value directness generally.

A very powerful expression of truthful but indirect confrontation comes from an ancient source. The prophet Nathan was called by God to confront King David with his sin in taking Bathsheba as his wife and in having her husband killed. Nathan tells David a story about a poor shepherd and his beloved lamb. David is outraged by the injustice of the wealthy, powerful man who takes the lamb for himself. He calls for severe punishment, to which Nathan responds, "You are the man." Nathan's approach was indirect, allowing the truth to catch David off-guard. David hears and repents (2 Sam. 12:1-15).

When truth is spoken in anger or out of long periods of suffering and injustice, it is often raw, intense, and even traumatizing. It can be difficult to hear and easy to dismiss because of the anger. In contexts of injustice, however, it is important that such truths be spoken. Despite the harshness or bitterness of the words, they can represent crucial opportunities for fidelity, repentance, and love.[13]

Drive-by Prophecy

Christians can misunderstand the prophetic task of speaking the truth. Sometimes those who take on the role of prophet in a community elevate themselves above the persons or community being exposed or criticized. Unlike the Hebrew prophets who wept as they challenged sins and hypocrisy, such critics stand at a distance and look down with judgment.[14]

When prophets or critics are committed to fidelity as well as to truthfulness, they do not "dump" their insights. A friend shared a disturbing story. A couple who had previously been part of his congregation felt led by God to point out his shortcomings. "We are here because the Spirit told us to come and vomit on you concerning your leadership. . . . You need to let go. . . . You need to be more prayerful. . . . We are here because we care." Later they warned him again about his inadequate prayer life. In looking back, the pastor acknowledged that some of their criticisms were on target, but he also realized that the best they had to offer him was mediated through their own brokenness.

Our fallenness means that we are not able to discern and speak the truth perfectly and that we need the help of God and others. Self-appointed prophets are often accountable to no one and are therefore especially vulnerable to grandiose displays and self-deception. Those persons who offer truth and light to others share their insights in the context of grace and humility.

God-talk can function as a trump card — a way to stop conversation or quickly win an argument. Claiming that God has "given me a word" or taking the mantle of prophet is sometimes used to further a person's purposes or to shore up contested authority. People who are able to claim charismatic gifts have a disproportionate ability to define truth in certain communities.

Many of us have been victims of what one pastor in the project called "drive-by prophecy" or "prophilying." At some time in our lives, a few of us have probably engaged in the practice. Cultivating a community that is wise enough to resist this behavior is important, but remaining open to a word from the Lord is crucial for people who value the role of prophecy in contemporary congregational life. Although we do not want to "silence the prophets," we can all grow in our capacity to discern and speak truth.

This does not mean that every spoken word should be nice or safe. It takes courage to offer an important message that is awkward, uncomfortable, or challenging. But speaking the truth in love means, as Frederick Buechner notes, speaking it "with concern not only for the truth that is being told but with concern also for the people it is being told to."[15]

Silence and Secrets

Obedience to the biblical command against lying "does not call us to be . . . blabbermouths. Truthfulness is demanded from us about the things that we ought to speak about at all," explains Lewis Smedes.[16] A commitment to truthfulness does not mean that we disclose everything to everyone. "Silence and discretion, respect for the privacy and for the feelings of others must naturally govern what is spoken."[17]

Voyeurism is not the same as seeking the truth. We do not need to know a good deal of the information that is "out there" today. Media scrutiny of public figures is unrelenting, and feeds a voyeuristic impulse in the larger culture. Many people assume they have a "right" to know about every detail of a person's life, no matter how private or irrelevant to their public role. In her important book on lying, Sissela Bok explains that refusing to give information about one's private life (marriage, children, plans) "is justifiable" for public figures, "but the right to withhold information is not the right to lie about it. Lying under such circumstances bodes ill for conduct in other matters."[18]

In situations of danger or malevolence directed at ourselves or others, we may need to "be truthful without revealing what . . . [persons] did not directly ask for."[19] If we value truthfulness but also are committed to protecting individuals who are very vulnerable, we sometimes struggle with the conflicting responsibilities. While it is possible to be truthful without disclosing everything, the need for secrecy is often a warning sign that truthfulness in the larger context is gravely endangered.

The Scriptures draw a close connection between truth and light. In Ephesians 5:8-9, we are invited to live as "children of light — for the fruit of the light is found in all that is good and right and true." Lives characterized by being "light" and living as "children of light" suggest behavior that is aboveboard and available to communal scrutiny. Little is done "in corners" or hidden from view.[20]

In Luke 12:1-3, Jesus warns that a time is coming when everything will be revealed and all that has been done in secret will be made public. Whatever has been said in the dark will be heard in the light. Although this is a terrifying warning about hypocrisy and deception, it can also help us see ourselves as living within God's gaze now. Our actions and motives are known to God, and falsehood and dishonesty will not be covered indefinitely. Living in and as light — living truthfully — means that we do not need to fear scrutiny now or in the future.

One pastor's story of the impact of secrets on long-term relationships is a reminder of the importance of bringing difficult truths into the light early. A woman who had joined a congregation a few months earlier told Steve, the pastor, that she had recently learned of the infidelity of her husband, Bob. She asked Steve never to tell anyone, especially Bob, that she had told him. Pastor Steve did not promise, but he did persuade the couple to begin counseling with his associate; their marriage moved forward well. Bob showed leadership potential and became increasingly involved in church activities.

Because the pastor knew about Bob's previous infidelity but had never discussed it with him, the relationship between them was built on a foundation of interpersonal dishonesty from the start. This created unacknowledged but ongoing tensions between them. Pastor Steve acknowledges that he may have set Bob up for failure. "While we recognized his native leadership talents, we questioned his character and never really trusted him. Since we did not speak the truth to Bob about our reservations, he was bound to experience frustration with the leadership team." Eventually the couple and their family left and spread terrible slander about the pastoral team and the church throughout the larger community.

We struggle with seeking to keep confidences and to be truthful. People sometimes share their secrets with us because they need a sounding board or a safe place to process their thoughts, or because they need moral guidance. In other cases, they just want to unload. Bok explains, "Difficult choices arise for all those who have promised to keep secret what they have learned from a client, a patient, or a penitent. . . . At stake is fidelity, keeping faith with those who have confided their secrets on condition that they not be revealed." In most cases, we choose to keep those secrets as professionals or as faithful friends.[21]

Certain requests for information based on what we have been told in confidence are wrong, inappropriate, or unjust. To refuse them is justified.[22] Some situations are more complicated, however. Bok discusses the problem of finding out about doctors who are incompetent and dangerous to their patients. She argues, "There can be no excuse for lying to protect anyone who places patients at such risk. And only an overwhelming blindness to the suffering of those beyond one's immediate sphere can lead colleagues simply to oust an incompetent and dangerous surgeon from their own hospital so quietly that he can continue his 'work' at another."[23] Her warning is important for the church to hear. It is wrong and irresponsible when colleagues, supervisors, or congregations allow a leader who has been involved in some form of grave misconduct to leave quietly and go to another congregation and continue ministry.

Some "secrets" are dangerous to the community because the information is circulating among members, but because it is "confidential," it is never brought into the light to be tested. Secrets can be awkward in fractured or fracturing communities for other reasons. If, as individuals, we generally keep our promises and are careful about our words, we are likely to know more than we should or want to because people turn to us in difficult circumstances. We struggle to figure out how to be truthful when we have relevant information but cannot reveal how we know it, or cannot contribute true information because we shouldn't actually have had access to it. These circumstances give added meaning and urgency to living in the light, creating safe places for truthfulness, and recognizing the importance of discernment.

Framing and Reframing the Situation

Truth-telling is affected by how we frame the situation we are addressing. Discussions about framing or reframing are not the same as our cultural obsession with spin, though it is easy to collapse the two into each other. Using a familiar illustration of framing and matting a picture, we are reminded how different-colored mats and different-sized frames draw out very different features. They don't change what is in the picture, only what we notice or see at the moment.

An incident in congregational life illustrates how much our truthfulness is shaped by what we allow ourselves to see. A pastor in the project explained, "Joe is known for his bluntness. . . . He thinks there's . . . too much tiptoeing around the truth for the sake of not hurting people. So he just says it like he sees it. He did so at worship team practice last week."

As a musician, Joe was concerned with excellence, and when another good musician came along, Joe was eager to immediately replace the faithful regulars with this new person who was much more talented. Joe believed that it was time for the church to move beyond the humble offerings of the regular band, and he announced his perspective to the group. This caused a flurry of hurt and an awkward time for everyone involved.

Which truths do we notice? In Joe's concern for musical excellence and speaking the truth, he failed to recognize the fidelity and commitment of the less-than-stellar musicians. The pastor reflected on what these tensions mean for ministry. "It reminds me of the need for clear communication of our philosophy of ministry. . . . If our view of excellence in worship is tied up with auditions, performance, and so on, we need to be clear about that; if, on the other hand, we see a valid place for incorporating many people's gifts, the talented and the not-so-talented, we need to express that."

We can miss the truth because our frames aren't large enough.[24] One congregation was discouraged by the failure of the youth program to minister to the church youth for whom it had been designed. But the leader worked hard to call their attention to what had actually happened. The youth program turned out to be a highly effective outreach to unchurched kids, and she described the impact on each child who had come. In doing so, she helped the congregation see a different part of the truth.

Pastors and leaders can help congregations see what God is doing even when it doesn't fit their expectations. A truthful reframing of a situation can move them toward gratitude. But reframing becomes dishonest when we use it to cover or hide aspects of truth we would prefer to over-look. The problem of numerous unpaid bills should not be hidden as we talk about God's blessing on a ministry. We do not need to save face for God by ignoring certain relevant but problematic aspects of truth or reality.

Reframing should be in the service of greater truth, and we need to be careful that we do not "misremember our history as being worse than it was, thus distorting our perception of how much we have improved, to feel better about ourselves now."[25] Sometimes we Christians fall prey to this in our conversion narratives as we exaggerate the details of our former "lostness" to make God's rescue even more compelling.

Dealing Redemptively with Wrongdoing

Discovering wrongdoing in a community brings concerns about truth-telling to the foreground immediately. Because we want to deal redemptively with situations, we struggle with how much to say and to whom we should say it.

When a church volunteer discovered several members of the youth group using drugs in one of the Sunday school rooms, he was uncertain about his next steps. Should he confront the teens directly? Tell their parents? Call the police? He told the pastor, and together they confronted the teens along with their parents. The young people denied it, and the parents and congregation members who heard about the incident directed all their anger at the pastor and the volunteer who reported it. Months later, one boy's addiction was revealed, but this story is revelatory. Communities can be very unwelcoming of truth, especially if truth is unpleasant or embarrassing. People often prefer silence and secrecy over redemptive but difficult interventions.

As noted previously, it can be difficult to know what is true when we enter a messy situation. If we come in as a new person, we often do not know where the landmines are, and we cannot always find out. Levels of mistrust are high, especially if we are entering a situation in which dishonesty has prevailed. Sometimes we need to name the uncertainty without expecting to have the opportunity to fully sort it out. We can, however, make it clear that we will take concrete steps together toward a new goal of better relationships and more truthful and open communication.

One of the most difficult issues in church and community life is how much people need to know about a bad situation. In one case, a church employee was found to be using church credit cards for his own expenses and also to be involved in adultery. His family was part of the congregation, and leaders wondered about how much should be said publicly. The person could be removed from his job, but obviously the congregation would have questions. Finding ways to limit the harm done to other family members made full disclosure problematic.

The situation becomes even more aggravated if the person who has been involved in the wrongdoing chooses to rally support by telling only a small part of the story. The congregation may be confused, family members hurt, and friends uncertain about the "injustice" or "drastic measures." Careful discernment and disclosing as much truth as possible seem important for the well-being of the community.

The complications we have reviewed in being truthful and living truthfully are often the result of human finiteness, misunderstandings, or brokenness. At times, the practice is situated within conflicting but important commitments. In some cases, however, our truthfulness is undone by conscious and deliberate sin at the personal or corporate level. We will explore these issues in the next chapter.

CHAPTER TEN

Going Deeper: Exploring What Weakens and What Strengthens Truthfulness

So then, putting away falsehood, let all of us speak the truth to our neighbors, for we are members of one another.

Ephesians 4:25

Exploring Deformations of Truthfulness

It seemed like the perfect job for someone who had been recently graduated from seminary. Presented with an opportunity to expand a Christian ministry to a new city, Adam was thrilled to be entrusted with the start-up work. His soon-to-be supervisor was very affirming of Adam's gifts and prospects and assured him that he'd be a rising star in the ministry. Adam could count on being able to forego jumping through many of the regular hoops. The supervisor also assured him of an adequate salary, start-up funds, and institutional support for three years. Based on these promises, Adam accepted the position and moved his young family to the other side of the country.

After about a year's work, Adam became increasingly worried. There was much less money than had been promised, surprising disagreement about what he had understood to be firm arrangements, and a lot more interpersonal difficulties than he'd expected. When Adam raised questions about the shortages, his supervisor blamed the board of directors. When more promises were ignored and Adam again raised concerns, his supervisor threatened to terminate his contract because of his disrespect toward authority. Adam had intended his comments as truthfulness rather than disrespect.

The most difficult part for Adam was that his supervisor kept asking him how he was feeling about what was happening — combining demands that he be "truthful" about his feelings with suggestions of pastoral concern and threats of job termination. After the supervisor's dishonesty became too obvious for it to be denied, he asked Adam for grace. The combination of power and powerlessness, encouragement and threat, religious language and dishonesty was difficult. Adam realized that he had been taken in by flattery and undone by the fact that all of the interactions between him and his supervisor had been one-on-one. There was no one to turn to because no one else knew the story. Little had been put in writing, and virtually nothing had been shared with the board.

Flattery, dishonesty, lying, and self-deception — all deformations of truthfulness — are elements of this story. With slight variations, we encounter these deformations in ministry fairly regularly. We may want to live truthfully, but we are often undone by some aspect of deception or dissimulation. The promises that for Adam turned out to be flimsy hopes and a dishonest means of recruitment show the familiar linkage of betrayal and deception.

Deception of Others

Just as truth and light are connected in Scripture, so deception is described as choosing darkness, hiding, and shadows. In John 3:19-21, we read that despite the light of Christ having come into the world, some people "loved darkness rather than light because their deeds were evil." "God is light and in him there is no darkness at all," proclaims John in 1 John 1:5; he further warns against "walking in darkness" where we "lie and do not do what is true" (v. 6).

We encounter various forms of deception in ordinary church life. Congregations are sometimes slow to embrace a new opportunity for ministry. In one church, a small group of folks within the congregation was very excited about a project and got it started. Things went well, and the ministry was making a positive impact in the neighborhood. But the leaders of the project kept encountering "roadblocks" from the congregation — first concerns about how church property was being used, then questions about how funds were raised and distributed, then more questions about the kinds of people that would be in the building. Each question raised was viewed as a hindrance to ministry, so in frustration, the project leaders concluded that the church "just didn't get it." The small group gradually chose to move ahead but limit what it shared with the larger congregation.

With that decision, the project was able to short-circuit established church processes and ignore larger questions of fidelity. The group's dishonesty was primarily manifested in how money was dispensed, and involved a series of small deceptions. The leaders did not benefit personally, but they overlooked certain details in their reports to the congregation. In the end it was the local bank (an outside authority) that required transparency in reporting and helped them move away from deception.

Ordinarily, deception involves more than words and can be accomplished by deeds, a combination of statements and deeds, or by not doing anything at all. "To deceive" means to cause others "to accept as true or valid what is false or invalid."[1] If a lie is understood as "any intentionally deceptive message which is stated,"[2] then deception "is at the heart of all lies."[3] When we deceive through deeds — we often create the false appearances associated with dissimulation and hypocrisy.[4]

It is possible to deceive with words without resorting to explicit lies. In an essay on lies and deception, philosopher J. L. A. Garcia provides two examples:

> I can deceive someone into judging your professional qualifications modest by pointedly praising only your manners and dress, in such a way that the listener, straining to see how in making these remarks I am observing the rules of relevance and truthfulness, infers that this is *all* I can truthfully say in your favor. People also mislead in a related way by saying too little, as in this one. All S tells T about U's well-received recent presentation (which S attended and T missed) is that U's paper was nicely printed.[5]

Deception and lying are obviously closely related, and when we suspect someone of lying, it is often because of nonverbal behavior usually associated with deception. We notice that they avoid making eye contact, or take a particular posture, or use a different tone of voice, or don't say anything at all.[6] Because we so often distrust people's words, we pay close attention to their body language.[7]

"When listening for the truth, most of the world counts on both lips and eyes to say the same thing," notes Diane Komp. She explains further, "Children and teenagers are rarely accomplished enough to carry off complete deceit. It takes years of experience to bring our subconscious language into conscious control. I suspect that one of the reasons we think that teenagers lie more often than adults is that teenagers have not yet mastered this double duplicity."[8]

Self-Deception

People who want to be good but also want to do what they want are ready targets for the temptation of self-deception. In his reflections on self-deception, ethicist Stanley Hauerwas notes that we choose to stay ignorant of certain things we are doing, and we "deliberately allow certain engagements to go unexamined, quite aware that areas left unaccountable tend to cater to self-interest. As a result . . . the condition of self-deception becomes the rule rather than the exception in our lives, and often in the measure that we are trying to be honest and sincere."[9]

For religious folks, the need to perceive ourselves as good or righteous is strong, and it can be painful to admit certain truths. In some cases, we "misremember" in order to protect our self-esteem or sense of being right. Self-deception is often a misguided effort to maintain personal integrity. If we've made a mistake or chosen wrongly, our impulse is to try to convince ourselves that it was for the best, especially if the choice was costly or irrevocable.[10]

Despite ready lip-service to human sin and fallenness, many Christians believe that they are incorruptible and are surprised when they end up in trouble. The plague of clergy misconduct is a constant reminder of the power of self-deception. How many of us have wondered, "How could he have done that? What was she thinking?" The answer in many situations is that he wasn't thinking; he had stopped thinking and reflecting. Instead, the person deliberately excluded a part of his or her life from spiritual and moral scrutiny. By compartmentalizing aspects of our actions or thoughts, we are able to ignore major inconsistencies and wrongdoing.

Certain behaviors foster self-deception, according to Mark Knapp: "We tend to attribute successes to our own abilities and blame our failures on external factors. We tend to view evidence depicting us unfavorably as flawed while viewing positive feedback uncritically." "We . . . think our good traits are unusual while our faults are common."[11] Self-deception flourishes when we offer rationalizations, blame others for our problems, and evade responsibility.[12]

Lying

Biblical texts connect idolatry, deceit, lying, and destruction.[13] Jesus describes the devil as a "liar and the father of lies" (John 8:44). Biblical teaching against deception and lying is explicit and strong, though not always as unyielding as some theological and philosophical traditions have maintained.

While we should be wary of developing norms directly from narratives, occasionally biblical characters seem to have lied without negative consequences. Hebrew midwives lied to Pharaoh to protect threatened children, and Rahab lied to protect the Hebrew spies.[14] Such stories, however, are rare and often involve protecting the lives of others from harm. In most of the texts, duplicity, lying, and deception are strongly condemned.

Major writers in the Christian tradition have emphasized different aspects of lying, deception, and truthfulness. As noted previously in Chapter 8, Augustine was one of the first theologians to provide a careful discussion of lying in light of larger theological themes. Paul Griffiths' book on an Augustinian theology of duplicity draws from many of Augustine's writings to develop his distinctive argument. Griffiths explains that for Augustine, lies are "deliberately duplicitous verbal claims," and "insincere speech that deliberately contradicts what its speaker takes to be true."[15]

For Augustine, whether one's intent is to deceive or to make someone happy, one should never lie. Lying is wrong, even to prevent a worse sin, and certainly not to prevent minor harms. "No supposed good that might come from a lie can . . . justify either lying or considering whether to lie."[16]

Rooted in his emphasis on rightly ordered desire, Augustine's exceptionless ban on lying was also connected to seeing duplicitous speech as a "rupture of the divine image." In lying, "you take to yourself and make your own what really belongs to God, and you do so out of a misunderstanding of what you are and what you take to be your relation to speech. The thing taken, expropriated, in this case is speech." Thus lying is a "theft of language."[17] Over the centuries, Augustine's views on lying have been influential but also contested.

Thomas Aquinas, in the medieval church, also argued that the primary character of lying is that "a person intends to say what is false."[18] He distinguished among three kinds of lies: those that are helpful or told for the "well-being and convenience" of another, those that are jokes or told in fun, and those that are malicious or mischievous. While he viewed all three types of lies as sins, only the malicious expressions were seen as mortal sins.[19]

Arguments that lying can never be justified are most closely associated with the eighteenth-century philosopher Immanuel Kant. He argued that truthfulness is an unconditional duty and no circumstances could justify lying, even to save an innocent life. For Kant, lying for any reason always does harm because it undermines or opposes one of the foundations of social life, "the trustworthiness of speech."[20]

As noted earlier, Dietrich Bonhoeffer approached the questions of lying and truthfulness from a different perspective and attempted to rework some of the earlier distinctions and definitions. In his view, "the usual definition of the lie as a conscious discrepancy between thought and speech" was "completely inadequate." Instead, he argued that "the essential character of the lie is to be found at a far deeper level."

> One might say that the man who stands behind the word makes his word a lie or a truth. But even this is not enough; for the lie is something objective and must be defined accordingly. . . . The lie is primarily the denial of God as He has evidenced Himself to the world. . . . The lie is a contradiction of the word of God, which God has spoken in Christ, and upon which creation is founded. Consequently the lie is the denial, the negation and the conscious and deliberate destruction of the reality which is created by God and which consists in God, no matter whether this purpose is achieved by speech or by silence.[21]

For Bonhoeffer, lying, like truth-telling, was closely tied to relationships and context.[22] He explained, "The question must be asked whether and in what ways a man is entitled to demand truthful speech of others." Other writers have also argued that "we owe the duty of speaking the truth only to those who have a right to the truth."[23] These arguments, while important, are also troubling. They introduce complex questions in deciding who has a right to truth and who does not. In addition, it is quite easy to move from wondering about a person's right to the truth to affirming one's own "right" to lie.[24]

Questions regarding whether every person has a "right" to the truth and whether it can ever be right to lie in the service of a good cause continue to challenge us. A student recently told me about his experience on a short-term mission trip. Participants had lied to corrupt authorities in order to bring in supplies to assist in much-needed relief work. The team had been coached in how to respond to questions before they arrived at the border. After the experience, the student continued to struggle and asked, "Lying to border patrol officials — is that okay?" Is it okay?

The biblical and historical traditions seem to move between the arguments of Augustine and Bonhoeffer, rejecting lying and yet occasionally allowing that particular circumstances or conditions challenge the moral wisdom of an exceptionless ban. The primary emphasis, however, is strongly on truthfulness.

What Happens When We Lie?

Those who lie "usually weigh only the immediate harm to others from the lie against the benefits they want to achieve. The flaw in such an outlook is that it ignores or underestimates two additional kinds of harm — the harm that lying does to the liars themselves and the harm done to the general level of trust and social cooperation."[25]

In many cases, the consequences of deception and lying are loss of trust and credibility, as well as betrayals and breaks in relationships. "Those who learn that they have been lied to in an important matter . . . are resentful, disappointed, and suspicious. They feel wronged; they are wary of new overtures."[26]

Lies, small or large, undermine integrity, discipleship, and fidelity to God's word. For those who lie, the personal consequences are significant and ongoing. In his book on dishonesty and deception, Ralph Keyes says, "Liars must play a continual game of I've got a secret. Eternal vigilance is the price of duplicity." "At a minimum, sustaining deceit levies a stressful tax of constant alertness. As an ancient proverb puts it, Liars need good memories."[27]

Keyes notes that lies "acquire lives of their own, and resist being killed off." Once they are told, we need more lies to keep the first ones going. To break the pattern is difficult because lies "can be retracted only if one is willing to confess to being a liar."[28]

Why We Lie

Mark Knapp identifies many of the reasons we tell lies:

> To avoid punishment. . . . To protect oneself from harm. . . . To obtain a reward for oneself. . . . To protect or help another person. . . . To win admiration from others. . . . To get out of an awkward or embarrassing social situation. . . . To maintain privacy. . . . To exercise power over others. . . . To fulfill social expectations. . . . To have fun.[29]

Some lies contribute to the rupturing of relationships, but others are efforts to sustain connections, even at the cost of the truth.[30] We often use small lies to impress or to oblige.[31] When we lie for "someone else's sake," we often compound "dishonesty with self-deception."[32]

Many of us tell numerous little "half-truths" throughout the day. "The strangest thing about half-truths," Komp explains, "is how easy it would be most times for us to simply tell the whole truth."[33] Sometimes half-truths smooth out social relations; often they are used to get out of awkward situations. Polite lies and those told to "oil the bearings of social relationships" usually involve euphemisms or exaggerations. Despite their seeming harmlessness, such lies erode truthfulness and help us evade difficult realities.[34]

For many of us, it would be hard to abandon the "little white lies" that seem so important in personal relationships. We wonder, "When someone plays a piano solo for the offertory and flubs a section royally, isn't it OK to tell her it was still beautiful? Should we hold our tongues when it's time to pass out praise if we can't sincerely state an unequivocal compliment?" Though occasionally quite challenging, usually it is possible to be appreciative without lying.

Lies to protect someone are sometimes called paternalistic or noble. Sissela Bok provides familiar examples of contexts for compassionate lying: "when an applicant is denied work, a request for money is turned down, [or] an offer of marriage is refused." She explains that paternalistic lies are often used to

> conceal the real reasons for the rejection, to retain the civility of the interaction, and to soften the blow to the self-respect of the rejected. It is easier to say that one cannot do something, or that the rules do not allow it, than that one does not want to do it; easier to say that there is no mar-

ket for a writer's proposed book than that it is unreadable; or that there is no opening for the job seeker than that he lacks the necessary skills.[35]

Lewis Smedes points out that even compassionate lies have troublesome implications, however, because "benevolent lying demeans the people deceived" by assuming that they are better off without the truth, and it "corrodes the character of the liar." Lies told for another person's benefit are not necessarily good, and "the evils that attend a general practice of benevolent lying outweigh the short-term good that loving lying might manage to promote."[36]

We tend to think that some truth is better than none, but half-truths presented as whole truths are lies, and "relying on false or misleading information is worse than having none at all."[37] "We treat deception via incomplete truth as distinct from falsehood, even though they have exactly the same impact upon the listener."[38]

Creating a community that lives truthfully necessarily involves individuals committed to the practice. Because it is relational practice, our efforts can be undermined when other persons make it clear that they do not want to know the truth. Lying is more likely when there is social pressure to lie about a particular topic to a particular audience, when lying has occurred in the same context previously, and when the rewards for lying "are greater than those for telling the truth."[39]

The most morally compelling lies have to do with saving the life of another, but they too are costly.[40] Falsehood comes into the heart of our identity. While we may conclude that lying is always wrong, it may still be a "preferable alternative" in certain desperate situations.[41] But even then, in our efforts to protect the life of another, we ought also to mourn the loss of truthfulness and our involvement in it.[42]

Sorting Out Hard Cases

When we reflect on the truly difficult cases, we can begin with "strong moral bias" against lying.[43] We can surely assume that "no lie is permissible if the same . . . goal can be achieved with a truthful statement."[44] Sissela Bok suggests that we ask three questions: (1) Can we resolve the difficulty without resorting to a lie? (2) What moral explanation or excuse will we offer for lying? and (3) How would other morally responsible persons evaluate this decision to lie?[45]

In difficult situations, then, we can ask ourselves if lying is truly a last resort. Further, we can use a test of "publicity," asking "which lies, if any, would survive the appeal for justification to reasonable persons." We can ask how we would react if the lie we are considering were told to us.[46] These questions would function in a way that rules out almost every consideration of lying except as a way to protect others from grave harm. They provide a framework for prayerful discernment.

Pseudo-Innocence

Individuals, communities, and congregations can make it clear that they do not want to hear the truth. They aren't interested, can't handle it, or don't have the time. The prophet Isaiah described the difficulty he faced in trying to speak hard truths into the lives of God's people: "They are a rebellious people, faithless children, children who will not hear the instruction of the LORD; who say to the seers, 'Do not see'; and to the prophets, 'Do not prophesy to us what is right; speak to us smooth things, prophesy illusions . . .'" (Isa. 30:9-10).

Attempting to avoid the truth by choosing not to know or not to notice is a common strategy. In the eighteenth century, John Wesley wondered how rich people of his day could know so little about the condition and needs of their destitute neighbors. He concluded that they "keep out of the way of knowing . . . and then plead their voluntary ignorance, as an excuse for their hardness of heart."[47]

If we have deliberately closed our eyes to what is going on, ignorance does not free us from responsibility. It is only a form of pseudo or false innocence. We might "overlook" the negative implications of a budget decision because we want the decision to go through. Later, in defending ourselves to those who recognize or experience the damage caused by the decision, we offer excuses and say, "We didn't know."

There is, of course, the possibility of being genuinely mistaken, and both pseudo-innocence and lying should be distinguished from mistakes. As Mark Knapp points out, "When people make honest or even careless mistakes, they may present false information but they believe it to be true. In such cases, we will often perceive the person to be misinformed, but not a liar."[48] Nevertheless, we might also consider what the misinformed person could reasonably have been expected to know.

Euphemisms

Because connections between love and truthfulness are important to us, we need to be careful not to confuse "speaking the truth in love" with euphemisms. In attempts to be nice or to be kind, sometimes we come very close to falsehood and deception by using language that covers over the real sin or the ugliness of the issue or circumstance. I was surprised by a young student's response to Neal Plantinga's book on sin, called *Not the Way It's Supposed to Be.* She complained that sections of the book were too raw and that she was offended by some of his stories about sin.

It is striking how often we Christians want our discussions of sin to be sanitized; we don't want to look at it in all its miserable evil and destruction. While we are often fascinated by the romance of evil on television or in film, we are simultaneously uncomfortable when other Christians name the real truth about sin; we confuse delicacy with holiness.

Euphemisms help those who use them to avoid thinking about what they are doing and to feel morally comfortable when the circumstances are problematic. A familiar example is the frequently used phrase "We want to help you to transition to the next phase of ministry" when, in fact, the person is being laid off. The individual losing his or her job knows what's happening and feels betrayed by the lack of truthfulness. Often it is important to ask ourselves about who benefits when we call things by "nicer" names.[49]

A combination of "euphemisms and passive voice" allows misconduct to be no one's fault.[50] In the face of serious wrongdoing, a generic admission that "mistakes were made" or "it happened" is a common way to avoid or obscure the truth about actual responsibility. Mistakes don't just happen, and a generalized observation about the problem does not help us to come to grips with significant moral failure.

Idle Chatter, Rumors, and Gossip

When trash talk and the lurid details of the lives of celebrities are served up as daily fare on television and the Internet, it's difficult to remember how seriously the biblical writers took the problem of unhelpful speech and unholy conversation.[51] In his own setting some seventy years ago, Dietrich Bonhoeffer warned that "genuine words are replaced by idle chatter. Words no longer possess any weight. There is too much talk. And . . . when words become rootless and homeless, then the word loses truth, and then indeed there must almost inevitably be lying."[52]

Often we repeat information that we would do better to simply absorb. Taking seriously the words of Ephesians 4:29 could transform our interactions and communities: "Let no evil talk come out of your mouths, but only what is useful for building up, as there is need, so that your words may give grace to those who hear." Such a discipline would be a strong antidote to the defiling impact of chatter, rumor, slander, and gossip.

Rumors — "talk or opinion widely disseminated with no discernible source"[53] — are common and facilitated by Internet technology. Told frequently enough, rumors become taken-for-granted bits of information that are difficult to challenge even when they are completely untrue. In disagreements within community, it is easy for rumors or half-truths to circulate and take on a life of their own.

Unless addressed as a problem, gossip — "rumors of a more intimate or personal nature"[54] — can sometimes become part of how a community shares its concerns. Gossip regularly appears in prayer requests when more information than is necessary is shared with an entire group. In efforts to live truthfully, sometimes we speak a particular and important truth, but to the wrong people. It is still gossip when we share true information with persons who are neither involved in the situation nor able to contribute to its resolution.

It is not always easy to distinguish gossip from expressions of concern and accountability, but we can discipline ourselves by regularly asking, "Do I have a legitimate reason for sharing this information with these people? What are my motives for making this information public? Have I considered the well-being of persons that will be affected by this information? Have I checked my facts? Is my timing right?"[55]

Living into the Practice of Truthfulness

As we draw closer to the source of truth and live gratefully in response to the one who has taken us from darkness to light, our desires and longings can be reshaped. We can grow into living truthfully and loving truth. While living truthfully involves self-discipline and thoughtful reflection, it is most fully linked to embracing God's desire for truth in our inward being (Ps. 51:6).

The Quaker tradition offers time-tested suggestions for fostering truthful living. They include these four: (1) Listen "for the truth in the words of others"; (2) Speak the truth as you understand it with "cordiality, kindness, and love"; (3) Avoid "gossip, tale bearing, breaking confidences, or the disparagement of others"; and (4) Resist "temptations to falsehood, coercion, and abuse."[56] Adopting these commitments would transform many interactions and communication patterns in our families and congregations.

When we think about truthfulness in relation to speech, we do not often assume that listening is a top priority. But listening is at the heart of wisdom and discernment. Additionally, truthful words cannot stand alone; they must be supported and sustained by a "congruent" life. If we begin with an inner commitment to "speak without deception," we will find that truthful speech and living become more natural.[57]

A community that loves the truth will understand the wisdom of silence. Speaking truthfully, as Mennonite theologian Alan Kreider notes, does not mean that we will "always say everything we think or know. There is ample room, in the truthful life, for silence, discretion, the keeping of confidences and even the pleasantries that lubricate social interchange. . . . But this does mean that we are committed to making the words that we utter true words."[58]

Congregations, families, or communities that want to grow in truthfulness might invite their members to monitor their speech for several days, keeping a diary of every time they said something that was not true. They could then reflect on the kinds of lies they told, the reasons they did so, and how they could have responded more truthfully.

L. Gregory Jones, ethicist and theologian, describes his experience with this exercise. He and his students decided to try to live a week without telling any lies. Soon they realized that "all of us would have to be quiet much more often as we discovered situations and relationships in which it is better not to speak than to utter statements that are not true."[59]

In Ephesians 4, we find that individual and communal maturity in Christ are closely connected to "speaking the truth in love" (Eph. 4:15). New life in Christ is characterized by speech that gives grace: "Let no evil talk come out of your mouths, but only what is useful for building up, as there is need, so that your words may give grace to those who hear" (Eph. 4:29). A check on our behavior might include regularly examining ourselves as to how our words are giving grace and how they reveal that we are being conformed to the image of God (see also Col. 3:9-10).

Communities that are concerned about truthfulness will be attentive to structures and patterns of life together that encourage or discourage truthful living. What do we do together that helps members learn to tell "tactful truths instead of reassuring lies"?[60] How are truthfulness and grace modeled by the leadership? What structures are in place to help us keep short accounts among ourselves? Where do we allow ourselves freedom to ask one another hard questions about important dimensions of our lives?[61]

In families and other close communities, sometimes we operate with a version of a "don't ask, don't tell" policy.[62] We overlook or accommodate patterns of behavior that ought to be challenged. Sometimes a caring outsider can see clearly and speak truthfully about difficulties within a community. Although we formalize this with "consultants," it can be more informal as well. A faithful friend who will speak truth to us is a precious gift. A person who loves us enough to name difficult truths and risk our response can keep us from self-destruction.

Jesus' teaching in Matthew 5:23-24 challenges us to take individual initiative in repairing damaged relationships by going directly to the other person involved to seek reconciliation. Within congregational life, Jesus also encourages direct and personal interaction, and only when that fails are other "witnesses" to be drawn in (Matt. 18:15-17).

Communities that love truth will make a safe place for the awkwardness of confession, forgiveness, and healing. Where truthfulness and confession are practiced, communities depend on fidelity, the assurance that members won't abandon one another as they reveal their sins and weaknesses and move toward maturity and holiness. Truthful communities are communities of encouragement and hospitality. As Miroslav Volf explains, "Without the will to embrace the other there will be no truth *between people,* and without truth between people there will be no peace."[63]

A Word Fitly Spoken: The Importance of Discernment

While the practice of discernment is important for every other practice, it is central to living truthfully. Communities that practice discernment are prayerful in seeking the best way to address important truths. They are attentive to details and to the processes that are needed to help people hear, receive, and speak truth. They notice small lies and deceptions early, and do not ignore the difficult issues.

No one speaks all the truth all the time; the practice of discernment assists us in knowing how and when to speak. Although we might attend to various aspects of a situation in order to be truthful, there is still a lot we do not say. For a number of reasons, we almost always need to select.[64] As noted previously, speaking truthfully is not the same as saying everything that comes into our heads.

Truth-telling should always include discernment, an element of the fitting. We don't tell children everything, and yet we still seek to be truthful with them. We hold some things back to protect their well-being, or because they lack the conceptual categories or experience to understand particular details. Under certain circumstances, even with adults, there are legitimate concerns about appropriateness, responsibility, and timing.

An interesting example of discernment and timing comes from John 16:12-13, when Jesus says to his disciples, "I still have many things to say to you, but you cannot bear them now. When the Spirit of truth comes, he will guide you into all the truth." The time would come for the disciples to be told additional truth, but until then, the words would be unbearable. "A word fitly spoken," as Proverbs 25:11 says, "is like apples of gold in a setting of silver."

Creating a culture of truthfulness involves knowing when we should speak, and when it is appropriate to conclude that God is at work and we do not need to say anything. It requires patience and wisdom to know what ought to be borne for a time, and what should be confronted.

Timeliness is an important aspect of discernment, however. If we wait too long to address certain difficulties or conflicts in community, they can reach a point where it is too late to repair them. Naming deception early or identifying disagreements quickly helps to keep us from walking down paths from which it is hard to return. A recognition of timeliness also means that we will not store up all our grievances and then dump them in one moment of aggravated "truth-telling."[65]

Discernment requires fidelity, staying with something long enough to understand it. It means noticing what others overlook, and often involves a capacity to see patterns or connections where others see only brokenness. But there are situations in which timeliness and taking time to understand and give a measured response are in tension. Circumstances as well as our own finiteness can require that we move ahead without having all of the details in place.

Handling Disagreements Redemptively

If our communities develop the habit of delighting in the truth, we will be in a better position to deal with the inevitable conflicts and disagreements that are part of shared life. As we face conflict, truth-telling should include remembering and rehearsing who we are. We do this in teaching, preaching, and liturgy, reminding ourselves of our identity, to whom we belong, and the common commitments we cherish.

In situations of major conflict, where interpretations of events and motives are highly contested, it can be helpful to name truthfully what we can agree on. We can learn to ask specific questions. Seeking and speaking the truth about particular matters helps with broader truth-telling regarding who we are and how we can move forward. And a truthful community resists the impulse to use pep talks to cover over major problems. Substituting enthusiasm for truthful reflection brings neither resolution nor freedom.

Whether in marital or congregational disagreements, it is hard to get to the root of the difficulty if the parties will not sit down together and talk with one another. Creating a place that is safe for each to hear the other requires establishment of ground rules and a loving and truthful guide. Addressing generalities can seem safer, but speaking truthfully to one another, whether in the form of affirmation or critique, is most helpful if it involves specifics.

Chris Rice recalls the advice that their beloved friend and advisor John Alexander gave to the members of the Antioch community about handling their disagreements, tensions, and sins. "One of the foundations of community is knowing that you will sin and be sinned against. It needs to be our daily expectation. But there also needs to be an expectation of forgiving others their sins and being forgiven." He continued, "Expecting ourselves to be bad can't be an excuse not to change and grow." He challenged them further, "You need to learn to confront openly and without apology. But also without dogma, without anger."[66]

In confrontation, it is generally best to speak about difficult matters face-to-face. Words of affirmation and encouragement can be reread and reinforced when put in writing, but when hard words are recorded, they are often read over and over again with little benefit and with increasingly less context.[67]

Practicing "Clear"

The Good Works community has developed a ritual that helps staff members address interpersonal tensions before they become major disruptions.

They recognize the central importance of walking together in truth and of following Jesus' teaching about laying our gift at the altar and seeking reconciliation and forgiveness from one another. They call the practice "Clear."[68]

At their weekly staff meetings, the first question they ask one another after the opening prayer is "Are we clear?" Keith Wasserman explains, "This has now become a code word for 'Do you have anything you need to say to me about how you and I are doing or about how we are getting along and working out this thing called salvation?'" Is there something that we need to talk about before we "move into the business of the ministry"?

He notes that this practice has deepened trust and established an accountability structure that "forces our lives into the light with one another." Their approach also recognizes that interpersonal tensions have a great impact on the entire community. "This kind of discipleship nurtures and rewards truth-telling," he concludes. "What holds our community together must be both truth and love."

The structure created by Good Works makes room for truthfulness and keeps conflicts from festering. The community has been able to avoid the downward spiral of resentment that is common among coworkers who serve in highly demanding ministries. Because being a whole and holy community is important to them, they allow the time needed for this process. If someone is not "clear," there is structure and support to work through a biblical framework for reconciliation based on Matthew 5:23-24.

Oaths and Word-Watching

When we want to assure someone that we are being truthful or sincere, we sometimes preface our comments with words like "To be perfectly honest . . ." or "Frankly . . ." or even "To tell you the truth. . . ." But, as Alan and Eleanor Kreider rightly point out, such statements bring all of our other speech into question: Are we not being truthful the rest of the time?[69] If we live and speak truthfully, such assurances will not be needed.

Another way we attempt to establish or guarantee truthfulness is through the use of oaths.[70] In their book *Kingdom Ethics,* Glen Stassen and David Gushee argue that oath-taking "has an inherent danger in it. It establishes a two-tier system of speech." Like the Kreiders, they wonder, "When I speak under oath or swear that my words are true, then you as my listener are supposed to be able to have confidence in my words. But what, then, is the status of what I say when I am not swearing or not under oath? . . . The very existence of an oath-level of speech threatens to render (or unveil) everyday speech as less trustworthy."[71]

While the Christian tradition is mixed in its response to oath-taking,[72] Jesus' command in Matthew 5:33-37 is at least a powerful check on the use of oaths. He affirms honest and straightforward speech: ". . . I say to you, do not swear at all. . . . Let your word be 'Yes, Yes' or 'No, No'; anything more than this comes from the evil one."

Alan Kreider argues that the most important reason to reject oaths is "to reassert the Christian concern for truth-telling. When Jesus repudiated the oath, his main concern was to call a halt to two-level truth-telling, to the 'differentiation between the words which have to be true, and those which don't have to be true.' . . . Our 'no' is thus to oath-taking; our corresponding 'yes' will be to truth-telling."[73] We would do well to see ourselves as "stewards" of words, recognizing that language is a treasure entrusted to our care.[74]

A deepened commitment to living truthfully could change our individual character and the quality of our common life. Truthful living in the context of grace, gratitude, fidelity, and hospitality gives powerful testimony to the one who is the way, the truth, and the life.

PART IV

Practicing Hospitality and Beyond

CHAPTER ELEVEN

Hospitality: Drawing the Practices Together

*Welcome is one of the signs that a community is alive. To invite
others to live with us is a sign that we aren't afraid, that we have a
treasure of truth and of peace to share.*

Jean Vanier, *Community and Growth*

Hermas, a writer from the early centuries of the church, declared that in
hospitality could be found the practice of good.[1] In the late twentieth century, ethicist Thomas Ogletree echoed a similar conviction that "to be
moral is to be hospitable to the stranger."[2] These are strong claims about
the moral significance of hospitality, but if we consider the many issues of
exclusion, abandonment, recognition, and welcome in contemporary life,
we might be inclined to agree.

Communities in which hospitality is a vibrant practice tap into deep
human longings to belong, find a place to share one's gifts, and be valued.
The practice of hospitality reflects a willingness on the part of a community of people to be open to others and to their insights, needs, and contributions. Hospitable communities recognize that they are incomplete without other folks but also that they have a "treasure" to share with them.[3]

Hospitality is at the heart of Christian life, drawing from God's grace
and reflecting God's graciousness. In hospitality, we respond to the welcome that God has offered and replicate that welcome in the world. While
many current understandings of hospitality are limited to the hospitality

industry of restaurants and hotels, coffee and donuts at church, or well-planned dinner parties, the practice itself is biblically, historically, and theologically much more substantive and significant.

The practice of hospitality is important for communities as they reach out to others and as they work to strengthen their internal relationships. A community is also important for the practice of hospitality. Those who welcome strangers from within a community can find friends with whom to share the work and the blessing, help in maintaining perspective, and opportunities for rest and renewal.

When we regularly offer hospitality to strangers, we quickly discover the importance of other practices. Living and speaking truthfully are central to the vulnerability and transparency associated with welcoming people into our lives and communities. But to live truthfully while offering welcome, a family, congregation, or community also depends on the practice of fidelity or promising. Together, truthfulness and fidelity help create a trustworthy environment into which we can welcome strangers and within which it is safe to be vulnerable.

Unless it is rooted in gratitude, the practice of hospitality quickly becomes grudging (1 Pet. 4:9). Hospitality is not easy, and guests are not always pleasant or grateful. To sustain hospitality over the long term, our gratitude needs to be cultivated in response to the love and grace of God. Fidelity, truthfulness, and gratitude make space for the practice of hospitality.

Communities of hospitality also learn how important it is to set aside time for rest and renewal. Without some form of Sabbath-keeping, communities burn out very quickly. And the practice of discernment becomes crucial because not everyone can be welcomed into every context, and knowing how and when to "close the door" is a requisite for survival.

Within hospitable families, communities, and congregations, the other practices are not only necessary; they are tested and refined. If the community is sustained over time, often people learn how to speak the truth in love, keep their promises, and renew their gratitude. Envy, deception, grumbling, and betrayal destroy community and undermine hospitality, so when they appear in community life, they often prompt efforts at discernment, confession, and forgiveness.

Because a detailed exploration of the practice of hospitality is available in my book *Making Room*,[4] I will not repeat that material in this chapter. Instead, I will build on it and allow particular reflections on hospitality to open up a fuller picture of how the practices work together and how their deformations undermine the practice of hospitality. But before that, a few comments about the place of hospitality in the Christian tradition will introduce the discussion.[5]

A Look at the Tradition

Hospitality and shared meals fill the pages of Scripture. In Genesis 18, we read of Abraham and Sarah and the strangers/angels they welcome; it is a story of hospitality that is rich with promise and blessing. In the historical books, we see that the Israelites, themselves strangers and sojourners, are frequently called upon by God to welcome and care for other strangers and sojourners.[6] At the end of the New Testament, Jesus speaks of himself as knocking at the door, and he promises to come in and eat with anyone who opens the door to him (Rev. 3:20).

In the Gospels, there are many stories of Jesus as a guest at dinner parties, family meals, and celebrations in various homes. He is also portrayed as a stranger who is sometimes welcomed but more often rejected. Frequently, he is pictured as a host who feeds hungry crowds, makes room for prostitutes and little children, and cooks breakfast for discouraged disciples.[7]

God is described as a host in the wilderness, supplying manna every day (Exod. 16). Later, Jesus reveals himself as the manna, the bread of life (John 6:32-35). Not only is he a host or a guest — Jesus is also the meal, the sustenance we need, the source of our lives. The centrality of hospitality is reinforced and regularly re-enacted in the Lord's Supper, the Eucharist, where we remember the costly welcome we have received into the kingdom, and where we are regularly welcomed to the table of the kingdom.

The earliest Christians understood the importance of hospitality. They knew that their welcome had come at a great cost, and that to be members of God's household, brothers and sisters of Jesus, they would need to practice the same kind of costly welcome. And so they welcomed one another into their homes when fleeing persecution or when traveling to share the gospel. They ate together regularly so that the poor would be fed and so that they could keep their new Christian identity alive in a hostile world (Acts 2:46). They worshiped in homes in the first centuries and depended on the hospitality of the homeowners. And, significantly, hospitality was the context within which they worked through complex and troubling ethnic and status differences.

The early church struggled to embody the belief that rich and poor believers were equals in the community of faith, and that Jews and Gentiles were one in Christ.[8] By God's grace and power, and because of the sacrificial welcome they had experienced in Christ, they learned to sit down at a table and share their homes and lives with people they had previously viewed as dirty or less than human. They sorted out this new way of living and valuing in the context of offering one another hospitality.

There were many failures. We see the struggles in the book of Acts and in Paul's letters to the churches in Corinth and Galatia. Nevertheless, in the first centuries, Christian hospitality was a central witness to the truth of the gospel and to its transforming power. Those who defended the faith before hostile rulers argued that Christian welcome to strangers and across social boundaries marked the gospel as authentic and true. Christians from different ethnic and socio-economic backgrounds ate together, loved and cared for one another, and shared one another's lives and homes.[9]

Jesus' message, as well as his life, death, and resurrection, have shaped Christian understandings of hospitality. Two of his teachings are particularly formative for the tradition. In Matthew 25:31-46, Jesus tells a story in response to his disciples' question about recognizing signs of "the end of the age" (Matt. 24:3). He describes a scene of final judgment in which the "sheep" and the "goats" are separated based on whether or not they had welcomed, fed, and clothed the Son of Man. "I was hungry and you gave me food . . . a stranger and you welcomed me" or "did not welcome me," explains Jesus. "Just as you did it to one of the least of these who are members of my family, you did it to me." This passage is central to almost every teaching and tradition related to hospitality because it so closely links care for those in need with care for the Son of Man himself. Our response to the "least" is tied to our response to Jesus and to his response to us.

Jesus' teaching on the kingdom in Luke 14:12-14 provides the basis for another distinctive understanding of hospitality. At a dinner party, he tells his host, "When you give a luncheon or a dinner, do not invite your friends or your brothers or your relatives or rich neighbors, in case they may invite you in return, and you would be repaid. But when you give a banquet, invite the poor, the crippled, the lame, and the blind. And you will be blessed, because they cannot repay you, for you will be repaid at the resurrection of the righteous."

Jesus calls for a practice that was as countercultural then as it is today. But based on these passages, the ancient church was convinced that

Christians had to open their doors to poor people and to strangers. The possibility of welcoming Jesus, as well as the importance of following his teaching, was reinforced by the writer of Hebrews, who brought to mind the blessing of Sarah and Abraham in welcoming strangers: "Do not neglect to show hospitality to strangers, for by doing that some have entertained angels without knowing it" (Heb. 13:2).

A particular vision for Christian hospitality developed in the fourth and fifth centuries of the church. Working with the biblical texts, writers argued that hospitality ought to be generous and uncalculating rather than "ambitious." Special attention should be given to people who did not appear to have the ability to repay the kindness. This was in contrast to other understandings of hospitality that offered it to "worthy" recipients, understood as persons who would be able to give something in return.[10]

For followers of Jesus, hospitality certainly included offering welcome to family, friends, and fellow believers. But it always involved more than that. The welcome and grace they had experienced in Christ was the model and the empowerment for their hospitality to strangers. As a result, believers made a special effort to welcome those who were poor, sick, and disabled. Although there were serious gaps in commitment and practice over the centuries, offering hospitality was an important part of Christian identity.

Hospitality was a central practice in the first fifteen hundred years of the church. During the Late Middle Ages, however, its special features were undermined for a variety of reasons, and hospitality came to be identified with lavish entertaining of the rich and powerful. Its practice often served to reinforce power and influence. The connection with poor people, with equality, and with crossing social and cultural boundaries was nearly lost.

A few communities, however, maintained a commitment to earlier understandings. Parts of the monastic tradition never lost their appreciation for hospitality, most evident in the Benedictine emphasis on welcome that goes back to the sixth century and continues today. Certain church traditions emphasized the importance of hospitality and sharing meals together; particular examples include Anabaptist and African-American church traditions.

In recent decades, attention to hospitality has increased, and its theological and human importance has again been recognized. Christian communities have formed around offering welcome to strangers. The Catholic Worker movement recovered the moral and practical significance of hospitality in the 1930s. L'Arche communities, founded by Jean Vanier around the world, create a life in community with people with severe disabilities. Other communities welcome homeless people, students and seekers, street children, and refugees.

The central importance of hospitality is also being recovered in congregations. We see fresh expressions of welcome when congregations make a place for unchurched children, international students, and isolated older people. Congregations are building bridges to their larger communities as they offer weekly neighborhood meals and find opportunities to come alongside troubled families.

As noted earlier, in the Christian tradition of hospitality the emphasis is on welcoming strangers.[11] But what makes someone a stranger? Who are the strangers in our world that need welcome? Strangers are people without a place, disconnected from life-giving relationships and networks.[12] Sometimes that's a literal condition — as in the case of refugees or homeless people. In other cases, as with alienated teens or people with disabilities, persons may have a place to live, but they do not necessarily have a place where they can contribute something, or where they are valued. Because hospitality is part of what it means to be human, every human being flourishes in the context of welcome.

In our society, even neighbors can be strangers. Small acts of hospitality can make a place for the lonely child down the street and the elderly neighbor whose relatives live across the country. International students, visiting speakers, and the new family in town need welcome. But strangers who are without resources and unable to purchase what they need are the most vulnerable.

In many societies, hospitality has provided the moral framework for protecting strangers and responding to their needs. Although sometimes contested, the practice of granting sanctuary or asylum remains part of moral and political conversations. As in ancient times, offering welcome to those that are vulnerable continues to be a sign of contradiction, a sign of hope "that love is possible" in a broken world.[13]

The practice is important not only for strangers and other vulnerable persons; it is also crucial for the life of a congregation itself. Hospitality is a means of grace for hosts as well as guests. Many people, after practicing hospitality, comment that they "got so much more than they gave" in welcoming a refugee family or in caring for a sick neighbor. One friend who has worked in hospice care for years describes the hospitality she experiences from patients and families as being holy ground. Hospitality is an invitation from God to grow deeper in love.

It is also an opportunity to reflect on and to participate in the mutual welcoming and love evident in the life of the Trinity. Miroslav Volf notes, "Inscribed on the very heart of God's grace is the rule that we can be its recipients only if we do not resist being made into its agents; what happens to us must be done by us. Having been embraced by God, we must make space for others and invite them in — even our enemies."[14]

Hospitality: Out of Step with Contemporary Culture

Today, many people in the United States have a limited view of hospitality even when they recognize the challenges of responding to "otherness" or seek practical ways to care for persons who are in need. Often, folks think of hospitality in terms of television shows and magazine articles about putting together a dinner party, or the graduate-school degrees related to the hospitality industry. Businesspeople take lessons in how to entertain, and churches develop hospitality programs for evangelism and church growth.

Because it is very effective in building and sustaining relationships, we can use hospitality to serve our own purposes. In many of the contemporary understandings noted above, we view hospitality as a means to another end — achieving business success, enhancing our image, or growing our numbers. Although Christians have always struggled with using hospitality for their own "advantage" or ambition, understandings today explicitly build on that expectation.

Another challenge to recovering a more generous approach to hospitality is that the practice does not fit well with our strong task orientation and emphasis on efficiency. Our practices become very unwelcoming when we try to develop structures that will anticipate every contingency. We overlook the centrality of relationships and crush the fragile expressions of respect and care when we only pay attention to how quickly and effectively tasks are accomplished. Congregations that value hospitality battle the demand for quick and measurable results. So entrenched is this mind-set that we frequently wonder, as an issue of stewardship, *Will hospitality work? What will it accomplish?*

When we orient our lives around tasks, opportunities for hospitality often appear in the form of interruptions. Because many of us are very busy, it is hard to imagine adding another thing to already out-of-control schedules. When tasks successfully completed become the measure of ministry, it is difficult to value relationships or small steps toward transformed identity. If we are to recover the practice of hospitality, we will need to do far more than clear our schedules for one more task or activity — we will need to reconsider how we live our lives.

Historically, homes have been a central location for hospitality, but in this society, we view our homes as very private space. They are a retreat from the world, our safe haven after a hard day's work. Our personal places are often quite isolated. When this isolation is combined with the increase in the number of adults working outside the home, and the small number of persons living in most households, it has a major impact on practicing hospitality. It is difficult to welcome people into our lives when no one is at home, when households are small, and when homes are very private. Risks are increased for hosts and guests unless there is a community to fall back on.

Complications and Deformations

Giving close attention to the other practices and their deformations can help us unpack the complications associated with practicing hospitality. The questions and fears that are commonly raised in relation to hospitality often reveal trouble with, or misunderstandings of, other practices.

I can't have people over when the house is such a mess. Besides, we've got our ups and downs as a family — it isn't always pretty. What would people think if we invited them in?

We often worry about appearances, and we work hard to project a particular image. One nine-year-old girl's observation spoke volumes as she helped her mother scramble to get the house ready for guests, "Mommy, you're trying to make the house look like children don't live here." If we work or wait until everything is perfect, we'll rarely offer welcome, and when we do, we're likely to be exhausted.

Hospitality is revelatory: if we invite people into our lives and homes, they'll see what's there. Hospitality and living truthfully meet here because welcome is not about putting on a show but about inviting people into our lives as we live them. When we truly make room for others, we cannot keep up false appearances for long; hospitality is an invitation to mutual truthfulness.

What if the strangers we welcome turn out to be dangerous? How can we know that their stories are true?

The tradition of hospitality is riddled with concerns about deception, about persons who "traffic" in Christ, and about those who are false teachers, frauds, unscrupulous vagabonds, or beggars who take all. Occasionally, a guest or host does not intend good. In certain circumstances, the other person becomes vulnerable to their deception. In the hospitality tradition, simple tests were developed to discern deception and dishonesty, so that communities would be protected from ongoing abuses. In general, truthfulness and intentions can be discerned more easily and safely in more communal or public settings. Threshold places (settings that are bridges between private and public space) are particularly helpful.

What about people who take advantage of our generosity? What if we are used?

Hosts in particular worry about being used. They fear being taken in by the deception of unscrupulous guests, or by their unrelenting demands. Because hospitality involves a relationship of at least two parties, it is vulnerable to implicit promises not to take advantage of one another. Sometimes it can be helpful to spell out expectations early in the relationship, but even when the practices function well, all the unpredictability cannot be removed from hospitality.

As part of their life together, one congregation gathered for a meal before worship each Sunday. It seemed like a great opportunity to build relationships within the community and with their new friends who lived on the street. As one member put it with a wry smile, "We were trying to make the tent larger" through the meals, but encountered a recurring problem with people "running away with pieces of the tent." Resistant to their church meal becoming another version of a soup kitchen, the congregation chose to suspend the meals, take time to reflect on how to build a deeper commitment among participants, and then begin again.

Fidelity, commitments, and implicit promises are also relevant to the form that our concerns take. We worry about offering hospitality, and ask "What if?" as we imagine every possible difficulty. Sometimes, in our fear, we overlook God's faithfulness and mistakenly think that being "used" is the biggest problem we can encounter. When we grow frustrated with the self-centeredness of some guests, it is easy for us to forget how often their behavior reflects the betrayals and infidelities many of them have previously experienced. If we try to have controls in place for all of the risks, we will miss out on much of the grace associated with the practice of hospitality.

What if hospitality doesn't work? What if people don't respond to our invitations?

When viewed as a strategy, hospitality is usually short-lived. Unless it becomes part of our DNA, we often abandon the practice when we meet resistance or when it does not quickly "bear fruit." Especially when there are significant social or cultural differences between them, potential guests can be very wary of the intentions of eager hosts. They do not respond positively until fidelity over time is evident. Gradually, very gradually, as one person put it, it is possible to weave a fabric of hospitality within a neighborhood. One pastor, who had planted a church among folks who had good reasons to be wary, lived and worked in the community for several years before anyone responded positively to his efforts. Only after they had discerned his family's fidelity to the community were the residents ready to partner together.

What if there isn't enough? What if we run out of . . . ?

Questions about limits come up often in hospitality. Resources of time, food, money, and energy are finite. Hospitality can be overwhelming if we are not careful to nurture our lives or if we try to do it alone. The practice of Sabbath-keeping helps us recognize our limits and God's sufficiency, and reminds us of a larger fidelity into which we fit our acts of hospitality.

As we welcome strangers, we can anticipate God's presence and supply. But we cannot therefore ignore our finiteness or our other responsibilities — to our children, our family, or other vulnerable persons we have already welcomed. Sabbath, discernment, and fidelity intersect with hospitality on the question of limits.

Is it wrong to expect guests to be grateful? Some act as if they are entitled to our hospitality. It's hard not to grow increasingly resentful.

In 1 Peter 4:9, as noted earlier, believers are urged to practice hospitality without complaining. Grudging hospitality is deadly; it humiliates the recipient while it adds to the weariness of the host. Gratitude is a necessary practice associated with hospitality, especially for hosts for whom gratitude to God is a wellspring of life and welcome.

In some cases, a guest's ingratitude is simply a violation of common courtesy. In other cases, however, guests struggle with circumstances that have put them into the role of being "needy" recipients. While most guests are grateful, some resent help even as they depend on it. When we find ourselves dismayed by the absence of gratitude, we need also to check our own thinking; difficulty in this area can be an invitation to truthful reflection. Hospitality should not function as a substitute for efforts at justice or equity.

If we welcome strangers into our community, couldn't they threaten our way of life?

This is a major tension in the tradition. Communities with a strong sense of identity and life-shaping commitments are often very good at offering hospitality, and they are the communities people generally want to join. But as we welcome people into community for more than a brief visit, issues of shared commitments and lifestyles become significant — whether for a nation, a church, or a household. Fidelity, truthfulness, and hospitality are complexly intertwined.

God's hospitality is inseparable from covenantal understandings of fidelity and truth.[15] There will be tensions in our practice of hospitality because the God of Scripture calls us to hospitality and also to faithfulness to a particular way of life. We've made promises to be true to God's ways, which include both welcoming strangers and living holy lives. Not every stranger we welcome will embrace that way of life or understand it in the same way. While this is sometimes an issue in brief acts of welcome, it is much more challenging in long-term relationships and as persons move from guests to members in our communities.

Discernment is also important as we struggle to determine which parts of our identity and commitments are central and which can or should be challenged. But learning to speak truthfully about "this is who we are" or "these are the minimal commitments which you must embrace to be part of this community" is not always easy, especially when the vision or the community itself is still evolving. It is often wise to start with what we know to be true, and to move from there to the more uncertain questions.

Inclusion and tolerance are important values to many people in contemporary society, though the rhetoric is complexly and unpredictably related to actual practice. Christians should be careful not to trade the capacity to make distinctions between good and evil for a notion of tolerance that is morally weak. At the same time, however, we must make sure that our fidelity and truth are situated in the primary call to love our enemies.

Most of our questions about inclusion and exclusion do not run so deep; they are often the result of fear, envy, or trying to protect what we have. Exclusion and inhospitality are sometimes the fruit of misplaced fidelity, where we define ourselves by whom we exclude. Communities will struggle with these issues, but a community that does not offer welcome at all is a community that is dying.[16] It has closed in on itself. In its misguided efforts at fidelity, it has been undone by its own fears.

Hospitality and Living into the Practices

As this book comes to a close, reflections on living into the practice of hospitality also give us opportunities to look again at how the practices are knit together in communities of faith and service.

Sharing Our Gifts

Communities that practice hospitality discover that one of the most precious resources they have to share with people is their fellowship and friendship. More than offering ministry or services to "those" in need, they welcome people into a common life. Many congregations, however, offer help without friendship. So, ironically, we find soup kitchens that are housed in churches, but those who eat lunch in the all-purpose room never experience the fellowship of the worshiping community.

Often, the best gift we can give another person is our time and attention. Human beings need a place in which they and their contributions are valued, and a hospitable community finds ways to value the gifts people bring. Few experiences are more lonely or isolating than finding oneself unwanted, unneeded, or unable to contribute. People come to life, however, when they and their offerings are valued. This means that communities and the folks within them must be willing to receive. Only as we recognize our own vulnerabilities and incompleteness are we open to what others can contribute.

Reconnecting Home and Church

In the history of Christian hospitality, the most important location for the practice was the overlap of home and church — a natural context for shared meals, conversation, and small-group gatherings. When we view our homes as personal spaces that are simultaneously crucial to God's work in the world, we discover many opportunities to create a place for healing, personal transformation, and community-building.

Some expressions of this are more personally demanding than others, but homes can become small outposts of God's kingdom. Through their hospitality, one couple at seminary created a community among students and neighbors where before there had been none. Their love for conversation and cooking was contagious, and for several years they welcomed many people into their small home once a week. Friendships were born and renewed at their gatherings. The couple was intentional about keeping the menu and format simple so that everyone would be comfortable taking their turn at cooking and hosting, and soon a second weekly meal was established in other nearby homes. Because of their model, the neighborhood potlucks continued when the couple finished seminary and, with their children, moved across the country.

Recently settled into a new place with new opportunities to offer hospitality, they sent me an e-mail:

> Shortly after arriving here in town, we met our neighbors. One family had recently lost their father; he killed himself after being diagnosed with cancer. The family fell into disarray following his death, and four weeks after we got here, they lost their home. The mother asked us if we could take . . . her children in. We prayed about it with [our children] and took in the two and later the third child.
>
> It was a very interesting experience — to say the least. Because this was supposed to be short-term (three weeks), we did not set up boundaries. And at the end of the three weeks, there was supposed to be a move to a new house within another three weeks. It went on like this for the entire time they were with us. . . .
>
> At week eleven, we set boundaries. In addition to the Wednesday dinner for the entire family, we said that we would like to know in advance when the mother would need her children, and we would like to be more involved with the search for a home. We, at times, felt like we were at the mother's mercy as far as planning anything. . . . Three days after meeting with the mother to set boundaries, she told us she found different housing arrangements for her kids, and they moved out.
>
> I know you do not know all the variables, but what should we have done differently? Should we have set boundaries regardless of the ex-

pected duration of the stay? We really wanted to allow for the mother's autonomy, but it appeared that without motivation (setting boundaries and being involved with her financial decisions) she did not move forward.

"What did we do wrong?" they wondered, as they reflected on questions of fidelity, hospitality, expectations, and limits. So much of what they had done was right. Our efforts at hospitality are often a mixture of blessing and difficulty, both imperfect and wonderful. They gave themselves, and in doing so, they provided three traumatized children with a model of a Christian family and a safe place to heal.

How many churches would be transformed if the households within them were encouraged to think differently about ministry? Many churches focus on programs, and given issues of scale, many of those may be necessary. But programs should open into relationships and help participants in building friendships and life-changing connections.

Speaking Truth in and about Hospitality

When we are betrayed by someone we have welcomed or when gratitude and truthfulness are missing in response to hospitality, we often feel hurt. If we are trying to encourage the practice of hospitality within a congregation, sometimes we hesitate to share our difficult experiences and disappointments. However, if we paint entirely rosy pictures and hide the costs, we are not being truthful or helpful. People do not initially understand how dependent they are on God's grace and on community support in the practice of hospitality, and are often surprised by the inevitable disappointments.

It is important to talk truthfully about all of the practices. Part of the challenge of recovering hospitality involves helping people to notice it and to tell stories about their experiences as guests, hosts, and strangers. Becoming more attentive to hospitality and story-telling allows us to recount the blessings of welcoming strangers and to learn from some of the challenges.

In hospitable settings, hard as well as helpful truths can be discovered and spoken. Many teachers can tell stories of students who have come to life in a classroom that felt safe and hospitable. One of my students recently told me about the "truths" that she had been told about her lack of academic ability. The words had profoundly limited her horizon and undermined her confidence. In a safe setting, she began to take risks and discover new abilities. She was able to offer gifts — significant intellectual insights — she had not known she had.

Good Endings

Mutual fidelity and hospitality are crucial as family and friends accompany a person through illness or the process of dying. In a story told in Chapter 2, several members of a congregation walked with a woman as she was dying of cancer. Her husband was unable to acknowledge her terminal condition and would not speak of it with his wife or with church members. In a sense, the congregation carried truthfulness for the couple; friends could see and respond to the woman's needs and talk with her where her husband could not.

This story gives us additional glimpses into how practices interact in the body of Christ. Sometimes a certain practice is so difficult for us in the moment that brothers and sisters must bear it for us.[17] But also in this account, the woman's husband was faithful to her, and his fidelity lessened the damage from his inability to be fully truthful in the situation.

Many practices come together in this experience. The woman invited her friends in to walk with her through this difficult event. She and her husband made room for them to offer their gifts. In a similar way, the church members walked with the couple in fidelity, truthfulness, and hospitality. Together they were able to experience grace, provide respite, and share hope.

Less significant "endings" or departures also demonstrate the power of hospitality. Drawing from the tradition of hospitality in Jewish life, one writer explains,

> How a guest leaves one's home can be the defining moment for the entire visit. . . . If [a guest] is walked out the door with warmth and friendliness, with sincere thanks for his presence and hopes for his return, the aftertaste of the visit will be sweet. For escorting a guest out of one's home and down the block . . . tells him that the host wishes to prolong the visit. It imparts the sense that the guest is valued as a person, and is not just the object of one's mitzvah.[18]

The wisdom of this teaching became very clear one Thanksgiving Day when my brother's family welcomed a friend to dinner. She was far from any family, and responded gladly to the invitation. As she was leaving, the four teenagers in the house got up with the rest of us and saw her to her car. All of us were surprised when she began to cry — she had been deeply touched by the sense that the teens had appreciated her presence.

Our cultural emphasis on efficiency and with "getting on with it" may account for some of our failures to acknowledge departures. Celebrations seem to serve little "purpose" when the person won't be returning, especially if the departure is irregular. While we might celebrate retirements, we are less likely to mark more awkward occasions, and yet these may be the most important times to acknowledge a person's contributions and what they have meant to the community. Instead, when a person leaves for another job, is laid off, or moves to another setting, we often allow or encourage them to slip away unnoticed.

Occasionally, we encounter communities that choose not to acknowledge any departures or accomplishments. Their work is "too important" for them to take time for celebrations or recognitions. Some fear that recognition will undercut humility. When an individual chooses not to be recognized, the community also loses an opportunity to celebrate its history with a person who helped to shape it.

Lukewarm Practices

I have assumed throughout this book that most Christians long for a fuller, more complete experience of life in community. Recently, however, I was reminded that some folks are content with a fairly thin version of it. There are church members who resist efforts to build stronger community because they are satisfied with Sunday-morning services and an occasional activity. In other cases, they are wary of a substantive recovery of particular practices, preferring more "moderate" versions in which practices are not too costly or personally inconvenient.

Part of the difficulty here is theological. Christian community is not optional — we are called to be part of the body of Christ. Lukewarm or half-hearted participation hurts the very thing necessary to our identity and flourishing. Mediocrity may be less demanding, but it is ultimately a spiritual and social disaster.[19] When communities choose a maintenance mode for extended periods, they are facilitating their own deaths.

Being content is different from being lukewarm. Patience and fidelity are important in troubling circumstances. Rooted in hope and sustained in gratitude, contentment allows us to move ahead toward a fuller life, despite major obstacles. In difficult situations, discernment may also require that we move slowly, sifting and weighing information or sorting out visions. This process, which can seem quite measured, is also different from being half-hearted.

A negative response to efforts at building community may, however, reflect a deep weariness which requires Sabbath rest. Alternatively, half-hearted responses may reflect boredom or frustration with one more program or project that congregational members are expected to embrace.[20] The goal in all of this is not to try harder to build community or to get the practices right. It is about living and loving well in response to Christ.

Subtle Idolatries

We are not saved by practices or by doing them well. Undoubtedly, paying attention to practices is a poor substitute for a relationship with the living God. And, strangely enough, we can make an idol out of a practice, imagining that if we live hospitably, keep our promises, or speak truthfully, we can define our identity or become good.

If, as a community, we see practices as the next skill set or framework for a program to make congregations work better, we will have missed the point. When we offer welcome or live with gratitude, when we make and keep promises or live truthfully, we are responding to the practices of God. Our experiences of community grow out of the practices through which we echo the goodness, grace, and truth we find in Jesus.

Distilling the Practices

After opening with music, prayer, and a sermon each week, the church I attend shares breakfast as part of our worship time. Community prayer follows our meal together, and we end each service with communion. We have drawn in a number of folks with serious disabilities who enjoy the combination of a more intimate worship with the fellowship of a regular meal.

One Sunday, a woman with a serious disability took bread and dipped it in the cup. A sudden jerk of her hand sent droplets of juice flying in every direction, but with obvious delight, she responded, "This is so good." She then said, with a sigh and a smile, "I like being next to Jesus." It was a beautiful and holy moment as she sprinkled those around her with grace.

Layers of gratitude, hospitality, fidelity, and truthfulness are drawn together in this communion ritual.[21] Sometimes the mystery leaks out in particularly startling or poignant ways, but always it helps us remember and experience again the welcome that Jesus offers us all.

Churches that practice hospitality have countless contexts in which to tell the story of God's welcome. When the Eucharist is more explicitly connected to regular expressions of hospitality in shared meals, caring, and friendship, a distinctive Christian identity and way of life are reinforced. As practices of hospitality, celebration, and Sabbath are taken seriously, they can become an invitation to joy and congregational renewal.

We are not called to create ideal families, communities, or congregations. Building faithful communities of truth and hospitality, however, is at the heart of our grateful response to the one who "became flesh and lived among us . . . full of grace and truth" (John 1:14). In the end, it is as simple and as complicated as "loving those whom God has set beside us today."[22]

Acknowledgments

Although writing is often a solitary activity, many individuals and communities helped to form, develop, and strengthen this book. I've located the acknowledgments at the end because I hoped that readers would more fully understand my words of gratitude and recognition if they had first encountered the fruit of this shared undertaking.

I am deeply grateful to the participants in the "Pastor in Community" project for all that they contributed to my life, the project, and the book. Wise and generous, they brought their experiences, gifts, and fidelity to our conversations and discussions. I cannot imagine this book without the insights of Linda Adams, Tim Blackmon, Nancy Frank, John Hay, Jr., Chris Heuertz, Maria Russell Kenney, Greg Leffel, Glenn Lorenz, Jeffrey Oglesby, Tiger Pennington, Ruth Anne Reese, Dan Schmitz, Keith Wasserman, Russell West, Jeff White, and Bud Woodward.

Pam Buck and Martin Gornik were central in the formation and leadership of the "Pastor in Community" project that is at the heart of *Living into Community*. We worked together over four years in developing the questions, readings, worship, and conversations for the project. Martin's enthusiasm about the value of the practices for congregational life and his liturgical gifts were crucial. Pam's capacity to bring visions to life and her commitment to building community made the project possible. We were ably assisted over the years by Catherine Driggers Gibbs, Tony Fox, and several volunteers.

The project itself would not have been conceivable without the generous support of the Lilly Endowment and without the encouragement and wisdom of Craig Dykstra and John Wimmer. I am very grateful for their thoughtful attention to practices and for their strong commitment to renewing the church, as well as for their friendship. More than a decade ago, Dorothy Bass first proposed that I write a second book on practices and provided initial support through the Valparaiso Project/Lilly Endowment. I am grateful for her support and for her own insightful work on practices.

Two other communities made important contributions to reflections on this topic. Church of the Apostles/Apostles Anglican Church initially hosted the project and contributed significantly to its development. Asbury Theological Seminary later became the host institution and helped bring the preliminary conversations to a wider audience. In both communities, attention to the practices has provided a grounded way to strengthen community and understand its challenges.

Students in my Ethics of Community courses at Asbury Theological Seminary were very responsive to the material that I first presented in class, and helpfully honed my reflections with their own studies and interests. Many of my faculty colleagues at Asbury provided encouragement and valuable suggestions from their research and ecclesial experience.

I'm also grateful for my connections with the communities of St. John's and St. Benedict's in Minnesota, and for the opportunity to present some of the material at the Monastic Institute several years ago.[1] The wisdom and honesty of people who are part of communities that have embodied fidelity and hospitality over centuries is priceless.

A number of friends, colleagues, and family members read and responded to the first drafts of the book by raising questions and clarifying arguments. My heartfelt thanks to Justin Barringer, Pam Buck, Nicola Hoggard Creegan, Martin Gornik, Maria Russell Kenney, Jeremy Pohl, Ron Pohl, and James Thobaben. Special thanks to my mother, Dorothy Pohl, who continues to delight in reading my work.

Jon Pott, editor-in-chief at William B. Eerdmans Publishing Company, was exceptionally supportive and patient over the years it has taken to finish this book. The opportunity to work with him is a gift in my life. In the editing process itself, Mary Hietbrink was a wonderfully collegial, skilled, and encouraging editor.

To my family, who provides my closest and most enduring experiences of community and the practices, I am, as always, deeply indebted and very grateful.

Notes

Chapter 1

1. This is a phrase used by Miriam Therese Winter, Adair Lummis, and Allison Stokes in their book *Defecting in Place: Women Claiming Responsibility for Their Own Spiritual Lives* (New York: Crossroad, 1994).

2. This definition is drawn from the explanation of practices offered by Craig Dykstra and Dorothy C. Bass in *Practicing Theology*, ed. Miroslav Volf and Dorothy C. Bass (Grand Rapids: Wm. B. Eerdmans, 2002), p. 18.

3. Stanley Hauerwas's impact through his writings and his students is noteworthy. Scholars and practitioners involved in the Ekklesia Project, the new monasticism, and the emerging church have made community central in their conversations. The work of N. T. Wright and others in biblical studies has also been very important.

4. Robert Webber, *Ancient-Future Faith* (Grand Rapids: Baker, 1999), p. 72.

5. See, for example, *Practicing Our Faith*, ed. Dorothy C. Bass (San Francisco: Jossey-Bass, 1997); *Practicing Theology*, ed. Volf and Bass; Dorothy C. Bass, *Receiving the Day* (San Francisco: Jossey-Bass, 2001); and Stephanie Paulsell, *Honoring the Body* (San Francisco: Jossey-Bass, 2003).

6. Participants in the Pastor in Community Project represented numerous denominational backgrounds. Their congregational contexts were diverse and included church plants, rural, suburban, and urban settings, and intentional communities.

7. Reading books and discussing them together in relation to community and practices proved very fruitful. We read Philip Hallie, *Lest Innocent Blood Be Shed* (New York: HarperPerennial, 1994); Dietrich Bonhoeffer, *Life Together* (New York: Harper & Row, 1954); Jean Vanier, *Community and Growth*, rev. ed. (New York: Paulist Press, 1989); Chris P. Rice, *Grace Matters* (San Francisco: Jossey-Bass, 2002); Christine D. Pohl, *Making Room: Recovering Hospitality as a Christian Tradition* (Grand Rapids: Wm. B. Eerdmans, 1999); Marilynne Robinson, *Gilead* (New York: Farrar, Straus & Giroux, 2004); and

L. Gregory Jones and Kevin R. Armstrong, *Resurrecting Excellence: Shaping Faithful Christian Ministry* (Grand Rapids: Wm. B. Eerdmans, 2006).

Chapter 2

1. Karl Barth, *Church Dogmatics*, Vol. IV: *The Doctrine of Reconciliation*, ed. G. W. Bromiley (Edinburgh: T&T Clark, 1956), Part 1 (Section 57.2), pp. 41-42.

2. Some theorists make the distinction between "personal" and "transpersonal" gratitude. "Personal gratitude is thankfulness toward a specific other person for the benefit that the person has provided (or just for their being). Transpersonal gratitude is a gratefulness to God, to a higher power, or to the cosmos." See Christopher Peterson and Martin E. P. Seligman, "Gratitude," in *Character Strengths and Virtues* (New York: Oxford University Press, 2004), p. 555.

3. Paul F. Camenisch, "Gift and Gratitude in Ethics," *Journal of Religious Ethics* 9 (Spring 1981): 23.

4. Consider what recent research findings and discussions in psychology suggest: "Compared with their less grateful counterparts, grateful people are higher in positive emotions and life satisfaction and also lower in negative emotions such as depression, anxiety, and envy" (Michael E. McCullough, Robert A. Emmons, and Jo-Ann Tsang, "The Grateful Disposition," *Journal of Personality and Social Psychology* 82, no. 1 [2002]: 124). And consider this observation: "A prevailing sentiment in both classical and popular writings on happiness is that an effective approach for maximizing one's contentment is to be consciously grateful for one's blessings" (Robert A. Emmons and Michael E. McCullough, "Counting Blessings versus Burdens," *Journal of Personality and Social Psychology* 84, no. 2 [2003]: 386). Those who work with the approach known as "Appreciative Inquiry" also give significant attention to the importance of gratitude.

5. This is a phrase used by Robert Hughes as the title of his book *Culture of Complaint* (New York: Grand Central Publishing, 1994).

6. See David W. Pao, *Thanksgiving: An Investigation of a Pauline Theme* (Downers Grove, Ill.: InterVarsity Press, 2002), pp. 96, 157, 162.

7. Martin Luther, *Luther's Works*, Vol. 25 (St. Louis: Concordia Publishing House, 1972), pp. 158-60.

8. Luther quotes a "well-known" proverb of his day: "If you call someone ungrateful, you mention all reproaches" (Martin Luther, *Luther's Works*, Vol. 7 [St. Louis: Concordia Publishing House, 1965], p. 83). See also Christopher Heath Wellman, "Gratitude as a Virtue," *Pacific Philosophical Quarterly* 80 (1999): 286, 294; and Terrance McConnell, *Gratitude* (Philadelphia: Temple University Press, 1993), p. 3.

9. Dietrich Bonhoeffer, *Life Together* (New York: Harper & Row, 1954), p. 29.

10. Kevin Rains, Vineyard Central Church, Cincinnati, Ohio.

11. Thomas à Kempis, *The Imitation of Christ*, Chapter 10: "Of Gratitude for God's Grace."

12. For an extraordinary reflection on "a culture of grace" as a "beautiful land," see Chris P. Rice, *Grace Matters* (San Francisco: Jossey-Bass, 2002).

13. Rice, *Grace Matters,* pp. 219-20.

14. Rice, *Grace Matters,* p. 257.

15. Rice, *Grace Matters,* pp. 259-60.

16. Rice, *Grace Matters,* p. 260.

17. Robert Raynolds, *In Praise of Gratitude* (New York: Harper & Brothers, 1961), p. 12.

18. Henri Nouwen, *Gracias!* (San Francisco: Harper & Row, 1983), pp. 21, 55.

19. See, for example, Psalms 100, 105, 106, 111.

20. I am indebted to Dr. Ruth Anne Reese for her Bible study on this passage during the Pastor in Community project.

21. Michael E. Williams, "Saying Grace: Living a Life of Gratitude," *Weavings* 7, no. 6 (November-December 1992): 33-34.

22. See Stephan Joubert, "Religious Reciprocity in 2 Corinthians 9:6-15: Generosity and Gratitude as Legitimate Responses to the *charis tou theou,*" *Neotestamentica* 33, no. 1 (1999): 79-90.

23. Pao, *Thanksgiving,* pp. 15, 79, 96. From his study of thanksgiving in the writings of Paul, Pao concludes that "the basis of community is the grace of God," and gratitude is significant in building up God's people (p. 118).

24. Nearly fifteen hundred years after the New Testament documents were written, the Heidelberg Catechism continued to teach the centrality of gratitude when it encouraged young believers to see that the motivation and substance of Christian living is gratitude. See Howard G. Hageman, "Guilt, Grace, and Gratitude," in *Guilt, Grace, and Gratitude,* ed. Donald J. Bruggink (New York: Half Moon Press, 1963), p. 9.

25. See Pao, *Thanksgiving,* pp. 86-89.

26. David A. deSilva, *Perseverance in Gratitude: A Socio-Rhetorical Commentary on the Epistle "to the Hebrews"* (Grand Rapids: Wm. B. Eerdmans, 2000), pp. 506-7; see Hebrews 13:15-16.

27. See John Wesley, *The Works of John Wesley* (1972; reprint, Grand Rapids: Zondervan, n.d.), Vol. 6, Sermon LXX: "The Case of Reason Impartially Considered," p. 359; and Vol. 7, Sermon XCIV: "Of Family Religion," p. 78. See also Vol. 6, Sermon LXI: "The Mystery of Iniquity," p. 256; and Vol. 7, Sermon CXIV: "The Unity of Divine Being," p. 269.

28. B. A. Gerrish, *Grace and Gratitude: The Eucharistic Theology of John Calvin* (Eugene, Ore.: Wipf & Stock, 2002), pp. 20, 43-44, 50.

29. Barth, *Church Dogmatics,* Vol. II: *The Doctrine of God,* ed. G. W. Bromiley and T. F. Torrance (Edinburgh: T&T Clark, 1957), first half volume (Sec. 31:3), p. 669.

30. Jonathan Edwards, *A Treatise on Religious Affections* (Grand Rapids: Baker, 1982), pp. 174, 186.

31. Henry H. Knight III, "The Relation of Love to Gratitude in the Theologies of Edwards and Wesley," *Evangelical Journal* 6 (1988): 5.

32. Knight, "The Relation of Love to Gratitude in the Theologies of Edwards and Wesley," p. 4.

33. Cicero, quoted in Peterson and Seligman, "Gratitude," in *Character Strengths and Virtues,* p. 555.

34. Adam Smith, *The Theory of Moral Sentiments* (Indianapolis: Liberty Fund, 1982), pp. 67-79, 94-96, 162, 174, 225.

35. See, for example, W. D. Ross, *The Right and the Good* (Oxford: Clarendon Press, 1930), pp. 21-23.

36. Mary Jo Leddy, *Radical Gratitude* (Maryknoll, N.Y.: Orbis Books, 2002), p. 51.

37. Echoing a number of key New Testament passages, John Wesley captures this combination of trust, gratitude, and contentment in writing about Christian character: "Whether in ease or pain, whether in sickness or health, whether in life or death, he giveth thanks from the ground of his heart to Him who orders it for good; knowing that as 'every good gift cometh from above,' so none but good can come from the Father of Lights. . . . He is therefore 'careful' (anxiously or uneasily) 'for nothing'; as having 'cast all his care on Him that careth for him,' . . . after 'making his request known to him with thanksgiving'" (Wesley, "The Character of a Methodist," Section 7 in *The Works of John Wesley,* Vol. 8, pp. 342-43).

38. Paul Tournier, *The Meaning of Gifts* (Richmond, Va.: John Knox Press, 1963), p. 32, quoted in Camenisch, "Gift and Gratitude in Ethics," p. 23.

39. Peterson and Seligman, "Gratitude," in *Character Strengths and Virtues,* p. 546.

40. For some remarkable expressions of entitlement, see episodes of "My Super Sweet Sixteen."

41. Robert J. Samuelson, *The Good Life and Its Discontents: The American Dream in the Age of Entitlement* (New York: Random House, 1995), pp. 5, 6, 15.

42. See Anthony B. Robinson, "Articles of Faith: The Unfortunate Age of Entitlement in America," *Seattle Post-Intelligencer,* 23 March 2007. Find it at this Web address: http://seattlepi.nwsource.com/local/308772_faith24.html.

43. Edward C. Vacek, S.J., "Gifts, God, Generosity, and Gratitude," in *Spirituality and Moral Theology,* ed. James Keating (New York: Paulist Press, 2000), p. 109.

44. See Leddy, *Radical Gratitude,* pp. 21, 23, 27.

45. Nouwen, *Gracias!* p. 187.

46. See Vacek, "Gifts, God, Generosity, and Gratitude," pp. 101-2.

Chapter 3

1. Paul F. Camenisch, "Gift and Gratitude in Ethics," *Journal of Religious Ethics* 9 (Spring 1981): 2. A similar description is offered by Michael E. McCullough, Robert A. Emmons, Shelley D. Kilpatrick, and David B. Larson in "Is Gratitude a Moral Affect?" *Psychological Bulletin* 127, no. 2 (2001): 252: "People are most likely to feel grateful when (a) they have received a particularly valuable benefit; (b) high effort and cost have been expended on their behalf; (c) the expenditure of effort on their behalf seems to have been intentional rather than accidental; and (d) the expenditure of effort on their behalf was gratuitous (i.e., was not determined by the existence of a role-based relationship between benefactor and beneficiary)." They note further that recipients are more likely to experience gratitude "toward benefactors from whom they would not expect benevolence" (p. 255).

2. McCullough, Emmons, Kilpatrick, and Larson, "Is Gratitude a Moral Affect?" p. 257.

3. Terrance McConnell, *Gratitude* (Philadelphia: Temple University Press, 1993), pp. 56-57.

4. Camenisch, "Gift and Gratitude in Ethics," pp. 2, 8-9.

5. Edward C. Vacek, S.J., "Gifts, God, Generosity, and Gratitude," in *Spirituality and Moral Theology,* ed. James Keating (New York: Paulist Press, 2000), pp. 103-4.

6. Robert A. Emmons and Michael E. McCullough, "Counting Blessings versus Burdens," *Journal of Personality and Social Psychology* 84, no. 2 (2003): 379.

7. David A. deSilva, *Perseverance in Gratitude: A Socio-Rhetorical Commentary on the Epistle "to the Hebrews"* (Grand Rapids: Wm. B. Eerdmans, 2000), p. 474, quoting Seneca, *Ben* 2.25.3.

8. Camenisch, "Gift and Gratitude in Ethics," p. 15. See also Christopher Peterson and Martin E. P. Seligman, *Character Strengths and Virtues* (New York: Oxford University Press, 2004), p. 556.

9. McConnell, *Gratitude,* pp. 75-76.

10. Vacek, "Gifts, God, Generosity, and Gratitude," p. 106.

11. See, for example, Philippians 1.

12. B. A. Gerrish, *Grace and Gratitude: The Eucharistic Theology of John Calvin* (Eugene, Ore.: Wipf & Stock, 2002), pp. 44-45.

13. Carol E. Becker, *Leading Women: How Church Women Can Avoid Leadership Traps and Negotiate the Gender Maze* (Nashville: Abingdon Press, 1996), pp. 93-96. She is quoting the work of Ann Huff.

14. Joyce Hollyday, "Gratitude: A Sermon on Giving Thanks," *Sojourners,* June 1987, p. 34.

15. Hollyday, "Gratitude," p. 34.

16. Bishop Tutu expressed concern in the South African situation that "by and large, the white community does not seem to have shown an appreciation for the incredible magnanimity of those who were the major victims of a system from which they [the whites] benefited so much" (Archbishop Desmond Tutu talking to the BBC's Peter Biles, BBC News Online, 1 May 2006).

17. Henri J. M. Nouwen, *Gracias!* (San Francisco: Harper & Row, 1983), pp. 16, 18-19.

18. Camenisch, "Gift and Gratitude in Ethics," p. 5.

19. Camenisch, "Gift and Gratitude in Ethics," p. 2.

20. Camenisch, "Gift and Gratitude in Ethics," p. 12.

21. deSilva, *Perseverance in Gratitude,* p. 474.

22. H. H. Guthrie Jr., *Theology as Thanksgiving: From Israel's Psalms to the Church's Eucharist* (New York: Seabury Press, 1981), pp. 56, 79, 148, 193, 214. See also David W. Pao, *Thanksgiving: An Investigation of a Pauline Theme* (Downers Grove, Ill.: InterVarsity Press, 2002), pp. 60-65, 71.

23. Psalm 106:7, 13; Pao, *Thanksgiving,* p. 151.

Chapter 4

1. David Hume, *A Treatise of Human Nature*, Bk. III, Pt. 1, Sec. 1, and Immanuel Kant, *Lectures on Ethics* (New York: Harper & Row, 1963), quoted in Christopher Heath Wellman, "Gratitude as a Virtue," *Pacific Philosophical Quarterly* 80 (1999): 294. See also Paul F. Camenisch, "Gift and Gratitude in Ethics," *The Journal of Religious Ethics* 9 (1981): 5; and Terrance McConnell, *Gratitude* (Philadelphia: Temple University Press, 1993), p. 3.

2. We addressed entitlement in the section on contemporary cultural challenges in Chapter 2.

3. Chris P. Rice, *Grace Matters* (San Francisco: Jossey-Bass, 2002), p. 90.

4. James Choung, "A Theology of Envy," *InterVarsity Library*, April 1996, p. 5. (You can access this article online at http://regions.ivcf.org/academic/1931.) See, for example, Romans 1:30, 1 Timothy 6:4, and Titus 3:3. See also Henry Fairlie, *The Seven Deadly Sins Today* (Washington, D.C.: New Republic Books, 1978), p. 78.

5. Will Willimon notes that "if Christianity is indeed a social, communal religion . . . then we ought to expect envy to thrive among the faithful." See William H. Willimon, *Sinning Like a Christian* (Nashville: Abingdon Press, 2005), p. 51.

6. Søren Kierkegaard, "The Sickness unto Death," quoted in Willimon, *Sinning Like a Christian*, p. 53. While various forms of media have changed our experience of proximity to the extent that now we are more likely to identify with (and envy) distant celebrities, the most virulent forms of envy still seem to flourish in face-to-face settings.

7. William F. May, "Envy: The Least Satisfying of the Seven Deadly Sins," *Christianity and Crisis*, 7 January 1963, p. 243.

8. Melanie Klein, *"Envy and Gratitude" and Other Works, 1946-1963*, vol. 3 of *The Writings of Melanie Klein* (New York: Free Press, 1975), pp. 217-19.

9. St. Basil, "On Envy," edited and condensed by Phyllis Graham, *The Angelus* 5, no. 5 (May 1982): 1.

10. May, "Envy," p. 242.

11. Related to envy is *Schadenfreude*, a German word for the "perverse delight" we find in the "failures and misfortunes of others." La Rochefoucauld observed, "In the misfortune of our best friends, we always find something that is not displeasing to us" (quoted in Willimon, *Sinning Like a Christian*, p. 59).

12. It is important to note the difference between envy and jealousy in the biblical tradition. God is described as a jealous God, but never as envious. Jealousy is tied to wanting to guard what is ours; envy is related to what belongs to others.

13. Basil, quoted by Vasiliki Limberis, "The Eyes Infected by Evil: Basil of Caesarea's Homily 'On Envy,'" *Harvard Theological Review* 84, no. 2 (1991): 175.

14. May, "Envy," p. 241.

15. Cornelius Plantinga Jr., *Not the Way It's Supposed to Be: A Breviary of Sin* (Grand Rapids: Wm. B. Eerdmans, 1995), p. 167. Because life is not fair, and the advantages that people gain are not always earned or given as gifts, and because we value equality so highly, anger at injustice needs to be distinguished from envy. Plantinga notes that those who are indignant at injustice "resent what is evil," while the envious "resent what is good" (p. 166).

16. Plantinga, *Not the Way It's Supposed to Be*, p. 162.

17. Don Herzog, "Envy: Poisoning the Banquet They Cannot Taste," in *Wicked Pleasures*, ed. Robert C. Solomon (Lanham, Md.: Rowman & Littlefield, 1999), p. 143.

18. Basil, "On Envy," p. 2.

19. Jean Vanier, *Community and Growth*, rev. ed. (New York: Paulist Press, 1989), p. 51.

20. Willimon, *Sinning Like a Christian*, p. 56.

21. See Plantinga, *Not the Way It's Supposed to Be*, p. 171. Also see Robert L. Perkins, "Envy as Personal Phenomenon and as Politics," *International Kierkegaard Commentaries* 14 (1984): 122-23.

22. Fairlie, *The Seven Deadly Sins Today*, p. 78. See also Plantinga, *Not the Way It's Supposed to Be*, p. 170.

23. Anselm C. Hagedorn and Jerome H. Neyrey, "'It Was Out of Envy that They Handed Jesus Over,'" *Journal for the Study of the New Testament* 69 (1998): 15-16. Envy is particularly dangerous in societies that are oriented toward honor. Hagedorn and Neyrey point out that Jesus addresses envy among the disciples (Mark 10:37, 43-45) by "disengagement from the whole world of honor. He effectively calls off the game of envy and declares the entire pursuit of honor off limits for the members of his group" (p. 49).

24. Henri J. M. Nouwen, *Sabbatical Journey* (New York: Crossroad, 1998), p. 216.

25. John Wesley, "A Farther Appeal to Men of Reason and Religion," Part II, Section III.16 in *The Works of John Wesley*, Vol. 8 (1872; reprint, Grand Rapids: Zondervan, n.d.), p. 194.

26. See David W. Pao, *Thanksgiving: An Investigation of a Pauline Theme* (Downers Grove, Ill.: InterVarsity Press, 2002), pp. 148, 151.

27. C. S. Lewis, *The Great Divorce* (New York: Macmillan, 1946), pp. 77-78.

28. Dietrich Bonhoeffer, *Life Together* (New York: Harper & Row, 1954), p. 29.

29. Wesley, "A Farther Appeal to Men of Reason and Religion," p. 194.

30. Researchers have found that "expressions of gratitude that are coupled with attempts to take advantage of the benefactor's generosity (e.g., following an expression of gratitude with an attempt to entice the customer to spend more money in the store) can produce reactance." See Michael E. McCullough, Shelley D. Kilpatrick, Robert A. Emmons, and David B. Larson, "Is Gratitude a Moral Affect?" *Psychological Bulletin* 127, no. 2 (2001): 259.

31. McCullough et al., "Is Gratitude a Moral Affect?" pp. 253, 260.

32. McCullough et al., "Is Gratitude a Moral Affect?" p. 259.

33. Bonhoeffer, *Life Together*, p. 28.

34. William Law, *A Serious Call to a Devout and Holy Life*, with an introduction by J. V. Moldenhawer (Philadelphia: Westminster Press, 1948), p. xx.

35. See Mary Jo Leddy's suggestions in *Radical Gratitude* (Maryknoll, N.Y.: Orbis Books, 2002), pp. 143-62.

36. Thomas Traherne, a poet from the seventeenth century, captures this beautifully: "Is not sight a jewel? Is not hearing a treasure? Is not speech a glory? O my Lord, pardon my ingratitude, and pity my dullness who am not sensible of these gifts. The freedom of Thy bounty hath deceived me. These things were too near to be considered. Thou

presentedst me with Thy blessings, and I was not aware. But now I give thanks and adore and praise Thee for Thine inestimable favors." See 165.13 in *The Westminster Collection of Christian Prayers,* compiled by Dorothy M. Stewart (Louisville: Westminster John Knox Press, 2002), p. 355.

37. Jean G. Fitzpatrick, "How Kids Learn Gratitude." You can access this article online at www.beliefnet.com/story/51/story_5119.html.

38. Marilynne Robinson, *Gilead* (New York: Farrar, Straus & Giroux, 2004), p. 52.

39. Rice, *Grace Matters,* p. 205.

40. Christopher Peterson and Martin E. P. Seligman, *Character Strengths and Virtues* (New York: Oxford University Press, 2004), p. 565.

41. Vanier, *Community and Growth,* p. 315.

42. Vanier, *Community and Growth,* pp. 313-15.

43. Joyce Hollyday, "Gratitude: A Sermon on Giving Thanks," *Sojourners,* June 1987, p. 34.

44. Vanier, *Community and Growth,* p. 314.

45. Bonhoeffer, *Life Together,* p. 67.

46. Bonhoeffer, *Life Together,* p. 68.

Chapter 5

1. Lewis B. Smedes, "The Power of Promises," in *A Chorus of Witnesses: Model Sermons for Today's Preacher,* ed. Thomas G. Long and Cornelius Plantinga Jr. (Grand Rapids: Wm. B. Eerdmans, 1994), p. 156.

2. Smedes, "The Power of Promises," p. 156.

3. Lewis B. Smedes, "Controlling the Unpredictable: The Power of Promising," *Christianity Today,* 21 January 1983, p. 19.

4. Margaret A. Farley, *Personal Commitments: Beginning, Keeping, Changing* (San Francisco: Harper & Row, 1986), pp. 12-13.

5. Stephen V. Doughty, *Discovering Community* (Nashville: Upper Room Books, 1999), p. 136.

6. Smedes, "Controlling the Unpredictable," pp. 18, 19. The Promise Keepers movement, so prominent in the 1990s, was a major effort to encourage men's fidelity to their wives and children, as well as to strengthen their commitments to their Christian faith.

7. David W. Pao, *Thanksgiving: An Investigation of a Pauline Theme* (Downers Grove, Ill.: InterVarsity Press, 2002), pp. 53-57, 60, 128, 148. See, for example, Psalm 116.

8. John R. Searle, "How to Derive 'Ought' from 'Is.'" *The Philosophical Review* (January 1964): 45.

9. Farley, *Personal Commitments,* p. 12.

10. Farley, *Personal Commitments,* pp. 16-17.

11. William Vitek, *Promising* (Philadelphia: Temple University Press, 1993), pp. 1, 3. Vitek explains further that promises are "double-tensed" in that they are made in the present but affect the future (p. 97).

12. Farley, *Personal Commitments,* pp. 34, 98.

13. Arendt, *The Human Condition* (Chicago: University of Chicago Press, 1958), p. 244.

14. Searle, "How to Derive 'Ought' from 'Is,'" pp. 51, 58.

15. Pall S. Ardal, "And That's a Promise," *The Philosophical Quarterly* 18 (July 1968): 225.

16. Vitek, *Promising*, pp. 191-92.

17. Vitek, *Promising*, pp. 20, 111.

18. Vitek, *Promising*, p. 220.

19. Farley, *Personal Commitments*, p. 20; W. D. Ross, *Foundations of Ethics* (Oxford: Clarendon Press, 1939), p. 96.

20. T. M. Scanlon, *What We Owe to Each Other* (Cambridge, Mass.: Belknap Press, 1998), p. 309.

21. Neil MacCormick and Joseph Raz, "Voluntary Obligations and Normative Powers," *Proceedings of the Aristotelian Society* 46 (1972): 72-73.

22. Gabriel Marcel, "Obedience and Fidelity," in *On Being Responsible*, ed. James M. Gustafson and James T. Laney (New York: Harper & Row, 1968), p. 84.

23. Vitek, *Promising*, p. 11. John Rawls explains: "The way in which the rule of promising specifies the appropriate circumstances and excusing conditions determines whether the practice it represents is just. For example, in order to make a binding promise, one must be fully conscious, in a rational frame of mind, and know the meaning of the operative words, their use in making promises, and so on. Furthermore, those words must be spoken freely or voluntarily . . . and in situations where one has a reasonably fair bargaining position. . . ." "In general the circumstances giving rise to a promise and the excusing conditions must be defined so as to preserve the equal liberty of the parties and to make the practice a rational means whereby men can enter into and stabilize cooperative agreements for mutual advantage." See John Rawls, *A Theory of Justice* (Cambridge, Mass.: Belknap Press, 1971), p. 345.

24. Rawls, *A Theory of Justice*, pp. 346, 349.

25. Michael H. Robins, *Promising, Intending, and Moral Autonomy* (Cambridge: Cambridge University Press, 1984), p. 2.

26. If what we promise is important to the other person, or if we have been emphatic in our promise by being explicit or by repeating it, we raise the level of expectation and of our responsibility to follow through. See Ross, *Foundations of Ethics*, pp. 100-101.

27. Robins, *Promising, Intending, and Moral Autonomy*, p. 85.

28. Craig Dykstra, *Growing in the Life of Faith: Education and Christian Practices*, 2nd ed. (Louisville: Westminster John Knox Press, 2005), pp. 106-7.

29. See Pao, *Thanksgiving*, p. 127.

30. Pao, *Thanksgiving*, pp. 60-61.

31. Farley, *Personal Commitments*, p. 119.

32. Pao, *Thanksgiving*, pp. 47-48. See also Hebrews 6:13-20; 8:6; 9:15.

33. The promises of Jesus "are connected to his divine power. . . . They are also connected to the example that Jesus gives us by means of his own glory and moral excellence. It is through these promises that believers participate with Jesus in the divine nature." I am grateful to Ruth Anne Reese for sharing some of her research on 2 Peter in a personal

e-mail to me. For a fuller account, see Ruth Anne Reese, *2 Peter and Jude,* The Two Horizons New Testament Commentary (Grand Rapids: Wm. B. Eerdmans, 2007).

34. Thomas Aquinas, *Summa Theologica,* Vol. 2, Question 88: "Of Vows," first and second articles (New York: Benziger Brothers, 1947), p. 1567.

35. Aquinas, *Summa Theologica,* Vol. 2, Question 88, p. 1568.

36. In recognizing the significance of this teaching, the Anabaptist tradition has rejected oath-taking. See also the discussion of oaths and word-watching in Chapter 10.

37. Craig Dykstra, "Family Promises," in *Faith and Families,* ed. Lindell Sawyers (Philadelphia: Geneva Press, 1986), pp. 137-63. See especially p. 142.

38. Dykstra, "Family Promises," p. 143.

39. Dykstra, "Family Promises," p. 145.

40. Dykstra, "Family Promises," pp. 152, 150.

41. Dykstra, "Family Promises," p. 149.

Chapter 6

1. John Rawls, "Two Concepts of Rules," *The Philosophical Review* 64 (1955): 17.

2. P. S. Atiyah, *Promises, Morals, and Law* (Oxford: Clarendon Press, 1981), p. 74, quoting David Lyons, *Forms and Limits of Utilitarianism* (Oxford: Oxford University Press, 1965), pp. 187-88.

3. W. D. Ross, *Foundations of Ethics* (Oxford: Clarendon Press, 1939), p. 90.

4. Thomas Aquinas, *Summa Theologica,* Vol. 2, Question 88: "Of Vows," third article (New York: Benziger Brothers, 1947), p. 1569.

5. See W. D. Ross, *The Right and the Good* (Oxford: Clarendon Press, 1930), p. 28.

6. Margaret Farley, *Personal Commitments: Beginning, Keeping, Changing* (San Francisco: Harper & Row, 1986), p. 99.

7. A. I. Melden, "On Promising," *Mind* 65 (1956): 59.

8. See parallel discussion in Edward C. Vacek, S.J., "Gifts, God, Generosity, and Gratitude," in *Spirituality and Moral Theology,* ed. James Keating (New York: Paulist Press, 2000), p. 107.

9. David P. Gushee, *Getting Marriage Right* (Grand Rapids: Baker, 2004), pp. 138-44.

10. For a recent discussion of a commitment to stability, see the book by Jonathan Wilson-Hartgrove, *The Wisdom of Stability* (Brewster, Mass.: Paraclete Press, 2010).

11. As noted in Chapter 1, this is a phrase used by Miriam Therese Winter, Adair Lummis, and Allison Stokes in their book *Defecting in Place: Women Claiming Responsibility for Their Own Spiritual Lives* (New York: Crossroad, 1994).

12. William Vitek, *Promising* (Philadelphia: Temple University Press, 1993), pp. 225-26. Situations become more complicated when we could have anticipated that we would not be able to fulfill a promise but chose to make the commitment anyway — for example, when we know we are at our limit, but still promise to lead another church program.

13. Vitek, *Promising,* p. 226.

14. T. M. Scanlon, *What We Owe to Each Other* (Cambridge, Mass.: Belknap Press, 1998), pp. 199-200; Farley, *Personal Commitments*, pp. 84, 108.

15. Raymond Avery Moody Jr., "Promising," M.A. thesis submitted to the University of Virginia (1967), pp. 43, 47, 51, 53. This thesis succinctly covers how promises are "abrogated."

16. Farley, *Personal Commitments*, p. 84.

17. Atiyah, *Promises, Morals, and Law*, pp. 143-46.

18. Vitek, *Promising*, pp. 102-8, 142.

19. Craig Dykstra, "Family Promises," in *Faith and Families*, ed. Lindell Sawyers (Philadelphia: Geneva Press, 1986), p. 161.

20. Martin Luther King Jr., "Letter from Birmingham Jail," in *Why We Can't Wait* (New York: Harper & Row, 1964), p. 86.

21. Chris P. Rice, *Grace Matters* (San Francisco: Jossey-Bass, 2002), pp. 148, 247, 252. Jean Vanier has noted, "A community has to learn how to be cheerful about letting people leave and how to trust that God will send other brothers and sisters." See *Community and Growth*, rev. ed. (New York: Paulist Press, 1989), p. 81.

22. Rice, *Grace Matters*, pp. 250, 289.

Chapter 7

1. John Calvin, *Institutes of the Christian Religion*, ed. John T. McNeill, trans. Ford Lewis Battles (Philadelphia: Westminster Press, 1960), Vol. 1, Book II, Ch. 1, p. 245.

2. Dante Alighieri, *The Divine Comedy: The Inferno:* Canto XXXI-XXXIII, trans. John Ciardi (New York: New American Library/Penguin, 2003), pp. 240-70.

3. John Calvin, in his commentary on Peter's betrayal, sees it as a warning by example to all of us. He notes that the disciples "advance with inconsiderate haste to boast of a constancy which they did not possess." See *Commentary on a Harmony of the Evangelists: Matthew, Mark, and Luke*, vol. 3 (Grand Rapids: Wm. B. Eerdmans, 1949), p. 221.

4. See "Lapsi," in *The Oxford Dictionary of the Christian Church*, ed. F. L. Cross (Oxford: Oxford University Press, 1983). The Donatist controversy in the fourth century was expressly related to these issues.

5. Eugene Peterson, *The Contemplative Pastor* (Grand Rapids: Wm. B. Eerdmans, 1993), p. 49.

6. See, for example, Matthew 10:11-15; Mark 6:10-11; and Luke 10:8-12.

7. See further discussion of discernment in Chapter 10.

8. See also Matthew 14:1-12.

9. In Judges 11:30-40, we find another example of a promise or vow that should not have been made. Thomas Aquinas quotes Jerome on Jephthah's vow: "In vowing he was foolish, through lack of discretion, and in keeping his vow he was wicked." See Thomas Aquinas, *Summa Theologica*, Vol. 2, Question 88: "Of Vows," second article (New York: Benziger Brothers, 1947), p. 1568.

10. In "A Paradox of Promising," Holly M. Smith explains, "Some promises convert an otherwise morally neutral act to an obligatory one, while others merely render more

obligatory an act that was already morally required." But "no promise to perform it can convert a really heinous act into a morally right one, since the obligation established by the promise would always be outweighed by the countervailing evil of the promised act." See her essay in *The Philosophical Review* 106, no. 2 (April 1997): 155, 157.

11. Richard M. Fox and Joseph P. DeMarco, *The Immorality of Promising* (Amherst, N.Y.: Humanity Books, 2000), p. 158.

12. Jean Vanier, *Community and Growth,* rev. ed. (New York: Paulist Press, 1989), pp. 31-32. See also Reinhold Niebuhr's classic work, *Moral Man and Immoral Society* (New York: Charles Scribner's Sons, 1932).

13. This is one reason why some denominations do not allow members to participate in secret societies. Secrecy, loyalty, and privilege combine in ways that can be very destructive, and loyalties can then compete with commitments to the larger Christian community.

14. "People who reveal to others things told to them in confidence, whether they do so for personal gain or for their own amusement, are clearly guilty of betrayal. Indeed, we say of such people that they have 'betrayed a confidence.'" See Leszek Kolakowski, *Freedom, Fame, Lying, and Betrayal* (Boulder, Colo.: Westview Press, 1999), pp. 74-75.

15. A fuller discussion of secrets will follow in Chapter 9.

16. See Barbara J. Blodgett, *Lives Entrusted: An Ethic of Trust for Ministry* (Minneapolis: Fortress Press, 2008), especially chapters 2 and 4.

17. Søren Kierkegaard, "Under the Spell of Good Intentions," pp. 13-14, in *Provocations: Spiritual Writings of Kierkegaard,* ed. Charles Moore (Maryknoll, N.Y.: Orbis Books, 2002).

18. Michael H. Robins, *Promising, Intending, and Moral Autonomy* (Cambridge: Cambridge University Press, 1984), p. 109.

19. Fox and DeMarco, *The Immorality of Promising,* pp. 41-42.

20. Vanier, *Community and Growth,* p. 63.

21. Vanier, *Community and Growth,* pp. 170, 152.

22. Edith Schaeffer, *What Is a Family?* (Grand Rapids: Baker, 1975, 1994), p. 201.

23. Vanier, *Community and Growth,* p. 169.

24. Vanier, *Community and Growth,* p. 300.

25. "The Order of Worship for such as would enter into or renew their Covenant with God," in *The Book of Offices, being the Orders of Service authorized for use in the Methodist Church* (London: Methodist Publishing House, 1936), pp. 130-31.

Chapter 8

1. See Luke Timothy Johnson, *The Acts of the Apostles,* Sacra Pagina, ed. Daniel J. Harrington, S.J. (Collegeville, Minn.: Liturgical Press, 1992), pp. 91-92. Johnson writes that what they did was an offense against God and the community, and a challenge to the apostles' authority.

2. Mark L. Knapp notes, "To reap the benefits of lying and deception, it has to be

performed within a social system that values and expects truthfulness." See *Lying and Deception in Human Interaction* (Boston: Pearson/Penguin Academics, 2008), p. 4.

3. Thomas Aquinas, *Summa Theologica,* Vol. 2, Question 109: "Of Truth," third article (New York: Benziger Brothers, 1947), p. 1662.

4. This quotation is from *Today's New International Version* (Grand Rapids: Zondervan, 2005).

5. Lewis B. Smedes, *Mere Morality* (Grand Rapids: Wm. B. Eerdmans, 1983), p. 213.

6. Margaret Lewis Furse, *Nothing But the Truth? What It Takes to Be Honest* (Nashville: Abingdon Press, 1981), p. 76.

7. See Diane M. Komp, *Anatomy of a Lie* (Grand Rapids: Zondervan, 1998), p. 162.

8. Komp, *Anatomy of a Lie,* pp. 162-63.

9. In Kierkegaard's brief essay "Under the Spell of Good Intentions," noted in Chapter 7, we see a very close connection between promising and truthfulness. See Søren Kierkegaard, "Under the Spell of Good Intentions," in *Provocations: Spiritual Writings of Kierkegaard,* ed. Charles Moore (Maryknoll, N.Y.: Orbis Books, 2002), p. 14.

10. "The Old English word *trouthe* signified loyalty, fidelity, and reliability. . . . A person who was 'true' was someone who could be counted on, whose word was good." See Ralph Keyes, *The Post-Truth Era* (New York: St. Martin's Press, 2004), p. 23.

11. Smedes, *Mere Morality,* p. 222.

12. See, for example, Psalms 25:10; 30:9; 57:3, 10; 61:7; 85:10; 89:14; and 138:2.

13. Smedes, *Mere Morality,* p. 222.

14. Miroslav Volf, *Exclusion and Embrace* (Nashville: Abingdon Press, 1996), pp. 258-59, quoting Alfred Jepsen, "Aman," in *Theological Dictionary of the Old Testament,* vol. 1 (Grand Rapids: Wm. B. Eerdmans, 1974), p. 313.

15. Volf, *Exclusion and Embrace,* p. 259.

16. Volf, *Exclusion and Embrace,* p. 262; see also Keyes, *The Post-Truth Era,* p. 23.

17. See Volf's discussion in *Exclusion and Embrace,* p. 255.

18. Dietrich Bonhoeffer, *Ethics* (New York: Macmillan, 1955), pp. 363, 364.

19. Charles Wellborn, "Truth-telling: An Exercise in Practical Morality," *Christian Ethics Today* 14, no. 6 (December 1998); access online in issue 19 (Spring 2004): 2: http://www.christianethicstoday.com.

20. Paul J. Griffiths, *Lying: An Augustinian Theology of Duplicity* (Grand Rapids: Brazos Press, 2004), pp. 14, 194, 225.

21. Aquinas, *Summa Theologica,* Vol. 2, Question 109, first article, pp. 1660-61, and third article, p. 1662.

22. Tristan Anne Borer, *Telling the Truths: Truth Telling and Peace Building in Post-Conflict Societies* (Notre Dame, Ind.: University of Notre Dame Press, 2006), pp. 20-22.

23. Here Borer is working with both Richard Wilson's and Thomas Nagel's distinction between "knowledge" and "acknowledgment." See Borer, *Telling the Truths,* p. 22.

24. Borer notes that "both knowledge and acknowledgment are important in different ways for fostering sustainable peace. Knowledge can be important for prosecutions and thus for furthering justice and the rule of law. Acknowledgment can contribute to the personal healing of victims. Both are necessary for peace." See Borer, *Telling the Truths,* p. 22.

25. See Keyes, *The Post-Truth Era,* p. 124.

26. Keyes notes, "All societies must reconcile the fact that lying is socially toxic with the fact that nearly all their members engage in this practice." See *The Post-Truth Era,* p. 27.

27. Carol Tavris and Elliot Aronson, *Mistakes Were Made (But Not by Me)* (Orlando: Houghton Mifflin Harcourt, 2007), p. 69.

28. See Keyes, *The Post-Truth Era,* p. 5.

29. Keyes, *The Post-Truth Era,* p. 13. See also Alan Kreider and Eleanor Kreider, "Economical with the Truth: Swearing and Lying — An Anabaptist Perspective," *Brethren in Christ History and Life* 24, no. 2 (August 2001): 154.

30. Keyes, *The Post-Truth Era,* p. 44, and Knapp, *Lying and Deception in Human Interaction,* pp. 150, 167.

31. Martin Luther King Jr., "Pilgrimage to Nonviolence," in *Stride Toward Freedom* (New York: Harper & Row, 1958), p. 92.

32. Complications in truth-telling, especially in terms of silence and styles of truthfulness, will be addressed in Chapter 9.

33. Alan Brinton, "St. Augustine and the Problem of Deception in Religious Persuasion," *Religious Studies* 19, no. 3 (September 1983): 445-49.

34. See Keyes, *The Post-Truth Era,* pp. 37, 41.

35. Keyes, *The Post-Truth Era,* p. 41.

36. When a parent's public image as virtuous leader does not match his or her behavior at home, children are often put in a position where they "cover" for the parent. When this involves an adult who is a clergyperson, the children's exposure to religious hypocrisy is particularly destructive.

37. Chris P. Rice, *Grace Matters* (San Francisco: Jossey-Bass, 2002), p. 184.

Chapter 9

1. Diane M. Komp, *Anatomy of a Lie* (Grand Rapids: Zondervan, 1998), p. 95.

2. Komp, *Anatomy of a Lie,* p. 69.

3. Elmer Ellsworth Brown, "Absolute Truthfulness," *Methodist Review,* January 1913, p. 39.

4. Paul J. Griffiths, *Lying: An Augustinian Theology of Duplicity* (Grand Rapids: Brazos Press, 2004), pp. 159-60.

5. Miroslav Volf, *Exclusion and Embrace* (Nashville: Abingdon Press, 1996), p. 243.

6. Volf, *Exclusion and Embrace,* pp. 261, 243, 247.

7. Volf, *Exclusion and Embrace,* pp. 248, 251, 247.

8. Volf, *Exclusion and Embrace,* p. 249.

9. Volf, *Exclusion and Embrace,* p. 236. See also Sissela Bok, *Lying: Moral Choice in Public and Private Life* (New York: Pantheon Books, 1978), p. 139.

10. Daniel Goleman, *Emotional Intelligence* (New York: Bantam Books, 1995), p. 97.

11. Paul L. Lehmann, "Telling the Truth," *The Princeton Seminary Bulletin* 15, no. 3 (new series) (1994): 255.

12. Emily Dickinson, Poem #1129, in *The Norton Anthology of Modern Poetry,* ed. Richard Ellmann and Robert O'Clair (New York: W. W. Norton, 1988), p. 41.

13. See Chris P. Rice, *Grace Matters* (San Francisco: Jossey-Bass, 2002).

14. Margaret Lewis Furse, *Nothing But the Truth? What It Takes to Be Honest* (Nashville: Abingdon Press, 1981), p. 33.

15. Frederick Buechner, *Telling the Truth,* quoted in Komp, *Anatomy of a Lie,* p. 153.

16. Lewis B. Smedes, *Mere Morality* (Grand Rapids: Wm. B. Eerdmans, 1983), p. 216.

17. Bok, *Lying,* p. 72.

18. Bok, *Lying,* p. 176.

19. Komp, *Anatomy of a Lie,* p. 167.

20. One of the criticisms leveled against false prophets in the first centuries of the church was that they taught or prophesied "in a corner." See the Shepherd of Hermas, *Mandate* 11:12-13, translated by Kirsopp Lake in *The Apostolic Fathers,* vol. 2, Loeb Classical Library (Cambridge, Mass.: Harvard University Press, 1912).

21. Bok, *Lying,* pp. 148-49.

22. Bok, *Lying,* p. 150.

23. Bok, *Lying,* p. 155.

24. The familiar poem about six blind men describing parts of an elephant as if they represented the nature of the whole animal captures this dilemma. See John Godfrey Saxe, "The Blind Men and the Elephant."

25. Carol Tavris and Elliot Aronson, *Mistakes Were Made (But Not by Me)* (Orlando: Houghton Mifflin Harcourt, 2007), p. 81.

Chapter 10

1. See "deceive" in *Webster's Ninth New Collegiate Dictionary* (Springfield, Mass.: Merriam-Webster, 1990).

2. Sissela Bok, *Lying: Moral Choice in Public and Private Life* (New York: Pantheon Books, 1978), pp. 13-14.

3. Lewis B. Smedes, *Mere Morality* (Grand Rapids: Wm. B. Eerdmans, 1983), p. 213.

4. See Thomas Aquinas, *Summa Theologica,* Vol. II, Question 111: "Of Dissimulation and Hypocrisy," second and fourth articles (New York: Benziger Brothers, 1947), pp. 1670, 1672.

5. J. L. A. Garcia, "Lies and the Vices of Deception," *Faith and Philosophy* 15, no. 4 (October 1998): 518.

6. Mark L. Knapp, *Lying and Deception in Human Interaction* (Boston: Pearson/ Penguin Academics, 2008), p. 10. Some of these patterns are culture-specific, and our assumptions can be very problematic if we are working with two or more cultures.

7. Diane M. Komp, *Anatomy of a Lie* (Grand Rapids: Zondervan, 1998), p. 144.

8. Komp, *Anatomy of a Lie,* pp. 142, 144.

9. Stanley Hauerwas, *Truthfulness and Tragedy: Further Investigation into Christian Ethics* (Notre Dame, Ind.: University of Notre Dame Press, 1977), p. 82.

10. See Knapp, *Lying and Deception in Human Interaction,* p. 125; Carol Tavris and

Elliot Aronson, *Mistakes Were Made (But Not by Me)* (Orlando: Houghton Mifflin Harcourt, 2007), pp. 71, 4, 22; and Hauerwas, *Truthfulness and Tragedy*, pp. 86-87.

11. Knapp, *Lying and Deception in Human Interaction*, p. 129.

12. Lloyd H. Steffen, "On Honesty and Self-Deception: 'You are the Man,'" *The Christian Century*, 29 April 1987, p. 404.

13. See, for example, Zechariah 10:2; Romans 1:18-32; and Revelation 21.

14. Exodus 1:19; Joshua 2:3-7. Both stories are discussed in Komp, *Anatomy of a Lie*, pp. 23-28. A compelling example of a Christian community's commitment to truthfulness and to protecting the vulnerable is the story of the village of Le Chambon as told by Philip Hallie in *Lest Innocent Blood Be Shed* (New York: HarperPerennial, 1994).

15. Paul J. Griffiths, *Lying: An Augustinian Theology of Duplicity* (Grand Rapids: Brazos Press, 2004), pp. 38, 31.

16. Griffiths, *Lying*, pp. 25-39, 96-97.

17. Griffiths, *Lying*, pp. 54, 183, 85-86.

18. Aquinas, *Summa Theologica*, Vol. 2, Question 110: "Of the Vices Opposed to Truth," first article, p. 1664.

19. Bok, *Lying*, p. 34; Aquinas, *Summa Theologica*, Vol. 2, Question 110, second article, p. 1665.

20. Bok, *Lying*, pp. 37-38; Griffiths, *Lying*, pp. 189-94.

21. Dietrich Bonhoeffer, *Ethics* (New York: Macmillan, 1955), pp. 368-69.

22. Bonhoeffer, *Ethics*, p. 363.

23. For example, see the work of Grotius, as noted in Bok, *Lying*, p. 37; see also discussion in Garcia, "Lies and the Vices of Deception," p. 520, and Smedes, *Mere Morality*, p. 233.

24. See Garcia, "Lies and the Vices of Deception," p. 521.

25. Bok, *Lying*, p. 24.

26. Bok, *Lying*, p. 20.

27. Ralph Keyes, *The Post-Truth Era* (New York: St. Martin's Press, 2004), p. 232.

28. Keyes, *The Post-Truth Era*, pp. 236, 78.

29. Knapp, *Lying and Deception in Human Interaction*, pp. 146-47.

30. Margaret Lewis Furse, *Nothing But the Truth? What It Takes to Be Honest* (Nashville: Abingdon Press, 1981), pp. 59, 74-75; Bok, *Lying*, p. 210.

31. Keyes reports on studies by Robert Feldman that differences in rates of lying between male and female college students were not significant. However, the lies were different in content. "Lies told by women were more often intended to smooth social situations, those told by men to impress others with dubious boasts." "To oversimplify, men lie to impress, women to oblige" (*The Post-Truth Era*, p. 97).

32. Keyes, *The Post-Truth Era*, p. 249.

33. Komp, *Anatomy of a Lie*, p. 37.

34. Smedes, *Mere Morality*, pp. 225-27.

35. Bok, *Lying*, p. 210.

36. Smedes, *Mere Morality*, pp. 231-32.

37. T. M. Scanlon, *What We Owe to Each Other* (Cambridge, Mass.: Belknap Press, 1998), p. 318.

38. Julia Fleming, "Deception by Means of Incomplete Truth: An Ethical Evalua- tion," *Josephinum Journal of Theology* 6, no. 1 (1999): 22. Fleming argues that the conclu- sion that deception by incomplete truth and lying are morally different operates exclu- sively "from the liar's perspective" and may be relevant in courts, but it is not a significant moral distinction. She concludes that no one can claim "moral superiority" for deceiving by incomplete truth over lying (pp. 26-28). Because much of the Christian tradition has accepted the Augustinian argument that lying was always wrong (in principle if not in practice), some have made this distinction between "lying and deception through incom- plete truth." The Catholic Church, during its persecution by Protestants, developed a practice of "mental reservation" in response (Fleming, pp. 22-23). "According to this con- cept, one might mislead persecutors with half-truths, retaining the more important half in one's heart." But over time, "it became an easy way to rationalize all manner of prevari- cation," according to Ralph Keyes. See *The Post-Truth Era*, p. 31.

39. Knapp, *Lying and Deception in Human Interaction*, pp. 13-14.

40. Smedes, *Mere Morality*, pp. 234, 237.

41. See the story of Le Chambon, where the people sought to be as truthful as pos- sible, risking their own lives but not necessarily those they were protecting (Hallie, *Lest Innocent Blood Be Shed*); Garcia, "Lies and the Vices of Deception," p. 531.

42. Komp writes, "Even if I saw no alternative in that situation other than to tell a lie to save a life, I would not later claim that any lie I told was justified" (*Anatomy of a Lie*, p. 167).

43. Smedes, *Mere Morality*, p. 232.

44. Knapp, *Lying and Deception in Human Interaction*, p. 49; Bok, *Lying*, pp. 30-31.

45. Bok, *Lying*, pp. 105-6.

46. Bok, *Lying*, p. 93; Knapp, *Lying and Deception in Human Interaction*, p. 49.

47. John Wesley, Sermon CIII: "On Visiting the Sick," in *The Works of the Rev. John Wesley*, Sermons, Vol. 2 (New York: Eaton & Mains, 1833), p. 330.

48. Knapp, *Lying and Deception in Human Interaction*, p. 12.

49. In her discussion of "no-fault syntax," Komp writes, "I like what Hannah More said about precision with words. 'Let us fortify our virtue by calling things by their proper names.'" See Hannah More, *Religion of the Heart* (Orleans, Mass.: Paraclete Press, 1996), p. 129), quoted in Komp, *Anatomy of a Lie*, p. 122.

50. Komp, *Anatomy of a Lie*, p. 121.

51. See, for example, Matthew 15:18-19 and Ephesians 5:4.

52. Bonhoeffer, *Ethics*, p. 367.

53. See "rumor" in *Webster's Ninth New Collegiate Dictionary.*

54. See "gossip" in *Webster's Ninth New Collegiate Dictionary.* See also Barbara J. Blodgett's chapter titled "Gossip" in *Lives Entrusted* (Minneapolis: Fortress Press, 2008), pp. 85-119.

55. These questions are modified from Komp, *Anatomy of a Lie*, pp. 106-7.

56. See http://www.nyym.org/quakerism/uqp.html.

57. Alan Kreider, "Christ, Culture, and Truth-telling," *Conrad Grebel Review* 15 (Fall 1997): 226-27.

58. Kreider, "Christ, Culture, and Truth-telling," pp. 226-27.

59. L. Gregory Jones, "Truth and Lies," *The Christian Century,* 11 March 1998, p. 263.

60. Knapp, *Lying and Deception in Human Interaction,* p. 57.

61. In the Methodist tradition, the questions used by John Wesley's bands were quite probing. See also the discussion titled "Practicing Clear" on pages 153-54 of this chapter.

62. See Chris P. Rice, *Grace Matters* (San Francisco: Jossey-Bass, 2002), p. 185.

63. Miroslav Volf, *Exclusion and Embrace* (Nashville: Abingdon Press, 1996), p. 258.

64. The impulse to say everything is more about "the need to express oneself" than it is about "what the recipient should hear and what effects it might have." See Knapp, *Lying and Deception in Human Interaction,* p. 34.

65. See Chris Rice's reflections on this danger in *Grace Matters,* p. 186.

66. Rice, *Grace Matters,* pp. 203-4.

67. There are numerous models for handling disagreements redemptively. One book that provides a helpful and detailed approach to difficult encounters is *Fierce Conversations* by Susan Scott (New York: Berkley Books, 2002).

68. Although they share some similar concerns, the practice of "Clear" should be distinguished from "Clearness Committees." Parker Palmer notes that as part of the Quaker practice of discernment, the community makes use of these committees. See his essay "The Clearness Committee: A Communal Approach to Discernment," The Center for Courage and Renewal, 2006. You can access this essay online at http://www.couragerenewal.org/parker/writings/clearness-committee.

69. Alan Kreider and Eleanor Kreider, "Economical with the Truth," *Brethren in Christ History and Life* 24, no. 2 (August 2001): 171.

70. See Scanlon, *What We Owe to Each Other,* p. 323.

71. Glen H. Stassen and David P. Gushee, *Kingdom Ethics: Following Jesus in Contemporary Context* (Downers Grove, Ill.: InterVarsity Press, 2003), p. 376.

72. See Kreider, "Christ, Culture, and Truth-telling," pp. 214-21.

73. Kreider, "Christ, Culture, and Truth-telling," p. 225.

74. See Marilyn Chandler McEntyre, *Caring for Words in a Culture of Lies* (Grand Rapids: Wm. B. Eerdmans, 2009), p. 20.

Chapter 11

1. Shepherd of Hermas, *Mandate* 8:8-10, translated by Kirsopp Lake in *The Apostolic Fathers,* vol. 2, Loeb Classical Library (Cambridge, Mass.: Harvard University Press, 1912). See also John Koenig, *New Testament Hospitality* (Eugene, Ore.: Wipf & Stock, 2001), p. 2.

2. Thomas Ogletree, *Hospitality to the Stranger* (Philadelphia: Fortress Press, 1985), p. 1.

3. Jean Vanier, *Community and Growth,* rev. ed. (New York: Paulist Press, 1989), p. 266.

4. Christine D. Pohl, *Making Room: Recovering Hospitality as a Christian Tradition* (Grand Rapids: Wm. B. Eerdmans, 1999).

5. Most of the participants in the Pastor in Community Project associated with this book had learned the importance and complexities of hospitality before we began working together. A commitment to the practice of hospitality united us and gave us a basis from which to think about how various practices intersect, undermine, and reinforce other practices. We did not begin our conversations with hospitality in a formal sense, but in our efforts to live out the practice of hospitality, each of us had discovered the necessity of other practices.

6. It is important to recognize that there are also accounts of exclusion in the Scriptures. Some of these issues will be addressed in the section on complications. The tensions related to boundaries and hospitality are discussed more fully in Chapter 7 of *Making Room.*

7. See, for example, Mark 2:15-17; Mark 6:1-6; Mark 10:13-16; Luke 7:36-50; Luke 9:10-17; Luke 14:1-24; Luke 18:15-17; Luke 19:1-10; John 1:10-13; and John 21:1-14.

8. See, for example, 1 Corinthians 11:17-22; Galatians 3:27-29; and James 2:1-13.

9. "First Apology of Justin," Chapter 14, *The Ante-Nicene Fathers: Translations of the Writings of the Fathers down to A.D. 325,* vol. 1, p. 167; Aristedes, "Apology," Chapter 15, *The Ante-Nicene Fathers,* vol. 9, p. 277.

10. See Lactantius, *The Divine Institutes,* bk. 6, ch. 12, *The Ante-Nicene Fathers,* vol. 7, pp. 176-77; John Chrysostom, "Homily 20 on 1 Corinthians," *A Select Library of the Nicene and Post-Nicene Fathers of the Church,* First Series, vol. 12, p. 117; and John Chrysostom, "Homily 45 on Acts," *A Select Library of the Nicene and Post-Nicene Fathers of the Church,* First Series, vol. 11, pp. 275-76.

11. One of the main Greek words for hospitality in the New Testament is *philoxenia,* which means "love of strangers."

12. Walter Brueggemann, *Interpretation and Obedience* (Minneapolis: Fortress Press, 1991), p. 294; and Pohl, *Making Room,* pp. 85-89.

13. Vanier, *Community and Growth,* pp. 311-12.

14. Miroslav Volf, *Exclusion and Embrace* (Nashville: Abingdon Press, 1996), p. 129.

15. See Reinhard Hütter, "Hospitality and Truth: The Disclosure of Practices in Worship and Doctrine," in *Practicing Theology,* ed. Miroslav Volf and Dorothy C. Bass (Grand Rapids: Wm. B. Eerdmans, 2002), pp. 206-27.

16. Vanier, *Community and Growth,* pp. 266-67.

17. In a wonderful article titled "Memory, Funerals, and the Communion of Saints," M. Therese Lysaught, in conversation with David Keck's work, suggests that when fellow believers are affected by Alzheimer's disease, a congregation can "believe for them" as it continues to remember and value them. See *Growing Old in Christ,* ed. Stanley Hauerwas, Carole Bailey Stoneking, Keith G. Meador, and David Cloutier (Grand Rapids: Wm. B. Eerdmans, 2003), p. 297.

18. You can access the piece titled "Tzedakah and Hospitality" online: http://www.shemayisrael.com/publicat/hazon/tzedaka/Tzedakah_and_Hospitality.htm. *Mitzvah* is defined as a "commandment of the Jewish law" and "a meritorious or charitable act." See *Webster's Ninth New Collegiate Dictionary* (Springfield, Mass.: Merriam-Webster, 1990).

19. See Revelation 3:14-22.

20. One place where we see congregation members individually embracing a deeper commitment and community even when the church congregation does not is in the remarkable growth of oblates — laypersons who attach themselves to monastic households. Desiring more than ordinary congregational life, but not in a position to embrace the full monastic experience, individuals choose a more substantive place in community while remaining in conventional life situations.

21. Theologian Reinhard Hütter explains, "In the proclamation of the word, the truth of God's hospitality in Christ is announced and promised; in the celebration of the Supper, the hospitality of this truth is concretely remembered and tangibly received. God's own truth grants itself, enacts its own hospitality whenever the Gospel is proclaimed and the Lord's Supper celebrated. They point to each other." See "Hospitality and Truth," p. 221.

22. Vanier, *Community and Growth*, pp. 45-46.

Acknowledgments

1. This preliminary material was published as "Practices at the Heart of Community Life" in *One Heart, One Soul, Many Communities,* ed. Mary Forman, OSB (Collegeville, Minn.: Saint John's University Press, 2009), pp. 69-93.

Bibliography

Gratitude

Ashwin, Mary. "'. . . Against All Other Virtue and Goodness': An Exploration of Envy in Relation to Concepts of Sin." *Psychoanalytic Studies* 1, no. 4 (1999): 421-34.

Basil of Caesarea. "On Envy." Condensed and edited by Phyllis Graham. *The Angelus* 5, no. 5 (May 1982).

Berger, Fred R. "Gratitude." *Ethics* 85, no. 4 (July 1975): 298-309.

Camenisch, Paul F. "Gift and Gratitude in Ethics." *Journal of Religious Ethics* 9 (Spring 1981): 1-34.

Choung, James. "A Theology of Envy." *InterVarsity Library,* April 1996. This can be accessed online at http://regions.ivcf.org/academic/1931.

Comte-Sponville, André. *A Small Treatise on the Great Virtues.* New York: Henry Holt, 2001. See the chapter on gratitude, pp. 132-39.

deSilva, David A. *Perseverance in Gratitude: A Socio-Rhetorical Commentary on the Epistle "to the Hebrews."* Grand Rapids: Wm. B. Eerdmans, 2000.

Dickie, Matthew W. "The Fathers of the Church and the Evil Eye." In *Byzantine Magic,* edited by Henry Maguire. Washington, D.C.: Dumbarton Oaks Research Library; distributed by Harvard University Press, 1995, pp. 9-34.

Emmons, Robert A., and Michael E. McCullough. "Counting Blessings versus Burdens: An Experimental Investigation of Gratitude and Subjective Well-Being in Daily Life." *Journal of Personality and Social Psychology* 84, no. 2 (2003): 377-89.

Epstein, Joseph. *Envy.* New York: Oxford University Press and the New York Public Library, 2003.

Fairlie, Henry. *The Seven Deadly Sins Today.* Washington, D.C.: New Republic Books, 1978.

Fitzgerald, Patrick. "Gratitude and Justice." *Ethics* 109 (October 1998): 119-53.

Gerrish, B. A. *Grace and Gratitude: The Eucharistic Theology of John Calvin.* Eugene, Ore.: Wipf & Stock, 2002; previously published by Fortress Press, 1993.

Hagedorn, Anselm C., and Jerome H. Neyrey. "'It Was Out of Envy that They Handed Jesus Over' (Mark 15:10): The Anatomy of Envy and the Gospel of Mark." *Journal for the Study of the New Testament* 69 (1998): 15-56.

Hageman, Howard G. "Guilt, Grace, and Gratitude." In *Guilt, Grace, and Gratitude: A Commentary on the Heidelberg Catechism,* edited by Donald J. Bruggink. New York: Half Moon Press, 1963, pp. 1-19.

Henking, Patricia E. "A Grateful Heart." *The Christian Ministry,* July-August 1993, pp. 8-10.

Herzog, Don. "Envy: Poisoning the Banquet They Cannot Taste." In *Wicked Pleasures: Meditations on the Seven "Deadly" Sins,* edited by Robert C. Solomon. Lanham, Md.: Rowman & Littlefield, 1999, pp. 141-60.

Hiltner, Seward. "Gratitude." *Pastoral Psychology,* November 1963, pp. 5-7.

Hollyday, Joyce. "Gratitude: A Sermon on Giving Thanks." *Sojourners,* June 1987, pp. 32-34.

Joubert, Stephan. "Religious Reciprocity in 2 Corinthians 9:6-15: Generosity and Gratitude as Legitimate Responses to the *charis tou theou.*" *Neotestamentica* 33, no. 1 (1999): 79-90.

Kerr, Hugh. "Grace and Gratitude." *Theology Today* 43, no. 2 (July 1986): 151-54.

Knight, Henry H., III. "The Relation of Love to Gratitude in the Theologies of Edwards and Wesley." *Evangelical Journal* 6 (1988): 3-12.

Leddy, Mary Jo. *Radical Gratitude.* Maryknoll, N.Y.: Orbis Books, 2002.

Limberis, Vasiliki. "The Eyes Infected by Evil: Basil of Caesarea's Homily, *On Envy.*" *Harvard Theological Review* 84, no. 2 (1991): 163-84.

McConnell, Terrance. *Gratitude.* Philadelphia: Temple University Press, 1993.

McCullough, Michael E., Robert A. Emmons, and Jo-Ann Tsang. "The Grateful Disposition: A Conceptual and Empirical Topography." *Journal of Personality and Social Psychology* 82, no. 1 (2002): 112-27.

McCullough, Michael E., Shelley D. Kilpatrick, Robert A. Emmons, and David B. Larson. "Is Gratitude a Moral Affect?" *Psychological Bulletin* 127, no. 2 (2001): 249-66.

May, William F. "Envy: The Least Satisfying of the Seven Deadly Sins." *Christianity and Crisis,* 7 January 1963, pp. 241-44.

Nouwen, Henri J. M. *Gracias!* San Francisco: Harper & Row, 1983.

Pao, David W. *Thanksgiving: An Investigation of a Pauline Theme.* New Studies in Biblical Theology 13. Downers Grove, Ill.: InterVarsity Press, 2002.

Perkins, Robert L. "Envy as Personal Phenomenon and as Politics." *International Kierkegaard Commentaries* 14 (1984): 107-32.

Peterson, Christopher, and Martin E. P. Seligman. *Character Strengths and Virtues: A Handbook and Classification.* New York: Oxford University Press and the American Psychological Association, 2004. See the chapter on gratitude, pp. 553-68.

Plantinga, Cornelius, Jr. *Not the Way It's Supposed to Be: A Breviary of Sin.* Grand Rapids: Wm. B. Eerdmans, 1995. See the chapter on envy, pp. 157-72.

Raynolds, Robert. *In Praise of Gratitude.* New York: Harper & Brothers, 1961.

Vacek, Edward C., S.J. "Gifts, God, Generosity, and Gratitude." In *Spirituality and Moral Theology,* edited by James Keating. New York: Paulist Press, 2000, pp. 81-125.

Wellman, Christopher Heath. "Gratitude as a Virtue." *Pacific Philosophical Quarterly* 80, no. 3 (1999): 284-300.

Willimon, William H. *Sinning Like a Christian: A New Look at the Seven Deadly Sins.* Nashville: Abingdon Press, 2005. See the chapter on envy, pp. 49-65.

Yarhouse, Mark A. "The Vice of Envy: Insights from the History of Pastoral Care." *Journal of Psychology and Christianity* 19, no. 1 (2000): 25-37.

Making and Keeping Promises

Arendt, Hannah. *The Human Condition.* Chicago: University of Chicago Press, 1958. See Chapter 33, "Irreversibility and the Power to Forgive," and Chapter 34, "Unpredictability and the Power of Promise," pp. 236-47.

Atiyah, P. S. *Promises, Morals, and Law.* New York: Oxford University Press, 1981.

Berry, Wendell. *Fidelity: Five Stories.* New York: Pantheon Books, 1992.

Downie, R. S. "Three Accounts of Promising." *The Philosophical Quarterly* 35, no. 140 (1985): 259-71.

Dykstra, Craig. "Family Promises: Faith and Families in the Context of the Church." In *Faith and Families,* edited by Lindell Sawyers. Philadelphia: Geneva Press, 1986, pp. 137-63.

Farley, Margaret A. *Personal Commitments: Beginning, Keeping, Changing.* San Francisco: Harper & Row, 1986.

Fox, Richard M., and Joseph P. DeMarco. "The Immorality of Promising." *The Journal of Value Inquiry* 27 (1993): 81-84.

Fox, Richard M., and Joseph P. DeMarco. *The Immorality of Promising.* Amherst, N.Y.: Humanity Books, 2000.

Grant, C. K. "Promises." *Mind* 58 (July 1949): 359-66.

Hare, R. M. "The Promising Game." In *The Is-Ought Question,* edited by W. D. Hudson. London: Macmillan, 1969, pp. 144-56.

Hume, David. *A Treatise of Human Nature.* New York: Oxford at the Clarendon Press, 1978. See Book III, Section V: "Of the Obligation of Promises," pp. 516-25.

Korn, Fred, and Shulamit R. Decktor Korn. "Where People Don't Promise." *Ethics* (April 1983): 445-50.

MacCormick, Neil, and Joseph Raz. "Voluntary Obligations and Normative Powers." *Proceedings of the Aristotelian Society* 46 (1972): 59-102.

Marcel, Gabriel. "Obedience and Fidelity." In *On Being Responsible: Issues in Personal Ethics,* edited by James M. Gustafson and James T. Laney. New York: Harper & Row, 1968, pp. 75-85.

Melden, A. I. "On Promising." *Mind* 65 (January 1956): 49-66.

Orbell, John, Robyn Dawes, and Alphons van de Kragt. "The Limits of Multilateral Promising." *Ethics* 100 (April 1990): 616-27.

Prichard, H. A. *Moral Obligation: Essays and Lectures.* Oxford: Clarendon Press, 1949. See "The Obligation to Keep a Promise," pp. 169-79.

Rawls, John. *A Theory of Justice.* Cambridge, Mass.: Belknap Press, 1971, pp. 344-49.

————. "Two Concepts of Rules." *The Philosophical Review* 64 (1955): 3-32.

Raz, J. "Promises and Obligations." In *Law, Morality, and Society: Essays in Honour of H. L. A. Hart,* ed. P. M. S. Hacker and J. Raz. Oxford: Clarendon Press, 1977, pp. 210-28.

Robins, Michael H. *Promising, Intending, and Moral Autonomy.* Cambridge: Cambridge University Press, 1984.

Ross, W. D. *Foundations of Ethics.* Oxford: Clarendon Press, 1939.

————. *The Right and the Good.* Oxford: Clarendon Press, 1930.

Scanlon, Thomas. "Promises and Practices." *Philosophy and Public Affairs* 19, no. 3 (Summer 1990): 199-226.

Scanlon, T. M. *What We Owe to Each Other.* Cambridge, Mass.: Belknap Press, 1998.

Searle, John R. "How to Derive 'Ought' from 'Is.'" *The Philosophical Review* (January 1964): 43-58.

————. *Speech Acts: An Essay in the Philosophy of Language.* Cambridge: Cambridge University Press, 1970, pp. 54-62.

Smedes, Lewis B. "Controlling the Unpredictable: The Power of Promising." *Christianity Today,* 21 January 1983, pp. 16-19.

————. "The Power of Promises." In *A Chorus of Witnesses: Model Sermons for Today's Preacher,* edited by Thomas G. Long and Cornelius Plantinga Jr. Grand Rapids: Wm. B. Eerdmans, 1994, pp. 156-62.

Smith, Holly M. "A Paradox of Promising." *The Philosophical Review* 106, no. 2 (April 1997): 153-96.

Tunick, Mark. *Practices and Principles: Approaches to Ethical and Legal Judgment.* Princeton, N.J.: Princeton University Press, 1998.

Vitek, William. *Promising.* Philadelphia: Temple University Press, 1993.

Living Truthfully

Bok, Sissela. *Lying: Moral Choice in Public and Private Life.* New York: Pantheon Books, 1978.

Bonhoeffer, Dietrich. *Ethics.* New York: Macmillan, 1955. See especially "What Is Meant by 'Telling the Truth'?" pp. 363-72.

Borer, Tristan Anne, ed. *Telling the Truths: Truth Telling and Peace Building in Post-Conflict Societies.* Notre Dame, Ind.: University of Notre Dame Press, 2006.

Brinton, Alan. "St. Augustine and the Problem of Deception in Religious Persuasion." *Religious Studies* 19, no. 3 (September 1983): 437-50.

Brown, Elmer Ellsworth. "Absolute Truthfulness." *Methodist Review* (1913): 35-45.

Carson, Thomas L. *Lying and Deception: Theory and Practice.* Oxford: Oxford University Press, 2010.

Caton, Hiram. "Truthfulness in Kant's Metaphysical Morality." In *Essays in Metaphysics*. Dublin: Blackrock, 1970, pp. 19-38.

Cousineau, Amy, Michael Chow, and Patricia Brezden. "'Worlds Apart': Truth-Telling in the Case of Mrs. VV." *The Journal of Pastoral Care and Counseling* 57, no. 4 (Winter 2003): 415-26.

Fleming, Julia. "Deception by Means of Incomplete Truth: An Ethical Evaluation." *Josephinum Journal of Theology* 6, no. 1 (1999): 21-30.

Furse, Margaret Lewis. *Nothing But the Truth? What It Takes to Be Honest*. Nashville: Abingdon Press, 1981.

Garcia, J. L. A. "Lies and the Vices of Deception." *Faith and Philosophy* 15, no. 4 (October 1998): 514-37.

Griffiths, Paul J. *Lying: An Augustinian Theology of Duplicity*. Grand Rapids: Brazos Press, 2004.

Hauerwas, Stanley. *Truthfulness and Tragedy: Further Investigation into Christian Ethics*. Notre Dame, Ind.: University of Notre Dame Press, 1977. See especially Chapter 5 with David B. Burrell: "Self-Deception and Autobiography: Reflections on Speer's *Inside the Third Reich*," pp. 82-98.

————. "Why the Truth Demands Truthfulness: An Imperious Engagement with Hartt." *Journal of the American Academy of Religion* 52, no. 1 (March 1984): 141-47.

Hütter, Reinhard. "Hospitality and Truth: The Disclosure of Practices in Worship and Doctrine." In *Practicing Theology*, edited by Miroslav Volf and Dorothy C. Bass. Grand Rapids: Wm. B. Eerdmans, 2002, pp. 206-27.

Jacobs, Alan. *Shaming the Devil: Essays in Truthtelling*. Grand Rapids: Wm. B. Eerdmans, 2004.

Jones, L. Gregory. "Truth and Lies." *Christian Century*, 11 March 1998, p. 263.

Keyes, Ralph. *The Post-Truth Era: Dishonesty and Deception in Contemporary Life*. New York: St. Martin's Press, 2004.

Knapp, Mark L. *Lying and Deception in Human Interaction*. Boston: Pearson/Penguin Academics, 2008.

Komp, Diane M. *Anatomy of a Lie: The Truth about Lies and Why Good People Tell Them*. Grand Rapids: Zondervan, 1998.

Kreider, Alan. "Christ, Culture, and Truth-Telling." *Conrad Grebel Review* 15 (Fall 1997): 207-33.

Kreider, Alan, and Eleanor Kreider. "Economical with the Truth: Swearing and Lying — An Anabaptist Perspective." *Brethren in Christ History and Life* 24, no. 2 (August 2001): 153-77.

McEntyre, Marilyn Chandler. *Caring for Words in a Culture of Lies*. Grand Rapids: Wm. B. Eerdmans, 2009.

Smedes, Lewis B. "Respect for Truthfulness." Chapter 8 in *Mere Morality: What God Expects from Ordinary People*. Grand Rapids: Wm. B. Eerdmans, 1983, pp. 211-38.

Smith, Wilfred Cantwell. "A Human View of Truth." *Studies in Religion: A Canadian Journal* 1, no. 1 (1971): 6-24.

Stassen, Glen H., and David P. Gushee. *Kingdom Ethics: Following Jesus in Contempo-*

rary Context. Downers Grove, Ill.: InterVarsity Press, 2003. See especially Chapter 18: "Truthtelling."

Steffen, Lloyd H. "On Honesty and Self-Deception: 'You Are the Man.'" *The Christian Century,* 29 April 1987, pp. 403-5.

Tavris, Carol, and Elliot Aronson. *Mistakes Were Made (But Not by Me).* Orlando: Houghton Mifflin Harcourt, 2007.

Ten Elshof, Gregg A. *I Told Me So: Self-Deception and the Christian Life.* Grand Rapids: Wm. B. Eerdmans, 2009.

Volf, Miroslav. *Exclusion and Embrace: A Theological Exploration of Identity, Otherness, and Reconciliation.* Nashville: Abingdon Press, 1996. See especially Chapter 6: "Deception and Truth."

Wellborn, Charles. "Truth-Telling: An Exercise in Practical Morality." *Christian Ethics Today* 14, no. 6 (December 1998). Access this essay online at http://www.christian ethicstoday.com, issue 19 (Spring 2004): 1-4.

Hospitality

Bretherton, Luke. *Hospitality as Holiness: Christian Witness amid Moral Diversity.* Burlington, Vt.: Ashgate, 2006.

Hershberger, Michele. *A Christian View of Hospitality.* Scottdale, Pa.: Herald Press, 1999.

Koenig, John. *The Feast of the World's Redemption.* Harrisburg, Pa.: Trinity Press, 2000.

————. *New Testament Hospitality.* Eugene, Ore.: Wipf & Stock, 2001.

LaVerdiere, Eugene. *Dining in the Kingdom of God.* Chicago: Liturgy Training Publications, 1994.

Mains, Karen Burton. *Open Heart, Open Home.* Elgin, Ill.: David C. Cook, 1987.

Newman, Elizabeth. *Untamed Hospitality: Welcoming God and Other Strangers.* Grand Rapids: Brazos Press, 2007.

Nouwen, Henri. *Reaching Out: The Three Movements of the Spiritual Life.* New York: Image Books, 1975.

Oden, Amy, ed. *And You Welcomed Me: A Sourcebook on Hospitality in Early Christianity.* Nashville: Abingdon Press, 2001.

Ogletree, Thomas W. *Hospitality to the Stranger: Dimensions of Moral Understanding.* Philadelphia: Fortress Press, 1985.

Pohl, Christine D. *Making Room: Recovering Hospitality as a Christian Tradition.* Grand Rapids: Wm. B. Eerdmans, 1999.

Pohl, Christine D., and Pamela J. Buck. *Study Guide for "Making Room."* Grand Rapids: Wm. B. Eerdmans, 2001.

Sutherland, Arthur. *I Was a Stranger: A Christian Theology of Hospitality.* Nashville: Abingdon Press, 2006.

Volf, Miroslav. *Exclusion and Embrace: A Theological Exploration of Identity, Otherness, and Reconciliation.* Nashville: Abingdon Press, 1996.

Webb-Mitchell, Brett. *Unexpected Guests at God's Banquet.* New York: Crossroad, 1994.

Practices in Community

Bass, Dorothy C., ed. *Practicing Our Faith: A Way of Life for a Searching People.* San Francisco: Jossey-Bass, 1997; second edition, 2010.

Benedict, Saint. *The Rule of St. Benedict in English* (1980). Edited by Timothy Fry, O.S.B. Collegeville, Minn.: Liturgical Press, 1982.

Bonhoeffer, Dietrich. *Life Together.* New York: Harper & Row, 1954.

Calhoun, Adele Ahlberg. *Spiritual Disciplines Handbook: Practices that Transform Us.* Downers Grove, Ill.: InterVarsity Press, 2005.

Doughty, Stephen V. *Discovering Community: A Meditation on Community in Christ.* Nashville: Upper Room Books, 1999.

Dykstra, Craig. *Growing in the Life of Faith: Education and Christian Practices,* 2nd ed. Louisville: Westminster John Knox Press, 2005.

Hallie, Philip. *Lest Innocent Blood Be Shed.* New York: HarperPerennial, 1994.

Rice, Chris P. *Grace Matters: A True Story of Race, Friendship, and Faith in the Heart of the South.* San Francisco: Jossey-Bass, 2002.

Robinson, Marilynne. *Gilead.* New York: Farrar, Straus & Giroux, 2004.

Smedes, Lewis. *Mere Morality: What God Expects from Ordinary People.* Grand Rapids: Wm. B. Eerdmans, 1983.

Vanier, Jean. *Community and Growth.* Revised edition. New York: Paulist Press, 1989.

Volf, Miroslav. *Exclusion and Embrace: A Theological Exploration of Identity, Otherness, and Reconciliation.* Nashville: Abingdon Press, 1996.

Volf, Miroslav, and Dorothy C. Bass, eds. *Practicing Theology: Beliefs and Practices in Christian Life.* Grand Rapids: Wm. B. Eerdmans, 2002.

Questions for Discussion and Reflection

Embracing Gratitude as a Way of Life

- What rituals or rhythms of gratitude could we establish that would keep us mindful of its importance?
- How can we work to create a culture of noticing what is good?
- Which complications of gratitude are most troublesome within community? How have we addressed them effectively? What else could be done?
- What attitudes and assumptions in our lives, congregation, or community support ingratitude and dissatisfaction? In what ways are we addressing personal and communal inclinations toward envy and grumbling?
- What are we doing in church, family, or community that we could build on to deepen the practice of gratitude?

Making and Keeping Promises

- In our congregational or community life, where have we seen specific expressions of fidelity or promise-keeping in the face of difficult challenges?
- What are we doing in our congregation or community to help people keep their promises and follow through on the commitments they have made?

- What contemporary issues or values do we need to confront in order to strengthen our fidelity to God and others?
- What are the most important promises we have made in shaping our families, churches, and communities?
- Are there tears in the fabric of our life together that have come from betrayals or deceptions? How are we moving toward repairing the damage? What resources do we have to help us move toward restoration?

Living Truthfully

- What features of our congregational or community life help us to be truthful?
- What dynamics make it hard for us to be truthful?
- What are we doing to become a truth-shaped community?
- How could we invite our community or congregation into a deeper or more mature level of truthfulness?
- What areas of dishonesty or self-deception do we need to address?
- What structures do we have in place to help us be more truthful about our struggles, situations, needs, and relationships?
- What structures could we establish?

Practicing Hospitality and Beyond

- Who are strangers in our community that need welcome?
- When we are offering or enjoying hospitality, which other practices are flourishing?
- As we think about difficulties we've encountered in offering or receiving hospitality, what other practices (or their deformations) have come into play? How might we address these difficulties?
- What are we — in our personal lives, families, congregation, or community — already doing to offer welcome? What could we build on to strengthen our practice of hospitality?

Index